i

Immigrating to Canada
and
Finding Employment

A Do-it-Yourself Kit
For Skilled Worker Class Applicants
Under the Latest Immigration Policy

A STEP–BY–STEP SETTLEMENT AND JOB SEARCH GUIDE

A 3 IN 1 PUBLICATION

by

Tariq Nadeem

iii

ISBN: 0-9734551-8-7 (Paperback)
ISBN: 0-9734551-9-5 (e-book)

Library and Archives Canada Cataloguing in Publication

Nadeem, Tariq, 1966-
    Immigrating to Canada and finding employment : a do-it-yourself kit for
skilled workers under the latest immigration policy : a step-by-step
settlement and job search guide : a 3-in-1 publication / Tariq Nadeem. --
2nd ed.

Includes bibliographical references and index.
ISBN 0-9734551-8-7

    1. Canada--Emigration and immigration--Handbooks, manuals, etc.
2. Alien labor--Canada--Handbooks, manuals, etc. 3. Job hunting-
Canada-Handbooks, manuals, etc. I. Title.

JV7274.N33 2005   325.71   C2005-904742-9

This book is printed on acid free paper.

This publication is designed to provide accurate and authoritative information that is up-to-date and current at the time of this publication. It is sold with the understanding that the publisher is not engaged in rendering any professional services.

Self-Help Publishers does not endorse any product or service in this publication. Any service or services provider listed in this publication assume full liability for their products and services and any claims direct or indirect arising from them.

Send your wholesale inquiries in U.S.A to Ingram Book Group, Baker & Taylor, and Nacscorp.
In United Kingdom and Europe send your wholesale inquiries to Bertram and Blackwell's.

For retail purchase visit your local Amazon and Barns and Nobles online bookstores or checkout with your local bookstore.

For reprint/co-publishing rights contact Self-Help Publishers at 3-445 Pioneer Dr. Kitchener ,ON, N2P 1L8 Canada or visit www.selfhelppublishers.com

Manufactured in United States of America and United Kingdom simultaneously by arrangements with Self-Help publishers.

Cover design and layout by Tariq Nadeem – Publishing date: August 15, 2005

ACKNOWLEDGEMENT & CREDITS

© Her Majesty the Queen in Right of Canada, represented by the Minister of Public works and Government Services, 2005.

Statistics Canada information is used with the permission of Minister of Industry, as Minister responsible for Statistics Canada. Information on the availability of the wide range of data from Statistics Canada can be obtained from Statistics Canada's Regional Offices, its World Wide Web site at http://www.statcan.ca and its toll-free access number 1-800-263-1136

Introduction to Canada, facts and figures – CIA -The world factbook
Fact sheet, http://www.cicic.ca/professions/indexe.stm
Cultural Shock: An introduction to KSA
Manage your impression – Put Your Best Foot Forward.
Top Ten Ways to Get Canadian Experience - Do You Have International Experience By Shawn Mintz of A.C.C.E.S www.accestrain.com.

I also thank Ms. Erum Chughtai for her assistance and help in dealing with technicalities of this publication.

All rights reserved. This information has been produced with the approval of Citizenship and Immigration Canada and with the authorization of Public Works and Government Services Canada 350 Albert Street, 4th Floor Ottawa ON K1A 0S5.

DISCLAIMER

DEDICATION

This book is dedicated to the late Dr. Val O'Donovan. He was a business and community leader, an innovator in satellite communications; the Chancellor Emeritus; a member of the Order of Canada, he also served as University of Waterloo's Chancellor for six years, was the recipient of the Laurier Outstanding Business Leader Award from Wilfrid Laurier University and the founder of Com Dev Ltd. in Canada. (www.comdev.ca)

His huge contributions in the space science and technology, as well as his pioneering vision of Canada in space will not be forgotten. With his exemplary leadership, dedication and passion, he used his success in the industry to build a better community around him. He committed himself towards communities to bring a positive change in the lives of people and their children. A man with a mind of an engineer and the soul of a poet will forever be remembered and recorded in history books of the Canadian space industry.

In fact, today, the people on planet earth are in desperate need of leaders like Dr. Val O'Donovan to make life better and peaceful.

A big salute to Dr. Val O'Donovan
and his wife Ms. Sheila O'Donovan !

PREFACE

Migrating from one country and culture to another is a giant and bold step in anyone's life. This publication is my humble effort to save the newcomer's hard earned money and time. I also wish to provide the prospective immigrants from around the world the necessary information and tools in advance to plan their new life well before arriving to Canada. Further, I am trying my best to well equip these perspective immigrants to meet the new challenges with courage, and to face the unexpected. in a professional manner.

Many new immigrants also come with horror stories. An example of those cited by our former Federal Minister of Citizenship and Immigration Canada, Honorable Mr. Denis Coderre who also was very well informed about all the complaints filed by prospective and new immigrants, especially about those unscrupulous immigration consultants who also undermined the reputation of honest and legitimate immigration consultants. Immigration Canada has thousands of complaints about these consultants. I would like to refer to a news article in the daily "Toronto Star" dated Sept.7, 2002. According to the newspaper, Mr. Coderre used a stopover in Hong Kong and cited horror stories of such consultants who urged their clients to lie on their applications, or who falsely claimed that extortionate fees often in excess of $ 10,000 – would guarantee a visa which has never been the case.

Our current Federal Minister of Citizenship and Immigration Honorable Mr. Joe Volpe and his staff is actively addressing the old and current issues to refine and harmonize the Canadian immigration policy to meet the challenges of 21st century .

I must thank and appreciate the cooperation of Ms. Nicole Hudon and Ms. Christine Way of Crown Copyright and Licensing who have guided me to obtain the necessary copyright clearance.

I am sure, you would like what you have in your hands. *Thanks for checking it out!*

CONTENTS

PART ONE

PART TWO

A NEW COMMER'S INTRODUCTION TO CANADA ___172

PART THREE

WORKING IN CANADA

CANADA
AN INTRODUCTION

Canada has a long tradition of welcoming immigrants. Home to two official languages, English and French, Canada is also a multicultural society, with more than 17% of the population reporting a mother tongue other than English or French. During the 1990s, Canada received between 200,000 and 250,000 immigrants per year. In 2001, Canada actually exceeded its target for the first time in years with 250,346 newcomers being granted permanent resident status. This limit has been increased up to 300,000 per year to offset Canada's aging population and to synchronize it with 1% of the total population. A total of 235,808 people immigrated to Canada in 2004, a seven percent increase over the previous year.

50% of all the newcomers come to Toronto, 15% go to Vancouver and 11% to Montreal. Canada is rich, according to World Wealth Report 2001 by Cap Gemini Ernst & Young, **31% of the world's millionaires live in North America** while 4% in Middle East, 24% in Asia Pacific, 36% in Europe and 1% in Africa. Canadians pay $138 Billion every year through their credit cards for their shopping.

UN SAYS CANADA IS THE BEST COUNTRY IN THE WORLD!

The United Nations has rated Canada several times the top country in the world for overall quality of life. Canadians enjoy a comfortable standard of living, good health care, social security, a high level of education, and a relatively safe and clean environment. The *Charter of Rights and Freedoms* entrenched in the Canadian constitution guarantees such fundamental rights as equality, mobility and legal rights, as well as freedom of speech, assembly and association. A 1997 survey of people in 20 countries found that the majority placed Canada in the top ten list of countries where they would like to live. Most consider Canada a generous, peaceful and compassionate nation, while they see Canadians as honest, friendly and polite.

1

Background: A land of vast distances and rich natural resources, Canada became a self-governing dominion in 1867 while retaining ties to the British crown. Economically and technologically the nation has developed in parallel with the US, its neighbor to the south across an unfortified border. Canada's paramount political problem is meeting public demands for quality improvements in health care and education services after a decade of budget cuts. The issue of reconciling Quebec's francophone heritage with the majority anglophone Canadian population has moved to the back burner in recent years; support for separatism abated after the Quebec government's referendum on independence failed to pass in October of 1995.

GEOGRAPHY

Location: Northern North America, bordering the North Atlantic Ocean on the east, North Pacific Ocean on the west, and the Arctic Ocean on the north, north of the conterminous US

Geographic coordinates: 60 00 N, 95 00 W

Map references: North America

Area:

total: 9,984,670 sq km
land: 9,093,507 sq km
water: 891,163 sq km

Area - comparative: somewhat larger than the US

Land boundaries:

total: 8,893 km
border countries: US 8,893 km (includes 2,477 km with Alaska)

Coastline: 202,080 km

Maritime claims - as described in UNCLOS 1982 :

territorial sea: 12 NM
continental shelf: 200 NM or to the edge of the continental margin
contiguous zone: 24 NM
exclusive economic zone: 200 NM

Climate: varies from temperate in south to subarctic and arctic in north

Terrain: mostly plains with mountains in west and lowlands in southeast

Elevation extremes:
lowest point: Atlantic Ocean 0 m
highest point: Mount Logan 5,959 m

Natural resources: iron ore, nickel, zinc, copper, gold, lead, molybdenum, potash, diamonds, silver, fish, timber, wildlife, coal, petroleum, natural gas, hydropower

Land use:
arable land: 4.94%
permanent crops: 0.02% *other:* 95.04% (1998 est.)
Irrigated land: 7,200 sq km (1998 est.)

Natural hazards: continuous permafrost in north is a serious obstacle to development; cyclonic storms form east of the Rocky Mountains, a result of the mixing of air masses from the Arctic, Pacific, and North American interior, and produce most of the country's rain and snow east of the mountains

Environment - current issues: air pollution and resulting acid rain severely affecting lakes and damaging forests; metal smelting, coal-burning utilities, and vehicle emissions impacting on agricultural and forest productivity; ocean waters becoming contaminated due to agricultural, industrial, mining, and forestry activities

Environment - international agreements: *party to:* Air Pollution, Air Pollution-Nitrogen Oxides, Air Pollution-Persistent Organic Pollutants, Air Pollution-Sulfur 85, Air Pollution-Sulfur 94, Antarctic-Environmental Protocol, Antarctic-Marine Living Resources, Antarctic Seals, Antarctic Treaty, Biodiversity, Climate Change, Climate Change-Kyoto Protocol, Desertification, Endangered Species, Environmental Modification, Hazardous Wastes, Law of the Sea, Marine Dumping, Ozone Layer Protection,

3

Ship Pollution, Tropical Timber 83, Tropical Timber 94, Wetlands *signed, but not ratified:* Air Pollution-Volatile Organic Compounds, Marine Life Conservation

Geography - note: second-largest country in world (after Russia); strategic location between Russia and US via north polar route; approximately 90% of the population is concentrated within 300 km of the US border

PEOPLE

Population: 32,805,041 (July 2005 est.)

Age structure:
0-14 years: 17.9% (male 3,016,032/female 2,869,244)
15-64 years: 68.9% (male 11,357,425/female 11,244,356)
65 years and over: 13.2% (male 1,842,496/female 2,475,488) (2005 est.)

Median age:
total: 38.54 years
male: 37.54 years
female: 39.56 years (2005 est.)

Population growth rate: 0.9% (2005 est.)

Birth rate: 10.84 births/1,000 population (2005 est.)

Death rate: 7.73 deaths/1,000 population (2005 est.)

Net migration rate: 5.9 migrant(s)/1,000 population (2005 est.)

Sex ratio: *at birth:*   1.05 male(s)/female

under 15 years: 1.05 male(s)/female
15-64 years: 1.01 male(s)/female
65 years and over: 0.74 male(s)/female
total population: 0.98 male(s)/female (2005 est.)

Infant mortality rate:
total: 4.75 deaths/1,000 live births
female: 5.21 deaths/1,000 live births (2005 est.)
male: 4.27 deaths/1,000 live births

Life expectancy at birth:
total population: 80.01 years
male: 76.73 years
female: 83.63 years (2005 est.)

Total fertility rate:
1.61 children born/woman (2005 est.)

HIV/AIDS - adult prevalence rate: 0.3% (2003 est.)

HIV/AIDS - people living with HIV/AIDS: 56,000 (2003 est.)

HIV/AIDS - deaths: less than 1,500 (2003 est.)

Nationality: *noun:* Canadian(s)
                   adjective: Canadian

Ethnic groups: British Isles origin 28%, French origin 23%, other European 15%, Amerindian 2%, other, mostly Asian, African, Arab 6%, mixed background 26%

Religions: Roman Catholic 42.6%, Protestant 23.3% (including United Church 9.5%, Anglican 6.8%, Baptist 2.4%, Lutheran 2%), other Christian 4.4%, Muslim 1.9%, other and unspecified 11.8%, none 16% (2001 census)

Languages: English 59.3% (official), French 23.2% (official), other 17.5%

Literacy: *definition:* age 15 and over can read and write
total population: 97% (1986 est.)
male: NA%
female: NA%

GOVERNMENT

Country name:
conventional long form: none
conventional short form: Canada

Government type: confederation with parliamentary democracy

Capital: Ottawa

Administrative divisions: 10 provinces and 3 territories*; Alberta, British Columbia, Manitoba, New Brunswick, Newfoundland and Labrador, Northwest Territories*, Nova Scotia, Nunavut*, Ontario, Prince Edward Island, Quebec, Saskatchewan, Yukon Territory*

Independence: 1 July 1867 (union of British North American colonies); 11 December 1931 (independence recognized)

National holiday: Canada Day, 1 July (1867)

Constitution: 17 April 1982 (Constitution Act); originally, the machinery of the government was set up in the British North America Act of 1867; charter of rights and unwritten customs

Legal system: based on English common law, except in Quebec, where civil law system based on French law prevails; accepts compulsory ICJ jurisdiction, with reservations

Suffrage: 18 years of age; universal (Right to vote)

Executive branch: *chief of state:* Queen ELIZABETH II (since 6 February 1952), represented by Governor General Adrienne CLARKSON (since October 7, 1999)

Elections: none; the monarchy is hereditary; governor general appointed by the monarch on the advice of the prime minister for a five-year term; following legislative elections, the leader of the majority party or the leader of the majority coalition in the House of Commons is automatically designated prime minister by the governor general

6

Head of government: Prime Minister Paul MARTIN (since 12 December 2003); Deputy Prime Minister Anne MCLELLAN (since 12 December 2003)

Cabinet: Federal Ministry chosen by the prime minister from among the members of his own party sitting in Parliament

Legislative branch: bicameral Parliament or Parlement consists of the Senate or Senat (members appointed by the governor general with the advice of the prime minister and serve until reaching 75 years of age; its normal limit is 105 senators) and the House of Commons or Chambre des Communes (308 seats; members elected by direct, popular vote to serve for up to five-year terms)

Elections: House of Commons - last held at June 28, 2004

Election results: **House of Commons - percent of vote by party -** Liberal Party 36.71%, Progressive Conservative Party 29.61% Bloc Quebecois 12.4%, New Democratic Party 15.6%; Other 4.8%

Seats by party: as of July 2004 - Liberal Party 135, Conservative Party 99, Bloc Quebecois 54, New Democratic Party 19 , Others 1.

Judicial branch: Supreme Court of Canada (judges are appointed by the prime minister through the governor general); Federal Court of Canada; Federal Court of Appeal; Provincial Courts (these are named variously Court of Appeal, Court of Queens Bench, Superior Court, Supreme Court, and Court of Justice)

Political parties and leaders: Bloc Quebecois [Gilles DUCEPPE]; Conservative Party of Canada (a merger of the Canadian Alliance and the Progressive Conservative Party) [Stephen HARPER]; Green Party [Jim HARRIS]; Liberal Party [Paul MARTIN]; New Democratic Party [Jack LAYTON]

Political pressure groups and leaders: NA

International organization participation: ACCT, AfDB, APEC, ARF, AsDB , ASEAN (dialogue partner), Australia Group, BIS, C, CDB, CE (observer), EAPC, EBRD, ESA (cooperating state), FAO, G-7, G-8, G-10, IADB, IAEA, IBRD, ICAO, ICC, ICCt, ICFTU, ICRM, IDA, IEA, IFAD, IFC, IFRCS, IHO, ILO, IMF, IMO, Interpol, IOC, IOM, ISO, ITU, MICAH, MONUC, NAM (guest), NATO, NEA, NSG, OAS, OECD, OPCW, OSCE, Paris Club, PCA, UN, UNAMSIL, UNCTAD, UNDOF, UNESCO, UNFICYP, UNHCR, UNMIK, UNMOVIC, UNTSO, UPU, WCL, WCO, WFTU, WHO, WIPO, WMO, WTO, ZC

Diplomatic representation in the US:
chief of mission: Ambassador Francis Joseph MCKENNA
chancery: 501 Pennsylvania Avenue NW, Washington, DC 20001
Fax: [1] (202) 682-7726
Telephone: [1] (202) 682-1740

Consulate(s) General: Atlanta, Boston, Buffalo, Chicago, Dallas, Detroit, Los Angeles, Miami, Minneapolis, New York, and Seattle

Consulate(s): Houston, Princeton, Raleigh-Durham, San Diego, San Francisco, and San Jose

Diplomatic representation from the US:
Chief of Mission: Ambassador David Wilkins (2005)
Embassy: 490 Sussex Drive, Ottawa, Ontario K1N 1G8

Mailing address: P. O. Box 5000, Ogdensburgh, NY 13669-0430
Telephone: [1] (613) 238-5335, 4470
Fax: [1] (613) 688-3097

Consulate(s) general: Calgary, Halifax, Montreal, Quebec, Toronto, and Vancouver

ECONOMY

Flag description: two vertical bands of red (hoist and fly side, half width), with white square between them; an 11-pointed red maple leaf is centered in the white square; the official colors of Canada are red and white

Economy – overview : As an affluent, high-tech industrial society, Canada today closely resembles the US in its market-oriented economic system, pattern of production, and high living standards. Since World War II, the impressive growth of the manufacturing, mining, and service sectors has transformed the nation from a largely rural economy into one primarily industrial and urban. The 1989 US-Canada Free Trade Agreement (FTA) and the 1994 North American Free Trade Agreement (NAFTA) (which includes Mexico) touched off a dramatic increase in trade and economic integration with the US. As a result of the close cross-border relationship, the economic sluggishness in the United States in 2001-02 had a negative impact on the Canadian economy. Real growth averaged nearly 3% during 1993-2000, but declined in 2001, with moderate recovery in 2002-03. Unemployment is up, with contraction in the manufacturing and natural resource sectors. Nevertheless, given its great natural resources, skilled labor force, and modern capital plant Canada enjoys solid economic prospects. Two shadows loom, the first being the continuing constitutional impasse between English- and French-speaking areas, which has been raising the specter of a split in the federation. Another long-term concern is the flow south to the US of professionals lured by higher pay, lower taxes, and the immense high-tech infrastructure. A key strength in the economy is the substantial trade surplus. Roughly 90% of the population lives within 160 kilometers of the US border.

GDP: purchasing power parity - $1.023 trillion (2004est.)

GDP - real growth rate:2.4% (2004 est.)

GDP - per capita: purchasing power parity - $31,500 (2004 est.)

GDP - composition by sector: *agriculture:* 2.3%, *industry:* 26.4% *services:* 71.3% (2004 est.)

9

Population below poverty line: NA% (1998 est.)

Household income or consumption by percentage share:

lowest 10%: 2.8%

highest 10%: 23.8% (1994)

Distribution of family income - Gini index: 31.5 (1994)

Inflation rate (consumer prices): 1.9% (2004 est.)

Labor force: 17.37 million (2004 est.)

Labor force - by occupation: services 74%, manufacturing 15%, construction 5%, agriculture 3%, other 3% (2000)

Unemployment rate: 7% (2004 est.)

Budget: *revenues:* $186 billion (2004)

expenditures: $144 billion, including capital expenditures of $NA (FY 2004 est.)

Public debt: $547.4 billion (2001-01)

Industries: transportation equipment, chemicals, processed and unprocessed minerals, food products; wood and paper products; fish products, petroleum and natural gas

Industrial production growth rate: 2% (2004 est.)

Electricity - production: 548.9 billion kWh (2002)

Electricity - production by source:

fossil fuel:	28%
hydro:	57.9%
other:	1.3% (2001)
nuclear:	12.9%

Electricity - consumption: 504.4 billion kWh (2001)

Electricity - exports: 38.4 billion kWh (2001)

Electricity - imports: 16.11 billion kWh (2001)

Oil - production: 3.11 million bbl/day (2004 est.)

Oil - consumption: 2.2 million bbl/day (2004est.)

Oil - exports: 1.37 million bbl/day (2004)

Oil - imports: 987,000 million bbl/day (2004)

Oil - proved reserves: 178.9 billion bbl (est 2004)

Natural gas - production: 165.8 billion cu m (2003 est.)

Natural gas - consumption: 55.8 billion cu m (2003 est.)

Natural gas - exports: 95.52 billion cu m (2003 est.)

Natural gas - imports: 8.73 billion cu m (2003 est.)

Natural gas - proved reserves: 1.691 trillion cu m (2004)

Agriculture - products: wheat, barley, oilseed, tobacco, fruits, vegetables; dairy products; forest products; fish

Exports: $315.6 billion f.o.b. (2004 est.)

Exports - commodities: motor vehicles and parts, industrial machinery, aircraft, telecommunications equipment; chemicals, plastics, fertilizers; wood pulp, timber, crude petroleum, natural gas, electricity, aluminum

Exports - partners: US 85.2%, Japan 2.1%, UK 1.6% (2004)

Imports: $256.1 billion f.o.b. (2004 est.)

Imports - commodities: machinery and equipment, motor vehicles and parts, crude oil, chemicals, electricity, durable consumer goods

Imports - partners: US 58.9%, China 6.8%, Mexico 3.8% (2004)

Economic aid - donor: ODA, $ 2 billion (2004)

Currency: Canadian dollar (CAD)

Currency code: CAD

Reserves of foreign exchange and gold: 36.27 billion (2003)

Exchange rates: Canadian dollars per US dollar – 1.3 (2004) 1.4 (2003), 1.57 (2002), 1.55 (2001), 1.49 (2000), 1.49 (1999)

Fiscal year: 1 April - 31 March

COMMUNICATIONS

Telephones - main lines in use: 19,950, 900 (2003)

Telephones - mobile cellular: 13,221,800 (2003)

Telephone system: *general assessment:* excellent service provided by modern technology

Domestic: domestic satellite system with about 300 earth stations *international:* country code - 1; 5 coaxial submarine cables; satellite earth stations - 5 Intelsat (4 Atlantic Ocean and 1 Pacific Ocean) and 2 Intersputnik (Atlantic Ocean region)

Radio broadcast stations: AM 245, FM 582, shortwave 6 (2004)

Television broadcast stations: 80 (plus many repeaters) (1997)

Internet country code: .ca

Internet hosts: 3,210,081 (2003)

Internet Service Providers (ISPs): 760 (2000 est.)

Internet users: 16.11 million (2002)

TRANSPORTAION

Railways: *total:* 48,909 km
standard gauge: 48,909 km 1.435-m gauge (2003)

Highways: *total:* 1,408,800 km
paved: 497,306 km (including 16,900 km of expressways)
unpaved: 911,494 km (2002)

Waterways: 3,000 km (including Saint Lawrence Seaway)

Pipelines: crude and refined oil 23,564 km; natural gas 74,980 km

Ports and harbors: Becancour (Quebec), Churchill, Halifax, Hamilton, Montreal, New Westminster, Prince Rupert, Quebec, Saint John (New Brunswick), St. John's (Newfoundland), Sept Isles, Sydney, Trois-Rivieres, Thunder Bay, Toronto, Vancouver, Windsor

Merchant marine: *total:* 119 ships (1,000 GRT or over) 1,784,229 GRT/2,657,499 DWT

By type: barge carrier 1, bulk 59, cargo 13, chemical tanker 6, combination bulk 2, combination ore/oil 1, passenger 2, passenger/cargo 1, petroleum tanker 18, rail car carrier 1,

Roll on/roll off 11, short-sea/passenger 3, specialized tanker 1

Registered in other countries: 43 (2003 est.)

Foreign-owned: Germany 3, Hong Kong 2, Monaco 18, United Kingdom 3, United States 2

Airports: 1,357 (2004est.)

Airports - with paved runways:

Total:	503
Over 3,047 m:	18
2,438 to 3,047 m:	16
914 to 1,523 m:	246
Under 914 m:	75 (2004 est.)
1,524 to 2,437 m:	150

Airports - with unpaved runways:

Total:	823
1,524 to 2,437 m:	67
914 to 1,523 m:	347
Under 914 m:	409 (2004 est.)
Heliports:	12 (2004 est.)

MILITARY

Military branches: Canadian Armed Forces: Land Forces Command, Maritime Command, Air Command

Military manpower - military age: 17 years of age (2004 est.)

Military manpower-availability: *males age 15-49:* 8,216,510 (2005 est.)

Military manpower - fit for military service:

Males age 16-49: 6,740,490 (2005 est.)

Military manpower - reaching military age annually: *males:* 223,821 (2005 est.)

Military expenditures - dollar figure:$9,801.7 million (2003)

Military expenditures - percent of GDP:1.1% (2003)

TRANSNATIONAL ISSUES

Disputes - international:

Managed maritime boundary disputes with the US at Dixon Entrance, Beaufort Sea, Strait of Juan de Fuca, and around the disputed Machias Seal Island and North Rock; uncontested dispute with Denmark over Hans Island sovereignty in the Kennedy Channel between Ellesmere Island and Greenland

Illicit drugs: illicit producer of cannabis for the domestic drug market and export to US; use of hydroponics technology permits growers to plant large quantities of high-quality marijuana indoors; transit point for heroin and cocaine entering the US market; vulnerable to narcotics money laundering because of its mature financial services sector

CANADIAN STUDENTS PERFORMANCE.

Canadian students are among top in the world survey. They are ranked fourth over-all in recent UNICEF report. Results reflects that immigrants do better in Canada then any other developed country offering immigration. According to UNICEF report following are the educational performance ranking in reading, math and science among 24 developed nations. They are the members of organization for economic cooperation.

1.   South Korea
2.   Japan
3.   Finland
4.   **Canada**
5.   Australia
6.   Austria
7.   United Kingdom
8.   Ireland
9.   Sweden
10. Czech Republic
11. New Zealand
12. France
13. Switzerland
14. Belgium
15. Iceland
16. Hungary
17. Norway
18. United States
19. Germany
20. Denmark
21. Spain
22. Italy
23. Greece
24. Portugal

Source: Canadian press

IMPORTANT **STATI**STICS **AB**OUT

CANADA

Population of Census Metropolitan Areas, (2001 Census Boundaries)					
	2000	**2001**	**2002**	**2003**	**2004**
	persons (thousands)				
Total census metropolitan areas	**19,332.2**	**19,959.7**	**20,285.3**	**20,526.2**	**20,754.8**
Toronto (Ont.)	4,747.2	4,883.8	5,020.4	5,114.5	5,203.6
Montréal (Que.)	3,471.3	3,507.4	3,547.1	3,577.4	3,607.2
Vancouver (B.C.)	2,040.3	2,076.1	2,111.3	2,140.6	2,160.0
Ottawa–Gatineau (Ont.–Que.)	1,078.5	1,102.9	1,118.8	1,131.6	1,142.7
Calgary (Alta.)	952.5	976.8	1,002.0	1,018.9	1,037.1
Edmonton (Alta.)	946.9	961.5	979.9	990.8	1,001.6
Quebec (Que.)	692.6	696.4	701.6	705.5	710.8
Hamilton (Ont.)	678.8	689.2	697.9	704.8	710.3
Winnipeg (Man.)	686.4	690.1	693.7	697.1	702.4
London (Ont.)	445.0	449.6	454.5	457.6	459.7
Kitchener (Ont.)	423.4	431.3	438.7	444.7	450.1
St. Catharines–Niagara (Ont.)	390.3	391.7	393.2	394.4	394.9
Halifax (N.S.)	366.3	369.1	373.8	376.9	379.8
Windsor (Ont.)	313.7	320.8	325.9	328.6	330.9
Victoria (B.C.)	321.8	325.4	326.8	328.2	330.2
Oshawa (Ont.)	301.8	308.5	315.8	324.0	332.0
Saskatoon (Sask.)	230.3	230.8	231.8	232.6	234.0
Regina (Sask.)	198.0	196.8	196.5	197.3	198.6
St. John's (N.L.)	175.9	176.2	177.5	178.7	179.9
Sherbrooke (Que.)	155.6	157.0	158.7	160.4	162.3
Greater Sudbury (Ont.)	162.2	161.5	161.0	161.1	161.1
Abbotsford (B.C.)[1]	'	SDR1DE	155.2	156.3	160.1
Kingston (Ont.)[1]	..	152.7	154.4	155.7	156.5
Saguenay (Que.)	159.4	157.8	156.2	155.0	154.2
Trois-Rivières (Que.)	140.6	140.1	140.0	140.4	141.2
Saint John (N.B.)	126.6	126.0	126.1	126.3	126.5
Thunder Bay (Ont.)	126.8	126.6	126.2	126.8	127.1

Note: Population as of July 1.

1. Abbotsford and Kingston became census metropolitan areas in 2001.

Source: Statistics Canada, CANSIM, table 051-0034 and Catalogue nos. 91-213-XIB and 91-213-XPB

Last modified: 2005-03-23.

19

Population By Mother Tongue, By Provinces And Territories (2001 Census)

	Canada	Newfoundland and Labrador	Prince Edward Island	Nova Scotia	New Brunswick
			number		
Total Population	29,639,035	508,080	133,385	897,570	719,710
Single responses[1]	29,257,885	507,425	132,855	893,195	713,770
English	17,352,315	499,750	125,125	832,660	465,170
French	6,703,325	2,110	5,665	34,025	236,665
Non-official languages	5,202,245	5,495	2,065	26,510	11,935
Chinese	853,745	520	130	2,125	1,215
Cantonese	322,315	50	0	425	190
Mandarin	101,790	25	20	115	105
Hakka	4,565	0	0	15	10
Chinese, n.o.s.	425,085	445	115	1,505	915
Italian	469,485	115	60	865	510
German	438,080	340	190	3,015	1,420
Polish	208,375	75	65	960	220
Spanish	245,495	55	55	700	510
Portuguese	213,815	105	15	355	150
Punjabi	271,220	90	0	275	80
Ukrainian	148,085	20	20	320	105
Arabic	199,940	215	145	4,035	535
Dutch	128,670	90	480	1,980	855
Tagalog (Pilipino)	174,060	130	20	335	150
Greek	120,360	35	0	1,110	165
Vietnamese	122,055	60	10	480	110
Cree	72,885	0	0	30	10
Inuktitut (Eskimo)	29,010	550	10	10	15
Other non-official languages	1,506,965	3,090	860	9,930	5,815
Multiple responses[2]	381,145	650	530	4,375	5,940
English and French	112,575	330	440	2,555	5,255
English and non-official language	219,860	310	85	1,660	550
French and non-official language	38,630	0	0	125	105
English, French and non-official language	10,085	10	0	35	35
Source: Statistics Canada, Census of population.					
Last modified: 2005-01-27.					

20

Population by mother tongue, by census metropolitan areas (2001 Census)					
	Toronto	Hamilton	St. Catharines–Niagara	Kitchener	London
	number				
Total Population	**4,647,955**	**655,055**	**371,400**	**409,765**	**427,215**
Single responses[1]	4,556,475	647,370	367,255	405,390	423,345
English	2,684,195	503,045	300,035	316,175	350,030
French	57,485	9,840	13,915	5,710	5,465
Non-official languages	1,814,795	134,485	53,295	83,515	67,850
Chinese	348,010	7,310	1,830	4,715	3,425
Cantonese	145,490	1,765	235	1,000	670
Mandarin	35,315	745	160	645	325
Hakka	2,085	0	15	20	0
Chinese, n.o.s.	165,120	4,795	1,420	3,055	2,420
Italian	195,960	22,680	13,760	2,165	4,075
German	43,665	7,720	7,550	15,090	4,835
Polish	79,875	11,565	4,485	5,525	7,015
Spanish	83,245	5,470	1,885	4,660	4,745
Portuguese	108,935	8,805	385	10,915	6,645
Punjabi	95,950	3,990	185	2,515	635
Ukrainian	26,675	3,680	2,335	765	1,375
Arabic	46,575	5,660	1,290	1,685	5,800
Dutch	13,565	5,895	4,490	2,090	5,300
Tagalog (Pilipino)	77,220	2,630	740	435	770
Greek	50,165	2,410	660	1,585	2,060
Vietnamese	36,555	2,810	500	2,935	1,720
Cree	110	20	10	10	0
Inuktitut (Eskimo)	10	0	0	0	0
Other non-official languages	608,280	43,840	13,200	28,415	19,435
Multiple responses[2]	91,480	7,685	4,150	4,375	3,865
English and French	7,810	1,265	1,315	600	795
English and non-official language	77,430	5,935	2,540	3,625	2,730
French and non-official language	4,585	370	210	95	225
English, French and non-official language	1,655	110	85	55	120

Source: Statistics Canada, Census of population.

Last modified: 2005-01-27.

Frequency of language of work in Toronto, by census metropolitan areas (2001 Census)					
Toronto	Total - Frequency of language of work	Only	Mostly	Equally	Regularly
	Number				
English	2,692,890	2,413,945	197,010	42,695	39,240
French	70,150	2,655	5,765	9,710	52,020
Chinese, not otherwise specified	42,565	12,940	7,735	4,110	17,780
Cantonese	33,375	10,495	6,770	2,770	13,340
Punjabi	15,230	2,325	1,485	2,615	8,805
German	4,075	110	220	580	3,165
Mandarin	8,015	2,090	1,420	655	3,850
Portuguese	23,560	4,335	3,590	2,880	12,755
Spanish	18,780	1,420	1,535	2,675	13,150
Vietnamese	5,275	910	570	575	3,220
Korean	6,820	1,265	1,470	675	3,410
Italian	32,285	1,890	2,030	4,630	23,735
Other languages	79,975	7,310	7,850	11,905	52,910
Source: Statistics Canada, Census of Population. Last modified: 2005-01-27					

Frequency of language of work in Montreal, by census metropolitan areas (2001 Census)					
Montréal	Total - Frequency of language of work	Only	Mostly	Equally	Regularly
	Number				
English	1,068,440	145,165	223,810	156,590	542,875
French	1,729,840	806,620	547,715	156,970	218,535
Chinese, not otherwise specified	7,275	2,885	1,150	1,095	2,145
Cantonese	1,020	395	175	50	400
Punjabi	1,140	200	95	285	560
German	1,615	45	160	240	1,170
Mandarin	470	125	175	30	140
Portuguese	3,365	240	395	635	2,095
Spanish	16,860	720	1,145	3,270	11,725
Vietnamese	2,195	555	300	325	1,015
Korean	290	65	45	15	165
Italian	18,165	885	1,485	4,535	11,260
Other languages	31,470	3,450	3,205	7,120	17,695
Source: Statistics Canada, Census of Population. Last modified: 2005-01-27					

Vancouver	Total - Frequency of language of work	Only	Mostly	Equally	Regularly
Frequency of language of work in Vancouver, by census metropolitan areas (2001 Census)					
		Number			
English	1,112,005	991,620	77,330	17,500	25,555
French	17,470	825	1,795	1,730	13,120
Chinese, not otherwise specified	38,215	11,110	7,515	4,050	15,540
Cantonese	31,475	9,930	6,130	2,560	12,855
Punjabi	18,920	4,970	2,055	3,040	8,855
German	2,575	135	240	355	1,845
Mandarin	14,400	3,705	2,900	1,400	6,395
Portuguese	610	95	75	50	390
Spanish	5,390	440	515	610	3,825
Vietnamese	3,360	900	465	480	1,515
Korean	5,230	1,325	1,155	490	2,260
Italian	1,580	15	120	195	1,250
Other languages	23,410	2,250	3,090	2,955	15,115

Source: Statistics Canada, Census of Population.
Last modified: 2005-01-27.

Definitions

Language of work: Refers to the language used most often at work by the individual at the time of the census. Other languages used at work on a regular basis are also collected.

Frequency of language of work: Indicates that a language is spoken at work by the respondent either most often or on a regular basis.

Only: Indicates that this is the only language spoken at work by the respondent.

Mostly: Indicates that this is the only language spoken most often at work while at least one other language is spoken on a regular basis by the respondent.

Equally: Indicates that this language has been reported with another language as the one spoken most often at work by the respondent.

Regularly: Indicates a language that was reported as being used on a regular basis at work. (A respondent must report a language spoken most often at work in order to have a language spoken regularly at work.)

Census metropolitan areas: Area consisting of one or more adjacent municipalities situated around a major urban core. To form a census metropolitan area, the urban core must have a population of at least 100,000.

23

Population projections for 2011 and 2016, at July 1

	2011			2016		
	Both sexes	Male	Female	Both sexes	Male	Female
	thousands			thousands		
All ages[1]	33,361.7	16,511.6	16,850.2	34,419.8	17,044.8	17,375.0
0–4	1,666.4	855.1	811.3	1,708.7	877.0	831.7
5–9	1,715.8	880.0	835.9	1,741.8	893.6	848.2
10–14	1,863.6	957.7	905.9	1,790.1	919.8	870.3
15–19	2,175.0	1,117.7	1,057.2	1,945.5	1,001.3	944.2
20–24	2,241.4	1,143.6	1,097.8	2,261.2	1,154.1	1,107.1
25–29	2,263.5	1,148.5	1,115.0	2,336.4	1,185.9	1,150.5
30–34	2,293.0	1,163.2	1,129.8	2,360.0	1,197.4	1,162.6
35–39	2,278.1	1,150.7	1,127.4	2,367.1	1,197.7	1,169.4
40–44	2,370.3	1,192.6	1,177.8	2,324.0	1,171.9	1,152.1
45–49	2,681.7	1,350.4	1,331.3	2,385.2	1,201.3	1,183.8
50–54	2,637.4	1,317.5	1,319.9	2,657.5	1,335.4	1,322.1
55–59	2,318.3	1,145.2	1,173.2	2,588.5	1,285.6	1,302.9
60–64	2,011.3	984.1	1,027.2	2,251.4	1,102.5	1,149.0
65–69	1,495.8	719.7	776.1	1,907.4	920.2	987.2
70–74	1,112.7	519.9	592.8	1,365.7	641.3	724.4
75–79	879.7	392.6	487.2	957.2	429.4	527.8
80–84	666.2	269.5	396.7	688.1	286.7	401.4
85–89	422.5	141.1	281.4	452.9	162.7	290.1
90 and over	269.0	62.6	206.4	331.0	80.7	250.2

Note: Figures represent the medium-growth projection and are based on 2000 population estimates.

1. Due to rounding, the totals may not always add up to the sum of the figures.

Source: Statistics Canada, CANSIM, table 052-0001.

Last Modified: 2005-02-01.

Population by religion, by provinces and territories (2001 Census)

	Canada	Quebec	Ontario	Manitoba	Saskatchewan
			number		
Total population	**29,639,035**	**7,125,580**	**11,285,550**	**1,103,700**	**963,150**
Catholic	12,936,905	5,939,715	3,911,760	323,690	305,390
Protestant	8,654,850	335,590	3,935,745	475,185	449,195
Christian Orthodox	479,620	100,375	264,055	15,645	14,280
Christian not included elsewhere	780,450	56,750	301,935	44,535	27,070
Muslim	579,640	108,620	352,530	5,095	2,230
Jewish	329,995	89,915	190,795	13,040	865
Buddhist	300,345	41,380	128,320	5,745	3,050
Hindu	297,200	24,525	217,555	3,835	1,585
Sikh	278,410	8,225	104,785	5,485	500
Eastern religions	37,550	3,425	17,780	795	780
Other religions	63,975	3,870	18,985	4,780	6,750
No religious affiliation	4,900,090	413,190	1,841,290	205,865	151,455

Source: Statistics Canada, Census of Population.
Last modified: 2005-01-25.

Population by religion, by provinces and territories (2001 Census)

	Canada	Alberta	British Columbia	Yukon
			number	
Total population	**29,639,035**	**2,941,150**	**3,868,875**	**28,520**
Catholic	12,936,905	786,360	675,320	6,015
Protestant	8,654,850	1,145,460	1,213,295	9,485
Christian Orthodox	479,620	44,475	35,655	150
Christian not included elsewhere	780,450	123,140	200,345	1,010
Muslim	579,640	49,040	56,220	60
Jewish	329,995	11,085	21,230	35
Buddhist	300,345	33,410	85,540	130
Hindu	297,200	15,965	31,500	10
Sikh	278,410	23,470	135,310	100
Eastern religions	37,550	3,335	9,970	190
Other religions	63,975	10,560	16,205	330
No religious affiliation	4,900,090	694,840	1,388,300	11,015

Source: Statistics Canada, Census of Population.
Last modified: 2005-01-25.

Consumer Price Index (monthly)

	February 2004	January 2005	February 2005	January 2005 to February 2005	February 2004 to February 2005
		1992 = 100		%	
Canada					
All items	**123.2**	**125.3**	**125.8**	**0.4**	**2.1**
Food	123.4	126.8	**126.6**	-0.2	2.6
Shelter	119.0	122.4	**122.6**	0.2	3.0
Household operations and furnishings	115.2	115.3	**115.5**	0.2	0.3
Clothing and footwear	104.0	100.0	**103.0**	3.0	-1.0
Transportation	141.9	146.3	**147.0**	0.5	3.6
Health and personal care	117.7	119.0	**119.7**	0.6	1.7
Recreation, education and reading	126.6	125.5	**126.3**	0.6	-0.2
Alcoholic beverages and tobacco products	141.1	145.1	**145.2**	0.1	2.9
Special aggregates					
All items excluding food	123.2	125.1	**125.7**	0.5	2.0
All items excluding energy	121.7	123.4	**123.7**	0.2	1.6
Energy	141.9	149.1	**152.3**	2.1	7.3

Sources: Statistics Canada, CANSIM, table 326-0001 and Catalogue nos. 62-001-XPB and 62-010-XIB.

Last Modified: 2005-03-22.

26

	January 2004	December 2004	January 2005	December 2004 to January 2005	January 2004 to January 2005
		1997 = 100		% change	
Canada	**119.9**	**125.8**	**126.1**	**0.2**	**5.2**
House only	127.1	134.1	**134.5**	0.3	5.8
Land only	106.0	110.0	**110.2**	0.2	4.0
Metropolitan areas (house and land)					
St. John's (N.L.)	114.5	122.3	**123.2**	0.7	7.6
Charlottetown (P.E.I.)	107.5	111.0	**111.0**	0.0	3.3
Halifax (N.S.)	121.1	121.8	**121.8**	0.0	0.6
Saint John, Fredericton and Moncton (N.B.)	103.6	107.2	**107.8**	0.6	4.1
Québec (Que.)	126.9	131.3	**131.8**	0.4	3.9
Montréal (Que.)	130.8	138.7	**139.4**	0.5	6.6
Ottawa–Gatineau (Ont.–Que.)[1]	141.7	151.0	**151.8**	0.5	7.1
Toronto and Oshawa (Ont.)	122.8	129.1	**129.2**	0.1	5.2
Hamilton (Ont.)	123.3	131.3	**131.6**	0.2	6.7
St. Catharines–Niagara (Ont.)	124.4	135.2	**136.0**	0.6	9.3
Kitchener (Ont.)[2]	122.4	129.3	**129.2**	-0.1	5.6
London (Ont.)	117.5	122.5	**123.3**	0.7	4.9
Windsor (Ont.)	102.1	103.0	**104.5**	1.5	2.4
Greater Sudbury and Thunder Bay (Ont.)[3]	96.7	99.0	**99.0**	0.0	2.4
Winnipeg (Man.)	116.4	125.6	**127.5**	1.5	9.5
Regina (Sask.)	128.5	136.9	**136.9**	0.0	6.5
Saskatoon (Sask.)	115.9	123.9	**123.9**	0.0	6.9
Edmonton (Alta.)	127.0	132.4	**132.6**	0.2	4.4
Calgary (Alta.)	135.3	140.2	**140.5**	0.2	3.8
Vancouver (B.C.)	99.0	102.7	**102.7**	0.0	3.7
Victoria (B.C.)	101.4	107.8	**108.4**	0.6	6.9

Construction price indexes, by selected metropolitan areas, New housing price indexes (monthly)

1. Formerly Ottawa–Hull.

2. Formerly Kitchener–Waterloo.

3. Formerly Sudbury–Thunder Bay.

Sources: Statistics Canada, CANSIM, table 327-0005 and Catalogue no. 62-007-XPB.

Last modified: 2005-03-09.

Employment by major industry groups, seasonally adjusted, by provinces (monthly)

	February 2004	January 2005	February 2005	January 2005 to February 2005	February 2004 to February 2005
	employment (thousands)			% change	
Canada – All industries	**15,844.4**	**16,057.4**	**16,084.0**	**0.2**	**1.5**
Goods-producing sector	3,943.5	4,037.0	4,006.7	-0.8	1.6
Agriculture	328.3	317.1	324.8	2.4	-1.1
Forestry, fishing, mining, oil and gas	281.6	297.2	300.6	1.1	6.7
Utilities	128.5	122.1	119.7	-2.0	-6.8
Construction	913.3	1,005.3	994.3	-1.1	8.9
Manufacturing	2,291.7	2,295.4	2,267.3	-1.2	-1.1
Services-producing sector	11,900.9	12,020.4	12,077.2	0.5	1.5
Trade	2,494.6	2,542.5	2,548.5	0.2	2.2
Transportation and warehousing	815.9	792.9	798.0	0.6	-2.2
Finance, insurance, real estate and leasing	923.0	985.1	989.2	0.4	7.2
Professional, scientific and technical services	1,002.5	1,030.1	1,032.9	0.3	3.0
Business, building and other support services[1]	627.4	622.4	635.8	2.2	1.3
Educational services	1,049.1	1,047.8	1,068.3	2.0	1.8
Health care and social assistance	1,724.1	1,722.1	1,732.0	0.6	0.5
Information, culture and recreation	735.2	721.0	736.0	2.1	0.1
Accommodation and food services	1,003.6	1,026.0	1,005.8	-2.0	0.2
Other services	702.1	708.5	707.6	-0.1	0.8
Public administration	823.3	821.9	823.2	0.2	0.0

1. Formerly Management of companies, administrative and other support services.

Source: Statistics Canada, CANSIM table 282-0088.

Last modified: 2005-03-11.

Average hourly wages of employees by selected characteristics and profession, unadjusted data, by provinces (monthly)

Canada	February 2004		February 2005		February 2004 to February 2005
	number of employees[1] (thousands)	average hourly wage ($)	number of employees[1] (thousands)	average hourly wage ($)	% change in hourly wage
15 years and over	**13,146.4**	**18.53**	**13,320.0**	**18.98**	**2.4**
15 to 24 years	2,157.9	10.56	2,210.6	10.79	2.2
25 to 54 years	9,550.1	20.08	9,569.9	20.57	2.4
55 years and over	1,438.3	20.18	1,539.5	20.85	3.3
Men	6,610.3	20.22	6,705.9	20.77	2.7
Women	6,536.1	16.82	6,614.1	17.17	2.1
Full-time	10,593.2	19.85	10,746.7	20.35	2.5
Part-time	2,553.2	13.05	2,573.3	13.28	1.8
Union coverage[2]	4,267.5	21.40	4,305.8	21.88	2.2
No union coverage[3]	8,878.9	17.15	9,014.2	17.60	2.6
Permanent job[4]	11,695.4	18.99	11,810.1	19.47	2.5
Temporary job[5]	1,451.0	14.84	1,509.9	15.13	2.0
Management occupations	947.5	29.12	912.3	30.14	3.5
Business, finance and administrative occupations	2,619.3	17.70	2,650.8	18.00	1.7
Natural and applied sciences and related occupations	860.7	26.28	927.7	26.79	1.9
Health occupations	796.8	21.98	823.6	22.05	0.3
Occupations in social science, education, government service and religion	1,133.7	24.41	1,169.7	24.37	-0.2
Occupations in art, culture, recreation and sport	291.3	18.58	309.7	19.85	6.8
Sales and service occupations	3,391.8	12.33	3,432.4	12.72	3.2
Trades, transport and equipment operators and related occupations	1,837.7	18.36	1,848.1	19.10	4.0
Occupations unique to primary industry	190.9	16.60	216.2	16.79	1.1
Occupations unique to processing, manufacturing and utilities	1,076.7	16.45	1,029.4	16.84	2.4

1. Those who work as employees of a private firm or business or the public sector.

2. Employees who are members of a union and employees who are not union members but who are covered by a collective agreement or a union contract.

3. Employees who are not members of a union or not covered by a collective agreement or a union contract.

4. A permanent job is one that is expected to last as long as the employee wants it, given that business conditions permit. That is, there is no pre-determined termination date.

5. A temporary job has a predetermined end date, or will end as soon as a specified project is completed. Includes seasonal jobs; temporary, term or contract jobs including work done through a temporary help agency; casual jobs; and other temporary work.

Sources: Statistics Canada, CANSIM tables 282-0069 and 282-0073.

Last modified: 2005-03-11.

Selected economic indicators, Canada and United States (monthly and quarterly)

	Latest period	Change from previous period	Annual change
Canada – Labour market [1,2]			
		thousands	%
Labour force(SA)	February 2005	17,293	0.2	1.2
Employment (SA)	February 2005	16,084	0.2	1.5
			%	
Unemployment rate (SA)	February 2005	7.0	0.0	-4.1
		$millions	%	
Gross Domestic Product at market prices (SAAR)[3] (Chained 1997 dollars)	4th quarter 2004	1,059,417	0.6	3.1
		index	%	
Consumer Price Index (1992=100)	February 2005	125.8	0.4	2.1
			%	
Stock market (closing quotations at month end)[4] (1975=1000)	February 2005	9,668.3	5.0	10.0

SA - seasonally adjusted

SAAR - seasonally adjusted at annual rates

1. Labour Force Survey for Canada, Payroll Survey for the United States.

2. Canadian estimates are drawn from a household survey while American estimates use a business survey and provide somewhat different coverage and definitions.

3. In Canadian dollars.

4. S&P/TSX Composite Index for Canada, and Dow Jones Composite Index for United States.

Sources: Statistics Canada, CANSIM, tables 176-0046, 282-0087, 326-0001, 379-0018, 451-0006, 451-0009 and 451-0010.

Last modified: 2005-03-22.

	Latest period	Change from previous period	Annual change
United States – Labour market [1,2]			
		thousands	%	
Labour force(SA)	February 2005	148,132	0.1	1.1
Employment (SA)	February 2005	140,144	-0.1	1.3
			%	
Unemployment rate (SA)	February 2005	5.4	3.8	-3.6
		$billion	%	
Gross Domestic Product at market prices (SAAR)[3] (Chained 2000 dollars)	3rd quarter 2004	10,891	1.0	4.0
		index	%	
Consumer Price index (1982-84=100)	February 2005	191.8	0.6	3.0
			%	
Stock market (closing quotations at quarter end)[3,4]	February 2005	10,766.2	2.6	1.7

SA - seasonally adjusted

SAAR - seasonally adjusted at annual rates

1. Labour Force Survey for Canada, Payroll Survey for the United States.

2. Canadian estimates are drawn from a household survey while American estimates use a business survey and provide somewhat different coverage and definitions.

3. In U.S. dollars.

4. S&P/TSX Composite Index for Canada, and Dow Jones Composite Index for United States.

Sources: Statistics Canada, CANSIM, tables 176-0046, 282-0087, 326-0001, 379-0018, 451-0006, 451-0009 and 451-0010.

Last modified: 2005-03-24.

Imports, exports and trade balance of goods on a balance-of-payments basis, by country or country grouping

	1999	2000	2001	2002	2003	2004
	\$ millions					
Exports	**369,034.9**	**429,372.2**	**420,657.1**	**413,795.3**	**400,010.0**	**430,357.6**
United States[1]	309,116.8	359,021.2	352,083.1	347,068.9	330,375.3	351,936.8
Japan	10,125.9	11,297.4	10,124.8	10,152.5	9,785.7	9,955.4
United Kingdom	6,002.9	7,273.3	6,912.9	6,184.8	7,697.8	9,447.1
Other European Economic Community countries	14,383.8	16,846.3	16,712.0	16,372.0	16,420.5	17,655.6
Other OECD[2]	9,947.2	12,059.0	12,129.2	12,174.1	12,668.6	14,211.6
Other countries[3]	19,458.4	22,875.1	22,695.0	21,843.0	23,062.1	27,151.0
Imports	**327,026.0**	**362,336.7**	**350,682.5**	**356,580.9**	**341,832.7**	**363,123.4**
United States[1]	249,485.3	266,511.1	254,949.4	255,093.2	239,870.7	249,981.3
Japan	10,592.2	11,729.8	10,572.0	11,732.9	10,644.9	10,029.4
United Kingdom	7,685.4	12,289.3	11,952.9	10,178.8	8,826.8	9,205.9
Other European Economic Community countries	20,765.8	21,136.5	23,197.0	25,860.8	25,982.7	27,052.5
Other OECD[2]	13,257.2	19,067.6	18,645.5	19,680.7	19,676.5	22,362.4
Other countries[3]	25,240.1	31,602.5	31,365.6	34,034.5	36,831.1	44,491.8
Balance	**42,008.9**	**67,035.5**	**69,974.6**	**57,214.4**	**58,177.3**	**67,234.2**
United States[1]	59,631.5	92,510.1	97,133.7	91,975.7	90,504.6	101,955.5
Japan	-466.3	-432.4	-447.2	-1,580.4	-859.2	-74.0
United Kingdom	-1,682.5	-5,016.0	-5,040.0	-3,994.0	-1,129.0	241.2
Other European Economic Community countries	-6,382.0	-4,290.2	-6,485.0	-9,488.8	-9,562.2	-9,396.9
Other OECD[2]	-3,310.0	-7,008.6	-6,516.3	-7,506.6	-7,007.9	-8,150.8
Other countries[3]	-5,781.7	-8,727.4	-8,670.6	-12,191.5	-13,769.0	-17,340.8

1. Includes also Puerto Rico and Virgin Islands.

2. Organisation for Economic Co-operation and Development excluding the United States, Japan, United Kingdom and the other European Economic Community.

3. Countries not included in the European Economic Community or the OECD.

Source: Statistics Canada, CANSIM, table 228-0003.

Last modified: 2005-02-10.

Immigrating to Canada and Finding Employment

Life expectancy at birth, by provinces

	Males	Females
	years	
Canada		
1920-22	59	61
1930-32	60	62
1940-42	63	66
1950-52	66	71
1960-62	68	74
1970-72	69	76
1980-82	72	79
1990-92	75	81
1990-92		
Newfoundland and Labrador	74	80
Prince Edward Island	73	81
Nova Scotia	74	80
New Brunswick	74	81
Quebec	74	81
Ontario	75	81
Manitoba	75	81
Saskatchewan	75	82
Alberta	75	81
British Columbia	75	81
Source: Statistics Canada.		
Last modified: 2005-02-17.		

33

Average weekly earnings, health care and social assistance, provinces and territories

	1999	2000	2001	2002	2003
	$\$^1$				
Canada	**544.79**	**562.39**	**581.34**	**605.12**	**612.92**
Newfoundland and Labrador	572.79	617.40	630.23	646.71	619.48
Prince Edward Island	521.90	542.49	569.18	599.49	602.10
Nova Scotia	508.16	525.72	555.00	581.66	599.76
New Brunswick	499.90	516.99	536.38	564.91	586.68
Quebec	529.55	543.53	562.77	587.15	591.40
Ontario	568.12	585.69	601.94	624.90	634.47
Manitoba	443.22	450.06	469.32	497.54	506.61
Saskatchewan	494.48	506.36	527.61	547.62	571.94
Alberta	543.64	565.06	590.89	615.84	617.75
British Columbia	574.97	595.07	612.49	634.62	642.55
Yukon	642.47	668.75	686.91	717.30	733.12
Northwest Territories including Nunavut	784.48	848.60	..	..	..
Northwest Territories	..	..	856.72	864.82	974.92
Nunavut	..	..	713.83	775.81	829.83
1. Unadjusted for seasonal variation.					
Source: Statistics Canada, CANSIM, table 281-0027 and Catalogue no. 72-002-XIB.					
Last Modified: 2005-02-18.					

Household size, by provinces and territories (2001 Census)

	2001				
	Canada	Quebec	Ontario	Manitoba	Saskatchewan
			number		
Total households[1]	**11,562,975**	**2,978,115**	**4,219,410**	**432,550**	**379,680**
1-person households	2,976,875	880,765	990,160	121,760	105,150
2-person households	3,772,430	981,660	1,327,325	139,535	127,270
3-person households	1,875,215	486,465	697,860	63,395	53,200
4-person households	1,843,800	427,695	737,405	64,185	54,430
5-person households	741,525	147,665	309,795	28,495	26,160
6-person or more households	353,135	53,860	156,870	15,185	13,470
Total persons in households	**29,522,300**	**7,097,850**	**11,254,730**	**1,090,625**	**956,630**
Average number of persons in household	**2.6**	**2.4**	**2.7**	**2.5**	**2.5**

Source: Statistics Canada, Census of Population.
Last modified : 2005-01-04.

Average weekly earnings (including overtime), educational and related services, by provinces and territories

	2000	2001	2002	2003
		$		
Canada	**673.88**	**694.30**	**725.27**	**747.88**
Newfoundland and Labrador	714.37	716.98	734.16	766.84
Prince Edward Island	705.42	699.68	709.18	708.35
Nova Scotia	606.49	653.34	697.12	693.92
New Brunswick	659.52	661.21	662.74	674.40
Quebec	663.50	708.53	745.02	780.89
Ontario	689.31	699.65	735.34	748.12
Manitoba	643.42	655.98	644.68	691.86
Saskatchewan	657.07	664.16	705.66	738.55
Alberta	620.22	638.99	679.87	713.51
British Columbia	712.46	729.71	740.92	759.71
Yukon	899.54	928.44	962.30	830.61

Note: Excludes owners or partners of unincorporated businesses and professional practices, the self-employed, unpaid family workers, persons working outside Canada, military personnel, and casual workers for whom a T4 is not required.
Source: Statistics Canada, CANSIM, table 281-0027 and Catalogue no. 72-002-X1B.
Last modified: 2005-02-18.

Average time spent on household activities, by sex

	1998		
	Total population[1]	Participants[2]	Participation rate[3]
	Both Sexes		
	hours per day		%
Activity group, total	**24.0**	**24.0**	**100**
Total work	**7.8**	**8.0**	**98**
Paid work and education	4.2	8.3	51
Paid work and related activites	3.6	8.3	44
Paid work	3.3	7.7	43
Activities related to paid work	0.0	0.6	8
Commuting	0.3	0.8	38
Education and related activities	**0.6**	**6.2**	**9**
Unpaid work	**3.6**	**3.9**	**91**
Household work and related activities	3.2	3.6	90
Cooking and washing up	0.8	1.0	74
Housekeeping	0.7	1.7	41
Maintenance and repair	0.2	2.5	6
Other household work	0.4	1.3	30
Shopping for goods and services	0.8	1.9	43
Child care	0.4	2.2	20
Civic and voluntary work	0.3	1.9	18
Personal care	10.4	10.4	100
Night sleep	8.1	8.1	100
Meals (excluding restaurant meals)	1.1	1.2	92
Other personal activities	1.3	1.3	95
Free time	**5.8**	**5.9**	**97**
Socializing including restaurant meals	1.9	2.9	66
Restaurant meals	0.3	1.6	19
Socializing in homes	1.3	2.4	55
Other socializing	0.3	2.6	12
Television, reading and other passive leisure	2.7	3.2	85
Watching television	2.2	2.8	77
Reading books, magazines, newspapers	0.4	1.3	32
Other passive leisure	0.1	1.1	9
Sports, movies and other entertainment events	0.2	2.7	6
Active leisure	1.0	2.4	40
Active sports	0.5	2.0	24
Other active leisure	0.5	2.3	22

Note: Averaged over a seven-day week.

1. The average number of hours per day spent on the activity for the entire population aged 15 years and over (whether or not the person reported the activity).

2. The average number of hours per day spent on the activity for the population that reported the activity.

3. The proportion of the population that reported spending some time on the activity.

Source: Statistics Canada, CANSIM, table 113-0001 . Last modified: 2004-09-02.

Average income after tax by economic family types

	1998	1999	2000	2001	2002
	\$ constant 2002				
Economic families[1], two people or more	54,600	55,800	57,600	60,300	60,500
Elderly families[2]	40,000	41,600	41,200	42,700	43,400
Married couples only	38,700	40,500	39,900	41,500	42,000
All other elderly families	44,700	45,200	45,700	47,300	48,400
Non-elderly families[3]	56,900	58,100	60,200	63,100	63,200
Married couples only	54,500	53,900	54,800	59,300	59,000
No earner	26,600	27,100	27,300	30,900	28,800
One earner	43,600	44,500	43,700	48,100	45,800
Two earners	61,800	60,800	61,400	65,500	65,700
Two parent families with children[4]	60,500	62,100	64,300	67,100	67,700
No earner	21,700	21,400	20,900	23,500	24,200
One earner	45,800	46,000	45,900	48,200	49,900
Two earners	61,600	62,500	64,900	67,000	67,200
Three or more earners	75,000	78,400	81,600	84,500	83,800
Married couples with other relatives	75,400	78,600	82,200	83,700	82,700
Lone-parent families[4]	29,500	29,900	32,600	34,100	33,000
Male lone-parent families	40,600	39,100	42,200	41,200	42,100
Female lone-parent families	27,500	28,200	30,600	32,500	30,800
No earner	15,500	16,100	15,600	16,600	15,800
One earner	28,400	28,900	30,400	31,600	30,400
Two or more earners	43,900	43,400	48,000	49,600	44,400
All other non-elderly families	51,300	52,400	53,700	56,400	58,000
Unattached individuals	22,800	23,600	24,100	25,300	25,900
Elderly male	24,300	23,900	23,200	25,200	24,600
Non-earner	21,800	22,300	21,400	23,000	22,500
Earner	38,700	33,200	31,500	35,200	32,400
Elderly female	19,800	19,900	20,300	21,400	21,900
Non-earner	19,200	19,400	19,600	20,500	21,500
Earner	27,400	26,900	28,600	31,700	26,800
Non-elderly male	25,200	25,700	27,300	28,200	28,400
Non-earner	9,600	9,300	9,200	10,800	10,100
Earner	28,200	28,700	30,000	30,800	31,300
Non-elderly female	21,200	23,000	22,600	23,900	25,200
Non-earner	9,900	9,600	9,500	11,000	11,300
Earner	24,700	27,000	26,200	27,200	28,300

Note: Average income after tax is total income, which includes government transfers, less income tax.

1. An economic family is a group of individuals sharing a common dwelling unit who are related by blood, marriage (including common-law relationships) or adoption.

2. Families in which the major income earner is 65 years of age and over.

3. Families in which the major income earner is less than 65 years of age.

4. With children less than 18 years of age.

Source: Statistics Canada, CANSIM, table 202-0603 and Catalogue no. 75-202-XIE. , Last modified: 2005-01-21.

Average household expenditures, by provinces and territories

	2003			
	Canada		**Newfoundland and Labrador**	
Household Characteristics				
Estimated number of households	11,803,420		193,690	
	Average expenditure per household	**Households reporting expenditures**	**Average expenditure per household**	**Households reporting expenditures**
	$	%	$	%
Total expenditures	**61,152**	**100.0**	**48,919**	**100.0**
Total current consumption	43,755	100.0	36,196	100.0
Food	6,791	100.0	6,147	100.0
Shelter	11,584	99.9	7,593	99.7
Household operation	2,870	100.0	2,564	100.0
Household furnishings and equipment	1,751	94.0	1,605	95.2
Clothing	2,436	99.1	2,442	98.5
Transportation	8,353	98.1	7,140	94.8
Health care	1,588	97.2	1,344	97.0
Personal care	834	99.4	722	99.9
Recreation	3,591	98.0	3,266	97.3
Reading materials and other printed matter	283	84.1	201	80.2
Education	1,007	44.5	790	43.5
Tobacco products and alcoholic beverages	1,489	84.7	1,470	85.8
Games of chance (net amount)	272	73.9	281	75.5
Miscellaneous	904	90.2	631	79.8
Personal income taxes	12,370	91.9	8,723	79.2
Personal insurance payments and pension contributions	3,505	81.2	2,986	73.9
Gifts of money and contributions	1,522	73.1	1,015	86.5

Source: Statistics Canada, CANSIM, table 203-0001.

Last modified: 2005-01-24.

Experienced labour force 15 years and over by industry, by census metropolitan areas (2001 Census)					

	2001				
	Toronto	Hamilton	St. Catharines–Niagara	Kitchener	London
	number				
Total labour force	**2,564,585**	**345,505**	**191,930**	**232,860**	**231,080**
All industries	2,522,020	340,295	189,285	229,885	227,010
Agriculture, forestry, fishing and hunting	9,425	4,320	5,435	2,160	4,200
Mining and oil and gas extraction	2,660	475	460	195	230
Utilities	15,765	1,825	1,435	860	1,000
Construction	124,395	19,565	10,575	12,970	11,970
Manufacturing	395,970	64,775	32,845	59,810	36,500
Wholesale trade	151,870	17,385	6,950	10,980	9,825
Retail trade	272,680	39,940	23,530	24,895	26,575
Transportation and warehousing	123,135	15,090	8,630	9,400	10,045
Information and cultural industries	100,760	8,005	2,940	4,650	5,010
Finance and insurance	177,210	15,500	5,875	12,365	12,075
Real estate and rental and leasing	56,890	6,125	2,445	3,190	4,045
Professional, scientific and technical services	246,655	17,990	7,150	12,570	11,435
Management of companies and enterprises	4,840	340	165	1,045	140
Administrative and support, waste management and remediation services	121,490	14,070	8,150	8,030	10,880
Educational services	143,985	23,710	11,695	16,200	17,145
Health care and social assistance	189,450	35,735	16,810	17,110	28,130
Arts, entertainment and recreation	47,870	5,990	7,960	3,400	3,900
Accommodation and food services	141,560	20,550	19,250	12,895	15,190
Other services (except public administration)	110,745	16,255	9,295	10,280	11,290
Public administration	84,655	12,645	7,695	6,880	7,425
Source: Statistics Canada, Census of Population.					
Last modified: 2005-02-17.					

39

Employed labour force by place of work, by provinces and territories (2001 Censuses)

	2001				
	Place of work status				
	Total	Worked at home	Worked outside Canada	No fixed workplace address	Usual place of work
	number				
Canada	**14,695,130**	**1,175,760**	**68,520**	**1,273,450**	**12,177,410**
Newfoundland and Labrador	188,815	11,570	590	15,865	160,790
Prince Edward Island	63,935	5,690	185	6,100	51,965
Nova Scotia	402,295	26,990	2,260	40,765	332,280
New Brunswick	325,335	20,215	1,520	30,050	273,545
Quebec	3,434,265	224,685	9,245	225,685	2,974,650
Ontario	5,713,900	406,230	33,930	466,945	4,806,790
Manitoba	549,990	54,310	1,605	43,335	450,730
Saskatchewan	479,735	86,500	870	40,370	352,000
Alberta	1,608,840	165,865	6,020	189,920	1,247,035
British Columbia	1,883,975	171,390	12,235	210,510	1,489,835
Yukon	15,860	1,065	35	1,605	13,155
Northwest Territories	18,810	795	15	1,435	16,565
Nunavut	9,380	455	10	855	8,065

Source: Statistics Canada, Census of Population.

Last modified: 2004-09-01.

40

Employed labour force by place of work, by census metropolitan areas (1996 and 2001 Censuses)

	2001				
	Place of work status				
	Total	Worked at home	Worked outside Canada	No fixed workplace address	Usual place of work
	number				
St. John's	80,090	4,015	335	5,695	70,040
Halifax	182,480	10,755	1,510	15,765	154,450
Saint John	55,865	2,645	170	4,930	48,120
Saguenay	65,520	2,685	65	3,915	58,850
Québec	343,745	17,895	840	22,130	302,875
Sherbrooke	74,960	4,430	165	4,675	65,685
Trois-Rivières	60,950	3,205	140	3,765	53,845
Montréal	1,678,715	93,120	5,325	107,745	1,472,530
Ottawa-Gatineau	561,870	34,435	2,365	35,275	489,795
Oshawa	150,690	7,860	400	11,770	130,660
Toronto	2,413,100	152,285	12,755	201,450	2,046,610
Hamilton	325,795	19,580	1,310	26,505	278,400
St. Catharines-Niagara	180,470	10,735	1,755	12,955	155,030
Kitchener	220,080	12,450	825	15,895	190,905
London	215,690	14,600	970	18,420	181,710
Windsor	149,810	5,245	6,975	7,645	129,950
Greater Sudbury	70,530	3,035	115	5,730	61,645
Thunder Bay	57,065	2,570	165	4,545	49,775
Winnipeg	345,730	17,035	955	25,655	302,085
Regina	100,465	5,945	235	7,515	86,780
Saskatoon	114,615	8,260	335	10,075	95,950
Calgary	540,370	38,600	2,725	61,085	437,965
Edmonton	503,355	32,325	1,810	54,130	415,090
Vancouver	995,320	80,285	9,040	102,590	803,400
Victoria	155,730	14,390	820	15,705	124,810
Source: Statistics Canada, Census of Population.					
Last modified: 2004-09-01.					

Exchange rates, interest rates, money supply and stock prices

	2000	2001	2002	2003	2004
	US$ per $ Canadian				
Exchange rate	**0.6732**	**0.6456**	**0.6368**	**0.7138**	**0.7685**
	%				
Selected interest rates					
Bank rate (last Wednesday of the month)	5.77	4.31	2.71	3.19	2.50
Prime business loan rate	7.27	5.81	4.21	4.69	4.00
Chartered bank typical mortgage rate					
1 year	7.85	6.14	5.17	4.84	4.59
3 years	8.17	6.88	6.28	5.82	5.65
5 years	8.35	7.40	7.02	6.39	6.23
Consumer loan rate	11.71	10.06	9.36	9.51	9.24
90 day prime corporate paper rate	5.71	3.87	2.66	2.94	2.31
	$ millions				
Money supply					
Gross M1	106,155	119,001	132,968	143,632	161,404
M2	491,645	517,448	550,030	581,721	617,337
M3	666,880	702,436	744,492	788,196	859,559
	1975 = 1000				
Toronto Stock Exchange 300 Index	**9,607.74**	**7,731.72**	**7,036.18**	**7,161.60**	**8,646.14**

Sources: Statistics Canada, CANSIM, tables 176-0036, 176-0043, 176-0047 and 176-0064; Bank of Canada, *Bank of Canada Review*, Ottawa.

Last modified: 2005-03-18.

TD Canada Trust Exchange Rate as of Friday July 29 16:09:08 EDT, 2005

Client Buys (Pays Canadian)		**Client Sells (Receives Canadian)**
US Dollar	1.24	1.197
Sterling Pound	2.188	2.110
Euro	1.521	1.443

Employment by industry

	2000	2001	2002	2003	2004
			thousands		
All industries	**14,758.6**	**14,946.7**	**15,307.9**	**15,665.1**	**15,949.7**
Goods-producing sector	3,826.0	3,779.4	3,881.4	3,930.6	3,992.7
Agriculture	373.7	322.7	324.2	328.3	324.1
Forestry, fishing, mining, oil and gas	276.0	279.6	271.0	281.1	285.7
Utilities	113.7	122.3	131.0	130.4	133.0
Construction	808.7	825.4	864.3	907.4	952.8
Manufacturing	2,253.9	2,229.5	2,291.0	2,283.4	2,297.0
Services-producing sector	10,932.6	11,167.3	11,426.5	11,734.4	11,957.0
Trade	2,303.3	2,363.9	2,401.6	2,457.6	2,503.6
Transportation and warehousing	773.8	779.3	760.3	789.3	809.3
Finance, insurance, real estate and leasing	861.2	878.2	891.1	912.2	955.0
Professional, scientific and technical services	937.4	985.5	985.5	1,000.7	1,010.1
Business, building and other support services[1]	533.0	535.7	579.6	607.9	630.1
Educational services	973.5	981.3	1,008.5	1,029.3	1,038.4
Health care and social assistance	1,499.6	1,543.1	1,622.2	1,683.2	1,736.7
Information, culture and recreation	664.9	711.6	714.2	714.2	732.7
Accommodation and food services	935.4	944.3	984.9	1,006.8	1,006.8
Other services	685.6	665.1	685.5	713.0	705.1
Public administration	765.0	779.2	793.0	820.3	829.2

1. Formerly Management of companies, administrative and other support services.

Source: Statistics Canada, CANSIM, table 282-0008 and Catalogue no. 71F0004XCB.

Last modified: 2005-02-17.

Crimes by type of offence

	1999	2000	2001	2002	2003
	rate per 100,000 population				
All incidents	8,530.4	8,432.6	8,453.7	8,507.0	8,884.8
Criminal Code offences (excluding traffic offences)	7,751.7	7,666.5	7,655.4	7,708.3	8,132.4
Crimes of violence	958.2	984.4	983.8	969.2	962.8
Homicide	1.8	1.8	1.8	1.9	1.7
Attempted murder	2.3	2.5	2.3	2.2	2.2
Assaults (level 1 to 3)[1]	728.0	761.6	763.9	751.6	746.5
Sexual assault	78.5	78.2	77.5	78.1	74.1
Other sexual offences	10.9	10.2	8.7	8.8	8.0
Robbery	94.5	88.1	88.0	85.0	89.6
Other crimes of violence[2]	41.3	41.3	41.1	40.8	40.7
Property crimes	4,275.7	4,080.9	4,003.5	3,974.5	4,121.4
Breaking and entering	1,046.1	955.9	900.9	878.7	899.5
Motor vehicle theft	530.8	522.4	543.5	516.3	540.7
Theft over $5,000	74.0	69.6	67.2	63.2	63.6
Theft $5,000 and under	2,231.2	2,160.5	2,126.3	2,127.8	2,220.4
Possession of stolen goods	96.4	93.0	86.9	95.8	103.6
Frauds	297.2	279.6	278.8	292.8	293.5
Other Criminal Code offences	2,517.9	2,601.2	2,668.1	2,764.6	3,048.3
Criminal Code offences (traffic offences)	387.0	366.4	387.6	374.9	366.3
Impaired driving	282.9	258.2	266.7	255.2	243.6
Other traffic offences[3]	125.4	124.9	123.0	122.9	122.7
Federal statutes	391.7	399.8	410.7	423.8	386.2
Drugs	263.6	287.0	288.2	295.8	271.8
Other federal statutes	128.1	112.7	122.5	127.9	114.4

1. "Assault level 1" is the first level of assault. It constitutes the intentional application of force without consent, attempt or threat to apply force to another person, and openly wearing a weapon (or an imitation) and accosting or impeding another person. "Assault with weapon or causing bodily harm" is the second level of assault. It constitutes assault with a weapon, threats to use a weapon (or an imitation), or assault causing bodily harm. "Aggravated assault level 3" is the third level of assault. It applies to anyone who wounds, maims, disfigures or endangers the life of complainant.
2. Includes unlawfully causing bodily harm, discharging firearms with intent, abductions, assaults against police officers, assaults against other peace or public officers and other assaults.
3. Includes dangerous operation of motor vehicle, boat, vessel or aircraft, dangerous operation of motor vehicle, boat, vessel or aircraft causing bodily harm or death, driving motor vehicle while prohibited and failure to stop or remain.

Source: Statistics Canada, CANSIM, table 252-0013.

Last Modified: 2004-11-18.

Weather conditions in capital and major cities

Definitions and notes	Annual Average		
	Snowfall	Total precipitation	Wet days
	cm	mm	number
St. John's	322.1	1,482	217
Charlottetown	338.7	1,201	177
Halifax	261.4	1,474	170
Fredericton	294.5	1,131	156
Québec	337.0	1,208	178
Montréal	214.2	940	162
Ottawa	221.5	911	159
Toronto	135.0	819	139
Winnipeg	114.8	504	119
Regina	107.4	364	109
Edmonton	129.6	461	123
Calgary	135.4	399	111
Vancouver	54.9	1,167	164
Victoria	46.9	858	153
Whitehorse	145.2	269	122
Yellowknife	143.9	267	118
International comparisons			
Beijing, China	30	623	66
Cairo, Egypt	...	22	5
Capetown, South Africa	...	652	95
London, England	...	594	107
Los Angeles, U.S.A.	...	373	39
Mexico City, Mexico	...	726	133
Moscow, Russia	161	575	181
New Delhi, India	...	715	47
Paris, France	...	585	164
Rio de Janeiro, Brazil	...	1,093	131
Rome, Italy	...	749	76
Sydney, Australia	...	1,205	152
Tokyo, Japan	20	1,563	104
Washington, D.C.	42	991	112

Sources: For Canada, *Climate Normals 1961–1990*, Climate Information Branch, Canadian Meteorological Centre, Environment Canada; for International data, *Climate Normals 1951–1980.*

Last modified: 2005-02-16.

Top 15 countries of origin for overnight visitors to Canada

	2003		
	Overnight trips		
Country of origin	Trips	Nights spent	Spending in Canada
		thousands	C$ millions
U.S.A.	14,232	56,723	7,288
United Kingdom	691	8,961	945
France	275	4,180	365
Germany	253	3,942	345
Japan	250	2,994	348
Australia	136	1,765	206
South Korea	133	3,341	222
Mexico	132	2,101	206
Netherlands	104	1,499	124
Hong Kong	87	1,623	106
Switzerland	83	1,605	150
Mainland China	77	2,329	143
Taiwan	68	1,079	78
India	67	1,297	57
Italy	57	727	68

Source: Statistics Canada, Culture, Tourism and the Centre for Education Statistics.
Last modified: 2004-10-15.

Top 15 countries visited by Canadians

	2003		
	Overnight visits		
Country visited	Visits	Nights spent	Spending in country
		thousands	C$ millions
U.S.A.	12,666	97,333	8,075
Mexico	716	7,375	790
United Kingdom	684	8,624	821
France	509	6,468	671
Cuba	495	4,408	451
Dominican Republic	415	3,983	403
Germany	331	3,297	278
Italy	248	3,279	384
Netherlands	165	1,401	110
Spain	154	2,017	199
Switzerland	125	911	98
Japan	122	1,643	193
Mainland China	115	2,245	197
Austria	109	586	77
Australia	99	2,685	195

Source: Statistics Canada, Culture, Tourism and the Centre for Education Statistics.
Last modified: 2004-10-15.

Household Internet use at home by Internet activity

	1999	2000	2001	2002	2003
	% of all households				
E-mail	26.3	37.4	46.1	48.9	52.1
Electronic banking	8.0	14.7	21.6	26.2	30.8
Purchasing goods and services	5.5	9.6	12.7	15.7	18.6
Medical or health information	15.6	22.9	30.1	32.8	35.6
Formal education/training	9.2	19.0	22.9	24.3	24.9
Government information	12.7	18.9	25.6	29.2	32.2
General browsing	24.3	36.2	44.3	46.1	48.5
Playing games	12.3	18.2	24.4	25.7	27.9
Chat groups	7.5	11.0	13.7	14.0	14.4
Other Internet services	10.0	17.7	21.1	24.8	23.5
Obtain and save music	7.8	17.8	23.3	24.3	20.6
Listen to the radio	5.0	9.3	12.3	12.3	13.1
Find sports related information	..	17.3	22.1	23.8	24.6
Financial information	..	18.5	22.8	23.5	25.0
View the news	..	20.4	26.2	27.2	30.2
Travel information/arrangements	..	21.9	27.4	30.4	33.6
Search for a job	..	12.2	16.2	18.0	19.6

Source: Statistics Canada, CANSIM, table 358-0006 and Catalogue no. 56F0003X (free).
Last modified: 2005-03-18.

Home Ownership Rate by Ethno-Racial Group in the City of Toronto, 1996

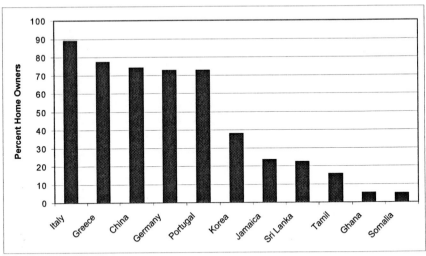

Source: Ornstein 2000

Home Ownership Rate of Immigrants Living in the Toronto CMA in 1996 by Period of Immigration

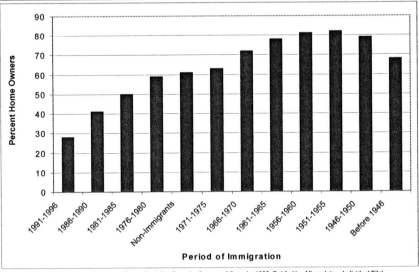

Source: Murdie and Teixeira, 2001 (Original Data - Statistics Canada, Census of Canada, 1996, Public Use Micro data – Individual File).

HOW TO **IMMIG**RATE

TO

CANADA

INTERNATIONAL CONTEXTS

The international environment has changed significantly in the wake of the terrorist attacks in the United States. There is a heightened awareness of the sophistication and geographic reach of terrorist activities, and the need to ensure that Canada's immigration and refugee protection programs are not seen as gateways to these activities in North America.

It is difficult to predict how the current campaign against terrorism will affect the global movement of people. Other factors that influence Canada's ability to attract and process immigrants and non-immigrants in an efficient and timely manner include the following:

- a significant increase in immigrant and non-immigrant applicants to Canada, including refugee claimants;
- a shift in source countries;
- the number of people on the move worldwide; and
- international skilled workers.

> **About 150 million people are on the move at any given time.**

A total of 235,808 people immigrated to Canada in 2004, a seven percent increase over the previous year. This number was within the 2004 planning target range of 220,000 to 245,000 new immigrants. Fifty-seven percent of immigrants were in the economic class. The provincial nominee program boosted immigration to a number of provinces that traditionally attract small immigration flows. For example, Manitoba's provincial nominee program helped boost immigration to the province to over 7,400 immigrants in 2004, the highest recorded level in the most recent 15-year period. Nevertheless, more than half of all immigrants continued to be destined to Ontario.

Thirty-eight percent of arriving immigrants between 25 and 64 years of age had a bachelor's degree as their highest level of education. At this level of education, there were an almost equal number of men and women immigrants. At the two extremes of the educational levels, however, women were overrepresented at the lower end and underrepresented at the higher end.

There has been a noticeable trend toward increasing skill levels among immigrants over the most recent 15-year period. Among immigrants 15 years of age or older whose skill level could be classified, 58% were professionals (skill level A), compared to only 17% in 1990. Together, the two lowest skill levels (intermediate and clerical, and elemental and labour) accounted for only 10% of immigrants in 2004 compared to 37% in 1990.

In 2004, 17% of all immigrants over the age of 15 (31,798) were classified as non-workers (a category that excludes students). Ninety-seven percent of these non-workers were female and a third declared no knowledge of English or French on landing. A high proportion (64%) was between the ages of 25 and 44.

The leading mother tongue of 2004 newcomers was Mandarin, followed by English and Arabic. A greater number of immigrants declared an ability to speak French so that in that year, one in seven immigrants had some knowledge of French on arrival in Canada.

Thirty-seven percent of new immigrants had no knowledge of English or French at arrival, but almost a third of these were children under the age of 10.

COUNTRIES OF ORIGIN

For the seventh year running, China and India were, respectively, the first and second leading countries of origin of new immigrants to Canada. In 2004, China accounted for 15% of immigrants (36,410) and India, for 11% (25,568). The Philippines (13,299) and Pakistan (12,796) were the third and fourth source countries, each accounting for around 5% of immigrants. The United States followed, with almost 7,500 immigrants or 3% of the national total.

Canada draws its immigrant population from a great number of countries, but over time, we have seen significant shifts in primary source countries. In 1990, the top two source countries were Hong Kong and Poland, which together accounted for some 20 percent of the movement in that year. In 2000, China and India were the two primary source countries, making up close to 30 percent of the movement.

Behind the interest in Canada as a migrant destination is the increasing worldwide mobility of people. It has been estimated that about 150 million people are on the move at any given time. Some flee persecution, civil strife, or severe political or economic upheaval; others are forced to leave as a result of natural disasters or environmental degradation; still others move primarily to seek a better way of life for themselves and their families. In short, migration as an aspect of globalization is accelerating. If it wishes to maximize the benefits of this movement, Canada cannot afford to stand still. We must proactively plan for the future.

In 2002, according to Statistics Canada, 328,302 babies were born in Canada. In 11 of the 12 years prior to 2002, Canadian birth numbers showed marked declines. Also in 2002 the number of live births in Canada fell to 10.5 babies for every 1,000 women. That actual births to women ratio was the lowest since 1921, the first year in which national statistics were kept.

The birth rate in Canada has fallen by 25% in the past decade. In fact the nation's fertility rate of 2.1 simply to replace and maintain its existing population: without immigration, without an influx of new Canadians, Canadian population would shrink.

The key to sustaining a robust immigration program hinges on striking the right balance between maximizing the benefits of immigration, such as economic growth and social development, and sustaining public confidence in the system by ensuring, through effective enforcement, that its generosity is not abused. Canada is not alone in facing increased pressures from irregular migration, including human trafficking and smuggling.

Currently, Canada, the United States, Australia and New Zealand are the only countries that encourage and plan for immigration. However, greater international economic integration and competition, ageing work forces and declining birth rates are leading countries of the European Union and Japan to reconsider their approach to the planned admission of foreign workers. It is anticipated that in the future, Canada will face serious competition in recruiting the highly skilled as most developed countries struggle with skill shortages and the effects of an ageing population.

For details about every class of immigrants please visit following link:

http://www.cic.gc.ca/english/monitor/issue09/05-overview.html

HOW ARE IMMIGRANTS CHOSEN ?

Since this book is designed to focus on skilled worker class immigrants who are the major source of immigration to Canada, so we will only touch other classes but master the skilled worker class.

Immigrating to Canada

Every year, Canada welcomes thousands of new residents to Canada. As someone interested in building a home for yourself in Canada, you have a number of options when applying for permanent residence status. Canada also fulfils its international humanitarian commitments by accepting a certain number of refugees each year. Read about these programs and decide which class suits you and your family best.

Skilled Worker Class Immigration

Canada values the skills and experiences that foreign professionals and workers bring with them. Check to see if your skills and experience qualify you to come to Canada as a skilled worker.

Business Class Immigration

Canada has a strong economic culture. If you have experience running or investing in businesses, you may qualify to come to Canada as a business immigrant. You can learn more by visiting this site. http://www.cic.gc.ca/english/business/index.html

Who is a Business Immigrant ?

Business immigrants are people who can invest in, or start businesses in Canada and are expected to support the development of a strong and prosperous Canadian economy. The Business Immigration Program seeks to attract people experienced in business to Canada.

Business immigrants are selected based on their ability to become economically established in Canada.

There are three classes of business immigrants:

1) Investors

The Immigrant Investor Program seeks to attract experienced persons and capital to Canada. Investors must demonstrate business experience, a minimum net worth of CDN $800,000 and make an investment of CDN $400,000.

2) Entrepreneurs

The Entrepreneur Program seeks to attract experienced persons that will own and actively manage businesses in Canada that will contribute to the economy and create jobs. Entrepreneurs must demonstrate business experience, a minimum net worth of CDN $300,000 and are subject to conditions upon arrival in Canada.

3) Self-employed persons

Self-employed persons must have the intention and ability to create their own employment. They are expected to contribute to the cultural, artistic or athletic life of Canada. They may create their own employment by purchasing and managing a farm in Canada.

Canada has Business Immigration Centres (BICs) specially staffed to assess potential business immigrants. You may wish to mail your application directly to a BIC to obtain a more specialized processing of your application. To do so, mail your completed application to one of the centres in Beijing, Berlin, Buffalo, Damascus, Hong Kong, London, Paris, Seoul and Singapore.

The application forms and guide can be downloaded from this site. *http://www.cic.gc.ca/english/applications/business.html*

Family Class Immigration

Family class immigration reunites families in Canadian homes. Learn how to sponsor your family member or come to Canada as a member of the family class from this website. *http://www.cic.gc.ca/english/sponsor/index.html*

International Adoption

Adopting children from abroad can be a long process. This is to protect children's rights. Learn about what you need to do to bring an adoptive child to Canada. You can learn more by visiting this website. *http://www.cic.gc.ca/english/sponsor/adopt-1.html*

Provincial Nomination

Most provinces in Canada have an agreement with the Government of Canada that allows them to play a more direct role in selecting immigrants who wish to settle in that province. If you wish to immigrate to one of Canada's provinces as a Provincial Nominee, you must first apply to the province where you wish to settle. The province will consider your application based on their immigration needs and your genuine intention to settle there.

Before applying to immigrate to Canada, Provincial Nominees must complete the provincial nomination process. Contact the province for more information.

Provincial Nominee Program - Contact Information

If you wish to come to Canada as a Provincial Nominee, you must first apply to the province to be nominated for immigration. Citizenship and Immigration Canada will process your application for permanent residence after the province sends a Certificate of Provincial Nomination to the <u>Visa Office</u> where you will send your forms.

Contact the provinces for more information on their Provincial Nominee Programs.

Alberta
Provincial Nominee Program
Economic Immigration
Alberta Economic Development
4th Floor, Commerce Place
10155-102 Street
Edmonton, Alberta
T5J 4L6
www.alberta-canada.com/pnp

British Columbia
Provincial Nominee Program
Ministry of Community, Aboriginal & Women's Service
P.O. Box 9915 Stn Prov Gov
Victoria, British Columbia
V8W 9V1
www.pnp.mi.gov.bc.ca

Manitoba
Provincial Nominee Program
Immigration Promotion & Recruitment Branch
Labour and Immigration Manitoba
9th Floor, 213 Notre Dame Avenue
Winnipeg, Manitoba
R3B 1N3
http://www.gov.mb.ca/labour/immigrate/english/immigration/1.html

New Brunswick

Provincial Nominee Program
Training and Employment Development
P.O. Box 6000
Fredericton, New Brunswick
E3B 5H1
www.gnb.ca/immigration/english/index.htm

Newfoundland and Labrador

Provincial Nominee Program
Industry, Trade and Technology
Confederation Building
West Block, 4th Floor
P.O. Box 8700
St. John's, Newfoundland
A1B 4J6
www.gov.nf.ca/itrd/prov_nominee.htm

Nova Scotia

Provincial Nominee Program
The Office of Economic Development
World Trade and Convention Centre
1800 Argyle Street
P.O. Box 519
Halifax, Nova Scotia
B3J 2R7
www.gov.ns.ca

Prince Edward Island

Provincial Nominee Program
Immigration and Investment Division
94 Euston Street, 2nd floor
Charlottetown, Prince Edward Island
C1A 7M8
www.gov.pe.ca

Saskatchewan

Provincial Nominee Program
Dept. of Government Relations and Immigration
Immigration Branch
2nd Floor - 1919 Saskatchewan Drive
Regina, Saskatchewan
S4P 3V7
www.immigrationsask.gov.sk.ca

Yukon
Provincial Nominee Program
Business Immigration, Industry Development
Business, Tourism and Culture
P.O. Box 2703
Whitehorse, Yukon
Y1A 2C6
www.btc.gov.yk.ca

Note: After you have been nominated by a province, you have to make a separate application to Citizenship and Immigration Canada (CIC) for permanent residence. A CIC officer will assess your application based on Canadian immigration regulations.

Provincial Nominees **are not** assessed on the six selection factors of the Federal Skilled Workers Program.

QUEBEC-SELECTED IMMIGRATION

Quebec is responsible for selecting immigrants who wish to settle in Quebec. Find out how to apply to be selected to settle in Quebec.

Immigrating to Quebec as a Skilled Worker

The Quebec government and the Government of Canada have an agreement that allows Quebec to select immigrants who best meet its immigration needs. Under the Canada-Quebec Accord on Immigration, Quebec is able to establish its own immigration requirements and select immigrants who will adapt well to living in Quebec.

To come to Canada as a Quebec Skilled Worker, you must first apply to the Quebec government for a *Certificat de selection du Québec*. Visit the Quebec Immigration Web site for more information.
http://www.immq.gouv.qc.ca/anglais/how_immigrate/workers/index .html

Note: After you have been selected by Quebec, you have to make a separate application to Citizenship and Immigration Canada (CIC) for permanent residence. A CIC officer will assess your application based on Canadian immigration regulations.

Quebec Skilled Workers **are not** assessed on the six selection factors of the Federal Skilled Workers Program.

Immigrating to Canada as a Skilled Worker

Since this book is designed to focus on the Federal Skilled Workers Program which is the major source of immigrants to Canada. (for more detailed facts and figures about this program, visit http://www.cic.gc.ca/english/pdf/pub/facts2001.pdf), so we will try to master every aspect under this category. This should enable potential candidates to not only evaluate their eligibility under the Federal Skilled Workers Program but to prepare their immigration application in a professional manner by themselves. This will save you thousands of dollars as professional fee that many candidates prefer to pay to consultants because of lack of confidence and knowledge.

Number of Permanent Residents by Top Source Countries

Source countries	1999	2000	2001	2002	2003
China, People's Republic of	29,119	36,723	40,328	33,237	36,116
India	17,430	26,103	27,869	28,822	24,560
Pakistan	9,297	14,196	15,345	14,156	12,330
Philippines	9,171	10,091	12,921	11,003	11,978
Korea, Republic of	7,216	7,635	9,604	7,324	7,086
United States	5,526	5,822	5,908	5,293	5,990
Iran	5,907	5,608	5,740	7,738	5,648
Romania	3,463	4,426	5,587	5,687	5,465
United Kingdom	4,478	4,648	5,355	4,719	5,194
Sri Lanka	4,723	5,843	5,515	4,962	4,442
Russia	3,776	3,522	4,071	3,675	3,520
Taiwan	5,464	3,511	3,114	2,906	2,123
Vietnam, Socialist Republic of	1,396	1,798	2,096	2,277	1,684
Hong Kong	3,664	2,862	1,965	1,538	1,466
Yugoslavia (former)	1,490	4,724	2,789	1,621	940
Bosnia-Herzegovina	2,808	981	870	465	264
Top 10 source countries	98,331	121,393	134,172	122,941	118,809
Other countries	91,632	106,066	116,444	106,095	102,543
Total	189,963	227,459	250,616	229,036	221,352

http://www.cic.gc.ca/english/pub/facts2003/permanent/16.html

For 2004 statistics please visit following:
http://www.cic.gc.ca/english/monitor/issue09/05-overview.html

Ranking of Permanent Residents by Top Source Countries

Source countries	1999	2000	2001	2002	2003
China, People's Republic of	1	1	1	1	1
India	2	2	2	2	2
Pakistan	3	3	3	3	3
Philippines	4	4	4	4	4
Korea, Republic of	5	5	5	6	5
United States	7	7	6	8	6
Iran	6	8	7	5	7
Romania	14	11	8	7	8
United Kingdom	10	10	10	10	9
Sri Lanka	9	6	9	9	10
Russia	12	13	13	14	13
Taiwan	8	14	19	19	21
Vietnam, Socialist Republic of	32	28	26	24	30
Hong Kong	13	17	29	32	32
Yugoslavia (former)	29	9	22	31	48
Bosnia-Herzegovina	17	49	52	70	87

http://www.cic.gc.ca/english/pub/facts2003/permanent/16.html

Who Are Skilled Workers

Skilled workers are people whose education and work experience will help them find work and make a home for themselves as permanent residents in Canada. Applying to come to Canada as a Skilled Worker is not difficult. You will find all the information and forms you need to make your application here. **http://www.cic.gc.ca/english/applications/index.html.**

Refer to www.cic.gc.ca often. The rules for applying as a Skilled Worker can change. Before you apply, make sure your application follows the current rules. After you apply, check back for information about the steps to follow. You can also check the status of your application while it is in process through this website. **http://www.cic.gc.ca/english/e-services/index.html**

Will You Qualify As a Skilled Worker?

Skilled workers are people who may become permanent residents because they are able to become economically established in Canada.

To be accepted as a Skilled Worker, applicants must:

- meet the minimum work experience requirements;
- prove that they have the funds required for settlement; and
- earn enough points in the six selection factors to meet the pass mark.

The following categories will help you determine if you can apply as Skilled Worker. You can assess your chances of being accepted. Consult each of the following areas for the current regulations regarding:

Minimum Work Experience Requirements

Skilled workers are people who may become permanent residents because they have the ability to become economically established in Canada.

You must meet the following minimum work experience requirements to allow you to apply as a skilled worker:

- You must have at least one year of full-time work experience. You must have been paid for this work.
- Your work experience must be in the category of **Skill Type 0**, or **Skill Level A or B** on the Canadian National Occupational Classification (NOC). (See below for instructions.)
- You must have had this experience within the last 10 years.

What are Skill Types

Skill Type 0 : These are the management occupations. All kinds of managers in their field of expertise fall under type 0.

Skill Level A: These are the occupations that required **university degree** at the bachelor's or master's or doctorate level for example Engineers, Physicians, Lawyers, Teachers.

Skill Level B: These are the occupations that requires college education or apprenticeship training for example 2 or 3 years diploma in the field of engineering / information technology or management sciences. Their designations may vary as Associate Engineer, Technologist and Technicians

- To know more about **Skill Type 0 or Skill Level A or B,** visit this link
  http://cnp2001noc.worklogic.com/e/matrix.pdf

67

National Occupation Classification (NOC)

The NOC is a classification system for jobs in the Canadian economy. It describes duties, skills, talents and work settings for occupations.

National Occupation Classification List

The following occupations are listed in Skill Type 0, Skill Level A or B of the National Occupation Classification List.

Code	A
0632	Accommodation Service Managers
5135	Actors and Comedians
1221	Administrative Officers
0114	Administrative Services Managers (other)
0312	Administrators - Post-Secondary Education and Vocational
2146	Aerospace Engineers
2222	Agricultural and Fish Products Inspectors
8252	Agricultural and Related Service Contractors and Managers
2123	Agricultural Representatives, Consultants and Specialists
2271	Air Pilots, Flight Engineers and Flying Instructors
2272	Air Traffic Control and Related Occupations
2244	Aircraft Instrument, Electrical and Avionics Mechanics, Technicians and Inspectors
7315	Aircraft Mechanics and Aircraft Inspectors
3234	Ambulance Attendants and Other Paramedical Occupations

Code	
5231	Announcers and Other Broadcasters
8257	Aquaculture Operators and Managers
2151	Architects
2251	Architectural Technologists and Technicians
0212	Architecture and Science Managers
5113	Archivists
5244	Artisans and Craftpersons
1235	Assessors, Valuators and Appraisers
5251	Athletes
5225	Audio and Video Recording Technicians
3141	Audiologists and Speech-Language Pathologists
5121	Authors and Writers
7321	Automotive Service Technicians, Truck Mechanics and Mechanical Repairers
Code	**B**
6252	Bakers
0122	Banking, Credit and Other Investment Managers
2221	Biological Technologists and Technicians
2121	Biologists and Related Scientists
7266	Blacksmiths and Die Setters
7262	Boilermakers
1231	Bookkeepers
7281	Bricklayers
5224	Broadcast Technicians
4163	Business Development Officers and Marketing Researchers and Consultants

Code	
0123	Business Services Managers (other)
6251	Butchers and Meat Cutters - Retail and Wholesale
Code	**C**
7272	Cabinetmakers
7247	Cable Television Service and Maintenance Technicians
3217	Cardiology Technologists
7271	Carpenters
9231	Central Control and Process Operators, Mineral and Metal Processing
6241	Chefs
2134	Chemical Engineers
2211	Chemical Technologists and Technicians
2112	Chemists
3122	Chiropractors
2231	Civil Engineering Technologists and Technicians
2131	Civil Engineers
6215	Cleaning Supervisors
5252	Coaches
4131	College and Other Vocational Instructors
7382	Commercial Divers
0643	Commissioned Officers, Armed Forces
0641	Commissioned Police Officers
4212	Community and Social Service Workers
0213	Computer and Information Systems Managers
2281	Computer and Network Operators and Web Technicians

2147	Computer Engineers (Except Software Engineers)
2174	Computer Programmers and Interactive Media Developers
7282	Concrete Finishers
5132	Conductors, Composers and Arrangers
1226	Conference and Event Planners
2224	Conservation and Fishery Officers
5112	Conservators and Curators
2234	Construction Estimators
2264	Construction Inspectors
0711	Construction Managers
7311	Construction Millwrights and Industrial Mechanics (Except Textile)
7215	Contractors and Supervisors, Carpentry Trades
7212	Contractors and Supervisors, Electrical Trades and Telecommunications
7217	Contractors and Supervisors, Heavy Construction Equipment Crews
7216	Contractors and Supervisors, Mechanic Trades
7214	Contractors and Supervisors, Metal Forming, Shaping and Erecting Trades
7219	Contractors and Supervisors, Other Construction Trades, Installers, Repairers
7213	Contractors and Supervisors, Pipefitting Trades
6242	Cooks
1227	Court Officers and Justices of the Peace
1244	Court Recorders and Medical Transcriptionists
7371	Crane Operators
1236	Customs, Ship and Other Brokers

Code	D
5134	Dancers
2172	Database Analysts and Data Administrators
2273	Deck Officers, Water Transport
3222	Dental Hygienists and Dental Therapists
3223	Dental Technologists, Technicians and Laboratory
3113	Dentists
3221	Denturists
3132	Dietitians and Nutritionists
2253	Drafting Technologists and Technicians
7372	Drillers and Blasters D Surface Mining, Quarrying and Construction
6214	Dry Cleaning and Laundry Supervisors
Code	**E**
4214	Early Childhood Educators and Assistants
4162	Economists and Economic Policy Researchers and Analysts
5122	Editors
4166	Education Policy Researchers, Consultants and Program Officers
4143	Educational Counsellors
7332	Electric Appliance Servicers and Repairers
2241	Electrical and Electronics Engineering Technologists and Technicians
2133	Electrical and Electronics Engineers
7333	Electrical Mechanics
7244	Electrical Power Line and Cable Workers
7241	Electricians (Except Industrial and Power System)

Code	
3218	Electroencephalographic and Other Diagnostic Technologists, n.e.c.
2242	Electronic Service Technicians (Household and Business
7318	Elevator Constructors and Mechanics
4213	Employment Counsellors
2274	Engineer Officers, Water Transport
2262	Engineering Inspectors and Regulatory Officers
0211	Engineering Managers
1222	Executive Assistants
6213	Executive Housekeepers
Code	**F**
0721	Facility Operation and Maintenance Managers
4153	Family, Marriage and Other Related Counsellors
8253	Farm Supervisors and Specialized Livestock Workers
8251	Farmers and Farm Managers
5222	Film and Video Camera Operators
1112	Financial and Investment Analysts
1111	Financial Auditors and Accountants
0111	Financial Managers
1114	Financial Officers (other)
0642	Fire Chiefs and Senior Firefighting Officers
6262	Firefighters
8261	Fishing Masters and Officers
8262	Fishing Vessel Skippers and Fishermen/women
7295	Floor Covering Installers

Code	
6212	Food Service Supervisors
2122	Forestry Professionals
2223	Forestry Technologists and Technicians
6272	Funeral Directors and Embalmers
Code	**G**
7253	Gas Fitters
2212	Geological and Mineral Technologists and Technicians
2144	Geological Engineers
2113	Geologists, Geochemists and Geophysicists
7292	Glaziers
0412	Government Managers - Economic Analysis, Policy Development
0413	Government Managers - Education Policy Development and Program Administration
0411	Government Managers - Health and Social Policy Development and Program Administration
6234	Grain Elevator Operators
5223	Graphic Arts Technicians
5241	Graphic Designers and Illustrators
Code	**H**
6271	Hairstylists and Barbers
3151	Head Nurses and Supervisors
3123	Health Diagnosing and Treating (Other Professional Occupations)
4165	Health Policy Researchers, Consultants and Program Officers
7312	Heavy-Duty Equipment Mechanics
0112	Human Resources Managers

Code	I
1228	Immigration, Employment Insurance and Revenue Officers
2141	Industrial and Manufacturing Engineers
2252	Industrial Designers
7242	Industrial Electricians
2233	Industrial Engineering and Manufacturing Technologists and Technicians
2243	Industrial Instrument Technicians and Mechanics
2171	Information Systems Analysts and Consultants
2263	Inspectors in Public and Environmental Health and Occupational Health and Safety
4216	Instructors (other)
4215	Instructors and Teachers of Persons with Disabilities
7293	Insulators
1233	Insurance Adjusters and Claims Examiners
6231	Insurance Agents and Brokers
1234	Insurance Underwriters
0121	Insurance, Real Estate and Financial Brokerage Managers
5242	Interior Designers
7264	Ironworkers
Code	J
7344	Jewellers, Watch Repairers and Related Occupations
5123	Journalists
4111	Judges

1227	Justices of the Peace
Code	**L**
2254	Land Survey Technologists and Technicians
2154	Land Surveyors
2225	Landscape and Horticultural Technicians and Specialists
2152	Landscape Architects
8255	Landscaping and Grounds Maintenance Contractors and Managers
4112	Lawyers and Quebec Notaries
1242	Legal Secretaries
0011	Legislators
5111	Librarians
5211	Library and Archive Technicians and Assistants
0511	Library, Archive, Museum and Art Gallery Managers
3233	Licensed Practical Nurses
1232	Loan Officers
8241	Logging Machinery Operators
Code	**M**
7316	Machine Fitters
7231	Machinists and Machining and Tooling Inspectors
0512	Managers - Publishing, Motion Pictures, Broadcasting and Performing Arts
0311	Managers in Health Care
0414	Managers in Public Administration (other)
0314	Managers in Social, Community and Correctional Services
0911	Manufacturing Managers

2255	Mapping and Related Technologists and Technicians
2161	Mathematicians, Statisticians and Actuaries
2232	Mechanical Engineering Technologists and Technicians
2132	Mechanical Engineers
3212	Medical Laboratory Technicians
3211	Medical Laboratory Technologists and Pathologists' Assistants
3215	Medical Radiation Technologists
1243	Medical Secretaries
3216	Medical Sonographers
3219	Medical Technologists and Technicians (other - except Dental Health)
2142	Metallurgical and Materials Engineers
2213	Meteorological Technicians
2114	Meteorologists
3232	Midwives and Practitioners of Natural Healing
2143	Mining Engineers
4154	Ministers of Religion
5226	Motion Pictures, Broadcasting (other Technical and Co-ordinating Occupations)
7322	Motor Vehicle Body Repairers
7334	Motorcycle and Other Related Mechanics
5212	Museums and Art Galleries (related Technical Occupations)
5133	Musicians and Singers
Code	**N**
4161	Natural and Applied Science Policy Researchers, Consultants and Program Officers
2261	Nondestructive Testers and Inspectors

8254	Nursery and Greenhouse Operators and Managers
Code	**O**
3143	Occupational Therapists
8232	Oil and Gas Well Drillers, Servicers, Testers and Related Workers
7331	Oil and Solid Fuel Heating Mechanics
3231	Opticians
3121	Optometrists
Code	**P**
7294	Painters and Decorators
5136	Painters, Sculptors and Other Visual Artists
9234	Papermaking and Coating Control Operators
4211	Paralegal and Related Occupations
5245	Patternmakers - Textile, Leather and Fur Products
5232	Performers (other)
1223	Personnel and Recruitment Officers
2145	Petroleum Engineers
9232	Petroleum, Gas and Chemical Process Operators
3131	Pharmacists
5221	Photographers
2115	Physical Sciences (Other Professional Occupations)
3112	Physicians - General Practitioners and Family Physicians
3111	Physicians - Specialist
2111	Physicists and Astronomers
3142	Physiotherapists

7252	Pipefitters
7284	Plasterers, Drywall Installers and Finishers and Lathers
7251	Plumbers
6261	Police Officers (Except Commissioned)
0132	Postal and Courier Services Managers
4122	Post-Secondary Teaching and Research Assistants
7243	Power System Electricians
7352	Power Systems and Power Station Operators
0811	Primary Production Managers (Except Agriculture)
7381	Printing Press Operators
4155	Probation and Parole Officers and Related Occupations
5131	Producers, Directors, Choreographers and Related Occupations
2148	Professional Engineers, n.e.c. (other)
1122	Professional Occupations in Business Services to Management
5124	Professional Occupations in Public Relations and Communications
4121	Professors - University
5254	Program Leaders and Instructors in Recreation and Sport
4168	Program Officers Unique to Government
1224	Property Administrators
4151	Psychologists
9233	Pulping Control Operators
1225	Purchasing Agents and Officers
0113	Purchasing Managers

Code	R
7361	Railway and Yard Locomotive Engineers
7314	Railway Carmen/women
7362	Railway Conductors and Brakemen/women
2275	Railway Traffic Controllers and Marine Traffic Regulators
6232	Real Estate Agents and Salespersons
0513	Recreation and Sports Program and Service Directors
4167	Recreation, Sports and Fitness Program Supervisors Consultants
7313	Refrigeration and Air Conditioning Mechanics
3152	Registered Nurses
4217	Religious Occupations (other)
0712	Residential Home Builders and Renovators
3214	Respiratory Therapists, Clinical Perfusionists and Cardio-Pulmonary Technologists
0631	Restaurant and Food Service Managers
6233	Retail and Wholesale Buyers
0621	Retail Trade Managers
6211	Retail Trade Supervisors
7291	Roofers and Shinglers
Code	S
0611	Sales, Marketing and Advertising Managers
0313	School Principals and Administrators of Elementary and Secondary
1241	Secretaries (Except Legal and Medical)
1113	Securities Agents, Investment Dealers and Brokers
0012	Senior Government Managers and Officials

0013	Senior Managers - Financial, Communications and Other Business
0016	Senior Managers - Goods Production, Utilities, Transportation and Construction
0014	Senior Managers - Health, Education, Social and Community
0015	Senior Managers - Trade, Broadcasting and Other Services, n.e.c.
6216	Service Supervisors (other)
0651	Services Managers (other)
7261	Sheet Metal Workers
7343	Shoe Repairers and Shoemakers
7335	Small Engine and Equipment Mechanics (other)
4164	Social Policy Researchers, Consultants and Program Officers
4169	Social Science, n.e.c. (Other Professional Occupations)
4152	Social Workers
2173	Software Engineers
1121	Specialists in Human Resources
5253	Sports Officials and Referees
7252	Sprinkler System Installers
7351	Stationary Engineers and Auxiliary Equipment Operators
7252	Steamfitters, Pipefitters and Sprinkler System Installers
7263	Structural Metal and Platework Fabricators and Fitters
9223	Supervisors, Electrical Products Manufacturing
9222	Supervisors, Electronics Manufacturing
9225	Supervisors, Fabric, Fur and Leather Products Manufacturing
1212	Supervisors, Finance and Insurance Clerks
9213	Supervisors, Food, Beverage and Tobacco Processing

9215	Supervisors, Forest Products Processing
9224	Supervisors, Furniture and Fixtures Manufacturing
1211	Supervisors, General Office and Administrative Support Clerks
8256	Supervisors, Landscape and Horticulture
1213	Supervisors, Library, Correspondence and Related Information Clerks
8211	Supervisors, Logging and Forestry
7211	Supervisors, Machinists and Related Occupations
1214	Supervisors, Mail and Message Distribution Occupations
9211	Supervisors, Mineral and Metal Processing
8221	Supervisors, Mining and Quarrying
7222	Supervisors, Motor Transport and Other Ground Transit Operators
9221	Supervisors, Motor Vehicle Assembling
8222	Supervisors, Oil and Gas Drilling and Service
9226	Supervisors, Other Mechanical and Metal Products Manufacturing
9227	Supervisors, Other Products Manufacturing and Assembly
9212	Supervisors, Petroleum, Gas and Chemical Processing and Utilities
9214	Supervisors, Plastic and Rubber Products Manufacturing
7218	Supervisors, Printing and Related Occupations
7221	Supervisors, Railway Transport Operations
1215	Supervisors, Recording, Distributing and Scheduling Occupations
9216	Supervisors, Textile Processing
5227	Support Occupations in Motion Pictures, Broadcasting and the Performing Arts
2283	Systems Testing Technicians

Code	T
7342	Tailors, Dressmakers, Furriers and Milliners
4142	Teachers - Elementary School and Kindergarten
4141	Teachers - Secondary School
6221	Technical Sales Specialists - Wholesale Trade
0131	Telecommunication Carriers Managers
7246	Telecommunications Installation and Repair Workers
7245	Telecommunications Line and Cable Workers
7317	Textile Machinery Mechanics and Repairers
5243	Theatre, Fashion, Exhibit and Other Creative Designers
3144	Therapy and Assessment (Other Professional Occupations)
3235	Therapy and Assessment (other Technical Occupations)
7283	Tilesetters
7232	Tool and Die Makers
7383	Trades and Related Occupations (other)
5125	Translators, Terminologists and Interpreters
0713	Transportation Managers
Code	**U**
8231	Underground Production and Development Miners
7341	Upholsterers
2153	Urban and Land Use Planners
2282	User Support Technicians
0912	Utilities Managers

Code	V
3114	Veterinarians
3213	Veterinary and Animal Health Technologists and

Code	W
7373	Water Well Drillers
2175	Web Designers and Developers
7265	Welders and Related Machine Operators

Determine Your NOC Category

Follow these steps to see if your work experience meets the requirements to apply as a skilled worker.

1. Find the title of any full-time jobs you had in the past 10 years using above <u>National Occupation Classification list</u>. This is a list of all jobs that are in Skill Type 0, Skill Level A or B on the NOC. **Write down the four-digit code located to the left of your job's title.**

2. Go to the <u>NOC Web site</u>:
(*http://cnp2001noc.worklogic.com/e/welcome.shtml*) and type your four-digit job-code in the "Quick Search" box. Make sure you press the "GO" button. A description of your occupation will appear. Make sure the description and "Main Duties" describe what you did at your last jobs.

Note: you do **not** have to meet the "Employment Requirements" listed in the description.

If the initial description and list of main duties **matches** what you did at your last jobs, you can count this experience as when you apply as a skilled worker. You can also earn points in <u>Factor 3</u> of the Selection Factors.

If the description **does not match** your work experience then you might not have the experience you need to apply as a skilled worker. Look through the <u>NOC list</u> to see if another occupation matches your experience. Check all of the jobs you had in the past 10 years to see if you have at least one year of work experience in a job that will qualify you as a skilled worker.

Check the list of <u>restricted occupations</u>. If your work experience is in a restricted occupation then you **cannot** use it to qualify for the Skilled Worker category.

What are restricted occupations: To protect the Canadian labour market, Citizenship and Immigration Canada has to make sure that Canada does not have too many people with the same skills.

There are no restricted occupations at the time of this publication

You do not meet the minimum requirements if:

- none of your work experience is listed in the NOC list;
- your experience did **not** occur in the 10 years before you applied; or
- your only work experience is in a restricted occupation.

If you do not meet the minimum work experience requirements, your application as a Skilled Worker will be refused.

Few examples of NOC Listed professions

6271   Hairstylists and Barbers

Hairstylists and barbers cut and style hair and perform related services. They are employed in hairstyling or hairdressing salons, barber shops, vocational schools, health care establishments and theatre, film and television establishments.

Example Titles

barber
barber apprentice
hair colour technician
hairdresser
hairdresser apprentice
hairstylist
hairstylist apprentice
wig stylist

Main duties

Hairstylists perform some or all of the following duties:

- Suggest hair style compatible with client's physical features or determine style from client's instructions and preferences
- Cut, trim, taper, curl, wave, perm and style hair
- Apply bleach, tints, dyes or rinses to colour, frost or streak hair
- Analyze hair and scalp condition and provide basic treatment or advice on beauty care treatments for scalp and hair
- May shampoo and rinse hair
- May train or supervise other hairstylists, hairstylist apprentices and helpers.

Barbers perform some or all of the following duties:

- Cut and trim hair according to client's instructions or preferences
- Shave and trim beards and moustaches
- May shampoo hair and provide other hair treatment, such as waving, straightening and tinting and may also provide scalp conditioning massages
- May train and supervise other barbers and barber apprentices.

Employment requirements for Hair Stylists

Some secondary school education is required.

- Completion of a two- or three-year hairstyling apprenticeship program or completion of a college or other program in hairstyling combined with on-the-job training is usually required.

87

- Several years of experience may replace formal education and training.
- Employers may require applicants to provide a hairstyling demonstration before being hired.
- There are various provincial/territorial certification and licensing requirements for hairstylists, ranging from trade certification to licensing by a provincial/territorial association. Interprovincial trade certification (Red Seal) is also available for qualified hairstylists. Barbers
- Some secondary school education is required.
- Completion of a two-year apprenticeship or other barber program is usually required.
- On-the-job training may be substituted for formal education.
- There are various provincial/territorial certification and licensing requirements for barbers, ranging from trade certification to licensing by a provincial/territorial association. Barbers can also obtain interprovincial trade certification (Red Seal) as qualified hairstylists.

Additional information

- Red Seal trade certification allows for interprovincial mobility.

2232   Mechanical Engineering Technologists and Technicians

Mechanical engineering technologists and technicians provide technical support and services or may work independently in mechanical engineering fields such as the design, development, maintenance and testing of machines, components, tools, heating and ventilating systems, power generation and power conversion plants, manufacturing plants and equipment. They are employed by consulting engineering, manufacturing and processing companies, institutions and government departments.

Example Titles

aeronautical technologist
heating designer
HVAC (heating, ventilating & air conditioning) technologist
machine designer
marine engineering technologist mechanical engineering technician
mechanical engineering technologist
mechanical technologist
mould designer
thermal station technician
tool and die designer
tool designer

Main duties

Mechanical engineering technologists perform some or all of the following duties:

- Prepare and interpret conventional and computer-assisted design (CAD) engineering designs, drawings, and specifications for machines and components, power transmission systems, process piping, heating, ventilating and air-conditioning systems

- Prepare cost and material estimates, project schedules and reports
- Conduct tests and analyses of machines, components and materials to determine their performance, strength, response to stress and other characteristics
- Design moulds, tools, dies, jigs and fixtures for use in manufacturing processes
- Inspect mechanical installations and construction
- Prepare contract and tender documents
- Supervise, monitor and inspect mechanical installations and construction projects
- Prepare standards and schedules and supervise mechanical maintenance programs or operations of mechanical plants.

Mechanical engineering technicians perform some or all of the following duties:

- Assist in preparing conventional and computer assisted design (CAD) engineering designs, drawings and specifications
- Carry out a limited range of mechanical tests and analyses of machines, components and materials
- Assist in the design of moulds, tools, dies, jigs and fixtures for use in manufacturing processes
- Assist in inspection of mechanical installations and construction projects
- Participate in the installation, repair and maintenance of machinery and equipment.

Employment requirements

- Completion of a two- or three-year college program in mechanical engineering technology is usually required for mechanical engineering technologists.
- Completion of a one- or two-year college program in mechanical engineering technology is usually required for mechanical engineering technicians.

- Certification in mechanical engineering technology or in a related field is available through provincial associations of engineering/applied science technologists and technicians and may be required for some positions.

- A period of supervised work experience, usually two years, is required before certification.

- In Quebec, membership in the regulatory body is required to use the title of Professional Technologist.

Additional information

- There is mobility to other related occupations such as technical sales or drafting technologists and technicians.

- Progression to supervisory occupations such as mechanical construction supervisor, manufacturing supervisor or operations maintenance manager is possible with experience.

2133 Electrical and Electronics Engineers

Electrical and electronics engineers design, plan, research, evaluate and test electrical and electronic equipment and systems. They are employed by electrical utilities, communications companies, manufacturers of electrical and electronic equipment, consulting firms, and by a wide range of manufacturing, processing and transportation industries and government.

Example Titles

avionics engineer
control systems engineer
design engineer, electrical
distribution planning engineer, electrical engineer
electrical network engineer
electronics engineer
instrumentation and control engineer
planning engineer, electrical systems
process control engineer, electrical

roadway lighting design engineer
television systems engineer
test engineer, electronics

Main duties

Electrical and electronics engineers perform some or all of the following duties:

- Conduct research into the feasibility, design, operation and performance of electrical generation and distribution networks, electrical machinery and components and electronic communications, instrumentation and control systems, equipment, and components

- Prepare material cost and timing estimates, reports and design specifications for electrical and electronic systems and equipment

- Design electrical and electronic circuits, components, systems and equipment

- Supervise and inspect the installation, modification, testing and operation of electrical and electronic systems and equipment

- Develop maintenance and operating standards for electrical and electronic systems and equipment

- Investigate electrical or electronic failures

- Prepare contract documents and evaluate tenders for construction or maintenance

- Supervise technicians, technologists, programmers, analysts and other engineers.

Electrical and electronics engineers may specialize in a number of areas including electrical design for residential, commercial or industrial installations, electrical power generation and transmission, and instrumentation and control systems.

Employment requirements

- A bachelor's degree in electrical or electronics engineering or in an appropriate related engineering discipline is required.

- A master's or doctoral degree in a related engineering discipline may be required.

- Licensing by a provincial or territorial association of professional engineers is required to approve engineering drawings and reports and to practise as a Professional Engineer (P.Eng.).

- Engineers are eligible for registration following graduation from an accredited educational program, and after three or four years of supervised work experience in engineering and passing a professional practice examination.

- Supervisory and senior positions in this unit group require experience.

Funds Required to Settle in Canada

The Government of Canada provides no financial support to new skilled worker immigrants. You must prove that you have enough money unencumbered by debts or obligations to support yourself and your family members after you arrive in Canada.

The required funds are equal to or greater than the amount listed below for each family size:

Number of family members	Funds required*
1	$9,897
2	$12,372
3	$15,387
4	$18,626
5	$20,821
6	$23,015
7+	$25,210

*Exception: If you have arranged employment as defined in Factor 5, you do not have to meet these financial requirements.

The minimum required funds may change at any time. Check CIC Web site to make sure you have the most recent information.

We strongly recommend that you research the cost of living in the region of Canada where you intend to live. Bring with you as much money as possible to make your establishment in Canada easier.

Disclosure of funds

You will have to tell a Canadian official if you carry more than $10,000 Canadian in cash funds upon your entry to Canada. This could be in the form of:

- money (coins or bank notes)
- securities in bearer form (stocks, bonds, debentures, treasury bills etc.)
- negotiable instruments in bearer form (bankers' drafts, cheques, travellers' cheques, money orders etc.)

Failure to disclose can result in fines and imprisonment

SIX SELECTION FACTORS AND PASS MARK

Self-Assessment Worksheet

This worksheet will help you to determine your chance of qualifying as a skilled worker. It explains the six factors on which points are awarded and helps you estimate how many points you may be awarded for each factor.

How to estimate your points

Read the explanation for each factor, then fill in your score on the worksheet.

If you have a spouse or common-law partner, you must decide which of you will be the principal applicant; the other person will be considered a family member. Use the self-assessment worksheet to determine which of you would score the most points. This person should be the principal applicant.

*Note: A **common-law partner** is a person of the same or opposite sex who has lived with you in a conjugal relationship for a period of at least one year.*

*A **family member** is a spouse, common-law partner or dependent child included in your application.*

FACTOR 1: Education (maximum 25 points)

Points are awarded for earned educational credentials as well as the number of years of full-time or full-time equivalent study. To be awarded points, you must meet **both** stated criteria.

*Note: **Full-time studies:** At least 15 hours of instruction per week during the academic year. This includes any period of workplace training that forms part of the course*

Full-time equivalent studies: If you completed a program of study on a part-time or accelerated basis, count the length of time it would have taken to complete the program on a full-time basis.

Instructions

Use the chart below to determine your points. If you have not completed the number of years of study that correspond to your highest educational credential, award yourself points based on the number of years of study.

Examples: If you have a Master's degree but have completed only 16 years of full-time study, award yourself 22 points. If you have a four-year Bachelor's degree and have completed 14 or more years of study, award yourself 20 points.

Master's or PhD **and** at least 17 years of full-time or full-time equivalent study	25
Two or more university degrees at the Bachelor's level and at least 15 years of full-time or full-time equivalent study; **or** A three-year diploma, trade certificate or apprenticeship and at least 15 years of full-time or full-time equivalent study	22
A university degree of two years or more at the Bachelor's level, and at least 14 years of full-time or full-time equivalent study; **or** A two-year diploma, trade certificate or apprenticeship and at least 14 years of full-time or full-time equivalent study	20
A one-year university degree at the Bachelor's level and at least 13 years of full-time or full-time equivalent study; **or** A one-year diploma, trade certificate or apprenticeship and at least 13 years of full-time or full-time equivalent study	15
A one-year diploma, trade certificate or apprenticeship and at least 12 years of full-time or full-time equivalent study	12
Secondary school (also called high school)	5
Your Score	

FACTOR 2: Language ability (maximum 24 points)

Points are awarded for proven ability in reading, writing, listening to and speaking English and/or French.

Instructions

STEP 1. If you have some abilities in both English and French, decide which of the two you are more comfortable using; this will be considered your **first official language**. The other will be your **second official language**.

STEP 2. Determine your points according to your ability to read, write, listen to, and speak these languages using the criteria in the Canadian Language Benchmarks.

Proficiency levels

The chart below contains basic descriptions of the proficiency levels you will be assessed against. These descriptions correspond to the Canadian Language Benchmarks and can be viewed in their entirety on CIC website by following the link to "How to Assess Your Language Skills".

Use this reference chart to find the Benchmark that best defines your language ability, or follow the link to "How to Assess Your Language Skills" on our Web site for direct links to each level.

Proficiency level	Ability			
	Speaking	Listening	Reading	Writing
HIGH: You communicate effectively in most social and work situations.	Benchmark 8: Pages 68-71	Benchmark 8: Pages 82-83	Benchmark 8: Pages 94-95	Benchmark 8: Pages 106-107
MODERATE: You communicate comfortably in familiar social and work situations.	Benchmark 6: Pages 60-63	Benchmark 6: Pages 78-79	Benchmark 6: Pages 90-91	Benchmark 6: Pages 102-103
BASIC: You can communicate in predictable contexts and on familiar topics.	Benchmark 4: Pages 12-13	Benchmark 4: Pages 24-25	Benchmark 4: Pages 36-37	Benchmark 4: Pages 48-49
NO: You do not meet the criteria for basic proficiency.	Do not meet Benchmark 4	Do not meet Benchmark 4	Do not meet Benchmark 4	Do not meet Benchmark 4

Calculating your language points

First official language	Read	Write	Listen	Speak
High proficiency	4	4	4	4
Moderate proficiency	2	2	2	2
Basic proficiency	1	1	1	1
No proficiency	0	0	0	0
Second official language	**Read**	**Write**	**Listen**	**Speak**
High proficiency	2	2	2	2
Moderate proficiency	2	2	2	2
Basic proficiency	1	1	1	1
No proficiency	0	0	0	0

Proof of Language Proficiency

The instructions above are meant to provide you with an informal self-assessment only. If you decide to apply to immigrate to Canada as a skilled worker, you must provide **conclusive proof** of your language abilities. There are two ways to provide this proof. Choose **one** of the options below to establish your proficiency in English and/or French.

Option 1: Take a language proficiency test from an approved organization

CIC strongly recommend that you take an official language test if you are claiming skills in a language that is not your native language.

Steps:	Results:
1. Make an arrangement for testing and pay test costs. A list of approved organizations can be found on our <u>Web site</u>. Follow the link to "How to Assess Your Language Skills". 2. Submit the assessment results with your immigration application.	• You test results must not be more than one year old at the time that you submit your immigration application. • Test results will be used as conclusive evidence of your language proficiency. • You will know **exactly** how many points you will receive for the language factor before you submit your application. To determine your points, see the test result equivalency charts that follow.

OPTION 2: Establish your proficiency levels through a written explanation and supporting documentation

Steps:	Results:
1. Gather material that supports your claim. This should include: • A submission written by you that details your training in, and use of, English and/or French • Official documentation of education in English and/or French • Official documentation of work experience in English and/or French 2. Determine what proficiency levels you wish to claim and indicate these levels clearly in your submission. 3. Submit these documents with your immigration application.	• CIC officers will **not** interview you to assess your proficiency levels. • Your submission must satisfy the officer that your language skills meet the benchmarks for the levels you are claiming. • A CIC officer will review the evidence you include with your application. • The officer will award points for your language ability based on what you send with your application. • You will not know in advance how many points the CIC officer will give you for your language skills.

Arranging A Language Test

If you choose Option 1, you must arrange a language test from any of the following approved organizations. For contact information, refer to our CIC Website and follow the link to "How to Assess Your Language Skills".

English language testing organizations	French language testing organizations
The University of Cambridge Local Examination Syndicate, Education Australia, and the British Council administer the **International English Language Testing System (IELTS).** **Note:** IELTS has "General Training" and "Academic" options for the reading and writing tests. If you choose to take an IELTS test, you must take the "General Training" option.	The Paris Chamber of Commerce and Industry administers the **Test d'Évaluation de Français (TEF).** **Note:** For immigration purposes, you must submit results for the following tests: - expression orale - compréhension orale - compréhension écrite - expression écrite
The University of British Columbia's Applied Research and Evaluation Services (ARES) administer the **Canadian International Language Proficiency Index Program (CELPIP).**	

Using your test results

Once you have taken a language test from an approved organization, you can determine how many points you will receive using one of the equivalency charts below:

International English Language Testing System (IELTS)

Level	Points (per ability)	Test results for each ability			
		Speaking	Listening	Reading (General Training)	Writing (General Training)
High	First official language: **4**	7.0 – 9.0	7.0 – 9.0	7.0 – 9.0	7.0 – 9.0
	Second official language: **2**				
Moderate	Either official language: **2**	5.0 – 6.9	5.0 – 6.9	5.0 – 6.9	5.0 – 6.9
Basic	Either official language: **1** (maximum of 2)	4.0 – 4.9	4.0 – 4.9	4.0 – 4.9	4.0 – 4.9
No	**0**	Less than 4.0	Less than 4.0	Less than 4.0	Less than 4.0

Canadian English Language Proficiency Index Program (CELPIP)

Level	Points (per ability)	Test results for each ability			
		Speaking	Listening	Reading	Writing
High	First official language: **4**	4H 5 6	4H 5 6	4H 5 6	4H 5 6
	Second official language: **2**				
Moderate	Either official language: **2**	3H 4L	3H 4L	3H 4L	3H 4L
Basic	Either official language: **1** (maximum of 2)	2H 3L	2H 3L	2H 3L	2H 3L
No	**0**	0 1 2L	0 1 2L	0 1 2L	0 1 2L

Test d'évaluation de français (TEF)

Level	Points (per ability)	Test results for each ability			
		Speaking (expression orale)	Listening (compréhension orale)	Reading (compréhension écrite)	Writing (expression écrite)
High	First official language: **4** / Second official language: **2**	Level 5 Level 6 (349-450 pts)	Level 5 Level 6 (280-360 pts)	Level 5 Level 6 (233-300 pts)	Level 5 Level 6 (349-450 pts)
Moderate	Either official language: **2**	Level 4 (271-348 pts)	Level 4 (217-279 pts)	Level 4 (181-232 pts)	Level 4 (271-348 pts)
Basic	Either official language: **1** (maximum of 2)	Level 3 (181-270 pts)	Level 3 (145-216 pts)	Level 3 (121-180 pts)	Level 3 (181-270 pts)
No	**0**	Level 0 Level 1 Level 2 (0-180 pts)	Level 0 Level 1 Level 2 (0-144 pts)	Level 0 Level 1 Level 2 (0-120 pts)	Level 0 Level 1 Level 2 (0-180 pts)

Add your points: Total of speaking + listening + reading + writing = _____ (both languages)

Your Score	

What Happens Next:

An officer from Citizenship and Immigration Canada will look at the evidence you include with your application.

- Your submission must satisfy the officer that your language skills meet the benchmarks for the level you are claiming.
- The officer does not have to ask you for more evidence so include as much evidence and documentation with your application as you can.
- The officer will not interview you to assess your language skills.
- The officer will award points for your language ability based on what you send with your application. You will not know how many points the CIC Officer gives you for your language skills or if the CIC Officer is satisfied that you have **clearly** demonstrated the level of language skills you claim on your application.

Canadian Language Benchmark 8

Speaking: High Level

Global Performance Descriptor

- Learner can communicate effectively in most daily practical and social situations, and in familiar routine work situations.
- Can participate in conversations with confidence.
- Can speak on familiar topics at both concrete and abstract levels (10 to 15 minutes).
- Can provide descriptions, opinions and explanations; can synthesize abstract complex ideas, can hypothesize.
- In social interaction, learner demonstrates increased ability to respond appropriately to the formality level of the situation.
- Can use a variety of sentence structures, including embedded and report structures, and an expanded inventory of concrete, idiomatic and conceptual language.
- Grammar and pronunciation errors rarely impede communication.
- Discourse is reasonably fluent.
- Uses phone on less familiar and some non-routine matters.

Performance Conditions

- Interaction is with one or more people, face to face or on the phone. It is often at a normal rate.
- Speech is partly predictable and does not always support the utterance.
- Considerable level of stress affects performance when verbal interaction may result in personal consequences (e.g. on the job).

- Audience is small familiar and unfamiliar informal groups.
- Setting and context are familiar, clear and predictable.
- Topic is familiar, concrete and abstract.
- Pictures and other visuals are used.
- Length of presentation is 15 to 20 minutes.

Interaction one-on-one

- Interaction is face to face or on the phone.
- Interaction is formal or semi-formal.
- Learner can partially prepare the exchange.

Interaction in a group

- Interaction takes place in a familiar group of up to 10 people.
- The topic or issue is familiar, non-personal, concrete and abstract.
- Interaction is informal or semi-formal.

Listening: High Level

Global Performance Descriptor

- Learner can comprehend main points, details, speaker's purpose, attitudes, levels of formality and styles in oral discourse in moderately demanding contexts.
- Can follow most formal and informal conversations, and some technical work-related discourse in own field at a normal rate of speech.
- Can follow discourse about abstract and complex ideas on a familiar topic.
- Can comprehend an expanded range of concrete, abstract and conceptual language.

- Can determine mood, attitudes and feelings.
- Can understand sufficient vocabulary, idioms and colloquial expressions to follow detailed stories of general popular interest.
- Can follow clear and coherent extended instructional texts and directions.
- Can follow clear and coherent phone messages on unfamiliar and non-routine matters.
- Often has difficulty following rapid, colloquial/idiomatic or regionally accented speech between native speakers.

Performance Conditions

- Tasks are in a standard format, with items to circle, match, fill in a blank, and complete a chart.
- Learner is adequately briefed for focused listening.
- Communication is face to face, observed live, or video- and audio-mediated (e.g., tape, TV, radio).
- Speech is clear at a normal rate.
- Instructions are clear and coherent.
- Listening texts are monologues/presentations and dialogues (five to 10 minutes), within familiar general topics and technical discourse in own field.
- Topics are familiar.
- Presentation/lecture is informal or semi-formal with the use of pictures, visuals (10 to 15 minutes).
- Learner is briefed for focused listening.
- Speech is clear, at a normal rate.

Reading: High Level

Global Performance Descriptor

- Learner can follow main ideas, key words and important details in an authentic two to three-page text on a familiar topic, but within an only partially predictable context.

- May read popular newspaper and magazine articles and popular easy fiction as well as academic and business materials.

- Can extract relevant points, but often requires clarification of idioms and of various cultural references.

- Can locate and integrate several specific pieces of information in visually complex texts (e.g., tables, directories) or across paragraphs or sections of text.

- Text can be on abstract, conceptual or technical topics, containing facts, attitudes and opinions. Inference may be required to identify the writer's bias and the purpose/function of text.

- Learner reads in English for information, to learn the language, to develop reading skills.

- Uses a unilingual dictionary when reading for precision vocabulary building.

Performance Conditions

- Text is one page, five to 10 paragraphs long and is related to personal experience or familiar context.

- Text is legible, easy to read; is in print or neat handwriting.

- Instructions are clear and explicit, but not always presented step by step.

- Pictures may accompany text.

- Context is relevant, but not always familiar and predictable.

- Text has clear organization.
- Text content is relevant (e.g., commercials/advertising features, business/form letters, brochures.)
- Informational text is eight to 15 paragraphs long with clear organization in print or electronic form.
- Pictures often accompany text.
- Language is both concrete and abstract, conceptual and technical.
- Text types: news articles, stories, short articles, reports, editorials, opinion essays.

Writing: High Level

Global Performance Descriptor

- Learner demonstrates fluent ability in performing moderately complex writing tasks.
- Can link sentences and paragraphs (three or four) to form coherent texts to express ideas on familiar abstract topics, with some support for main ideas, and with an appropriate sense of audience.
- Can write routine business letters (e.g., letters of inquiry, cover letters for applications) and personal and formal social messages.
- Can write down a set of simple instructions, based on clear oral communication or simple written procedural text of greater length.
- Can fill out complex formatted documents.
- Can extract key information and relevant detail from a page-long text and write an outline or a one-paragraph summary.
- Demonstrates good control over common sentence patterns, coordination and subordination, and spelling and mechanics. Has occasional difficulty with complex structures (e.g., those

reflecting cause and reason, purpose, comment), naturalness of phrases and expressions, organization and style.

Performance Conditions

- Circumstances range from informal to more formal occasions.
- Addressees are familiar.
- Topics are of immediate everyday relevance.
- Text is one or two short paragraphs in length.
- Text to reproduce is one or two pages in legible handwriting or print, or may be a short oral text (10 to 15 minutes).
- Texts are varied and may be of a specialized or technical nature.
- Learner may fill out a teacher-prepared summary grid to aid note taking or summarizing.
- Forms have over 40 items/pieces of information.
- Messages are two or three paragraphs in length.
- Brief texts required in pre-set formats are one to several sentences, up to one paragraph long.
- Learner text is three or four paragraphs long, on non-personal, abstract but familiar topics and issues.
- Where necessary for the task, learners must include information presented to them from other sources (e.g., photographs, drawings, reference text/research information, diagrams).

FACTOR 3: Work Experience (maximum 21 points)

Calculate your points by adding all of the years of full-time, paid work experience you have that:

- occurred within the past 10 years
- is **not** listed as a restricted occupation (follow the link to "Will You Qualify?" on our Web site to check)
- occurred in occupations listed in Skill Type 0 or Skill Level A or B of the NOC

Years of experience	Points
1	15
2	17
3	19
4+	21

If your work experience does not meet all of the above conditions, you may not count this experience.

Your Score

FACTOR 4: Age (maximum 10 points)

Points are given for your age at the time your application is received.

Age	Total Points
16 or under	0
17	2
18	4
19	6
20	8
21-49	10
50	8
51	6
52	4
53	2
54 and over	0

Your Score	

Factor 5: Arranged employment (maximum 10 points)

Determine your points based on the chart below:

If:	And:	Points
You are currently working in Canada on a temporary work permit (including sectoral confirmations).	Your work permit is valid for 12 or more months **after** the date you apply for a permanent resident visa; Your employer has made an offer to give you a permanent job if your application is successful.	10
You are currently working in Canada in a job that is HRDC confirmation-exempt under an international agreement or a significant benefit category (e.g. intra-company transferee).	Your work permit is valid for 12 or more months **after** the date you apply for a permanent resident visa; Your employer has made an offer to give you a permanent job if your application is successful.	10
You do not currently have a work permit and you do not intend to work in Canada before you have been issued a permanent resident visa.	You have a full-time job offer that has been confirmed by Human Resources Development Canada (HRDC); Your employer has made an offer to give you a permanent job if your application is successful. You meet all required Canadian licensing or	10

| | regulatory standards associated with the job.

Note:
- You cannot arrange for an HRDC confirmation. Your employer must do this.

- HRDC will confirm job offers for occupations listed in Skill Type 0 or Skill Level A or B of the NOC. | |

Your Score

FACTOR 6: Adaptability (maximum 10 points)

Points are awarded for certain adaptability elements based on the experience of the principal applicant and/or his or her spouse or common-law partner.

Instructions:

Use the chart below to determine your points. If you have a spouse or common-law partner, points for each element can be awarded only once, either for you **or** your spouse or common-law partner.

Adaptability criteria	Points
A. Spouse or common-law partner's level of education - Secondary school (high school) diploma or less: **0 points** - A one-year diploma, trade certificate, apprenticeship, or university degree and at least 12 years of full-time or full-time equivalent studies: **3 points** - A diploma, trade certificate, apprenticeship, or university degree of two years or more and at least 14 years of full-time or full-time equivalent studies: **4 points** - A Master's or PhD and at least 17 years of full-time or full-time equivalent studies: **5 points**	3-5
B. Previous study in Canada: - You or your accompanying spouse or common-law partner studied at a post-secondary institution in Canada for at least two years on a full-time basis. This must have been done after the age of 17 and with a valid study permit.	5
C. Previous work in Canada: - You or your accompanying spouse or common-law partner completed a minimum of one year of full-time work in Canada on a valid work permit.	5
D. Arranged employment: - You earned points under Factor 5: Arranged Employment.	5

E. Relatives in Canada: - You or your accompanying spouse or common-law partner has a relative (parent, grandparent, child, grandchild, child of a parent, sibling, child of a grandparent, aunt/uncle, or grandchild of a parent, niece or nephew) who lives in Canada and is a Canadian citizen or permanent resident.	5

Your Score

Your Score

Use this worksheet to calculate your total score. A visa officer will assess your application and will make the final decision; if there is a difference between the points you give yourself and the points the officer awards you, the officer's assessment will prevail.

	Factor	Maximum points	Your score
1	Education	25	
2	Language proficiency	24	
3	Work experience	21	
4	Age	10	
5	Arranged employment	10	
6	Adaptability	10	
	Total	**100**	

The pass mark

The pass mark was last set on September 18, 2003, at 67 points. To learn the current pass mark, consult CIC website

If:	Then:
Your total score is equal to or greater than the pass mark...	- You may qualify for immigration to Canada as a skilled worker. Read the rest of this guide to decide if you wish to apply under the Federal Skilled Worker Class.
Your total score is less than the pass mark...	- You are not likely to qualify for immigration to Canada as a skilled worker. We recommend that you do not apply at this time; - However, you may apply if you believe there are other factors that would help you to become economically established in Canada. Send a detailed letter with your application explaining these factors. Include any documents that support your claim.

Principal Applicant

If you are married or living with a common-law partner, you and your spouse or common-law partner must decide who will be the principal applicant. The other person will be considered the dependant in the applications.

Note: A common-law partner is the person who has lived with you in a conjugal relationship for at least one year. Common-law partner refers to **both opposite-sex and same-sex couples.**

Use the self-assessment test to help you determine which person would earn the most points. The person who would earn the most points should apply as the principal applicant.

You can also take the <u>on-line Self-Assessment</u> at this site http://www.cic.gc.ca/english/skilled/assess/index.html to see how many points you would earn in the six selection factors explained above.

Application Fees

A number of cost recovery and administrative fees are payable by applicants for processing applications of various types and for certain citizenship and immigration procedures. However, all fees are subject to change without notice. In general, fees are payable at the time of application. Please check with your nearest Citizenship and Immigration Canada office or Canadian mission abroad for confirmation.

Fees

There are two fees: the **processing fee** and the **right of permanent residence fee**.

The processing fee:

- **is non**-refundable whether your application is approved or not;
- must be paid when you send your application to the visa office;
- must be paid by the principal applicant and each accompanying family member.

The right of permanent residence fee:

- **is refundable** if a permanent resident visa is not issued or used, or if you withdraw your application;

- can be paid at any time during the application process, but must be paid before a permanent resident visa can be issued. If you do not pay the fee when you submit your application, the visa office will contact you when it is time to pay;

- must be paid by principal applicant and his or her spouse or common-law partner (if applicable).

The tables below show you how to calculate the amount required in Canadian dollars. You may have the option of paying in another currency. For information on how to pay your fees, consult **Appendix A: Checklist.**

Immigration and right of permanent residence fees

A. PROCESSING FEE	Number of Persons	Amount per Person	Amount Due
Principal applicant	1	x $550	$550
Spouse or common-law partner		x $550	
Each dependent child 22 years and over		x $550	
Each dependent child under 22 years		x $150	
		Total A	

B. RIGHT OF PERMANENT RESIDENCE FEE	Number of Persons	Amount per Person	Amount Due
Principal applicant	1	x $975	$975
Spouse or common-law partner		x $975	
Applicant's dependent children		Not applicable	
		Total B	
		Total A+B	

Note: All amounts are in Canadian dollars.

Additional fees

You must also pay for the following for yourself and your family members (if applicable):

- medical examinations
- police certificates
- language assessments

Medical and Security Requirements

Medical requirements

You and your family members, whether accompanying you or not, must undergo and pass a medical examination in order to come to Canada. To pass the medical examination you or your family members must not have a condition that:

- is a danger to public health or safety
- would cause excessive demand on health or social services in Canada. Examples of "excessive demand" include ongoing hospitalization or institutional care for a physical or mental illness.

Instructions

Instructions on how to undergo the medical examination will normally be sent to you after you submit your application to the visa office. For further instruction, see **Appendix D.** (For information on printing the appendices, visit:

http://www.cic.gc.ca/english/applications/guides/EG78.html#wp655525

Exam validity

The medical examination results are valid for 12 months from the date of the first medical examination. If you are not admitted as a permanent resident during this time, you must undergo another complete medical examination.

Authorized doctors

Your own doctor cannot do the medical examination. You must see a physician on Canada's list of <u>Designated Medical Practitioners</u>. Note that the physician is only responsible for conducting a medical examination; he or she cannot give you any advice on the immigration process.

Security requirements

Police certificates and clearances

You and your family members must provide us with a police certificate issued by the authorities of each country in which you have lived for six (6) months or more since reaching the age of 18. Certificates must be originals and issued within the last three months.

If you have been convicted of a criminal offence in Canada, your application cannot be approved unless you receive a pardon. To avoid the unnecessary payment of processing fees for an immigration application that will be refused, you should first apply for a pardon to the:

Clemency and Pardons Division
National Parole Board
410 Laurier Avenue West
Ottawa, ON, Canada
K1A 0R1
Fax: 1-613-941-4981

Web site: www.npb-cnlc.gc.ca (application forms can be downloaded from the site)

Appendix B - Checklist. (included in application forms)

WHO MAY REPRESENT YOU

A representative may be a lawyer, a consultant or any other person, including a friend, whom you hire for a fee or ask to help you do any of the following at no charge: (1) apply for permanent residence or a temporary stay in Canada; (2) submit a refugee claim; (3) appear in front of an adjudicator; (4) appeal a decision; (5) apply for citizenship; or (6) request information on matters dealing with the *Immigration Act* or the *Citizenship Act.*

What you should know before seeking the services of someone to help with your application

Do you need a representative?

- Citizenship and Immigration Canada (CIC) **does not require** you to have a representative. CIC have tried to make the application kits as simple as possible so that you can complete them yourself. You can get additional information on how to complete an application from the CIC Web site at **http://www.cic.gc.ca/english/contacts/call.html** or from a CIC Call Centre

- If you decide to use the services of a representative, you are free to do so.

- **CIC treats all applicants equally and does not provide preferential service to applicants with representatives.**

Who can act as a representative?

- Anyone can act as a representative.

- Only lawyers licensed to practise in Canada can represent you at the Federal Court.

- CIC can provide information on your file only to people who are either (1) Canadian citizens, (2) permanent residents of Canada or (3) physically present in Canada. Representatives who live outside Canada and are neither Canadian citizens nor permanent residents might be unable to help you.

- Volunteer and non-governmental organizations that deal with immigrants may provide free services.

General points

- CIC cannot recommend representatives or vouch for their honesty or skills. It is your responsibility to make sure that the representative you choose is ethical and competent to perform the services required. You should not be afraid to ask the representative (whether a lawyer or a consultant) for references or for other proof that he or she has the necessary skills.

- **Beware of representatives who claim that you will get a visa, obtain citizenship or benefit from special treatment from the Canadian government by using their services. CIC is not associated with any representatives.**

- Be cautious when dealing with foreign-based representatives. Such companies or individuals may be outside the reach of Canadian law, and there may be no protection or remedy available in Canada to a dissatisfied client.

Lawyers

- Lawyers practising in Canada are regulated by provincial regulatory bodies. Only a lawyer who is a member in good standing of a provincial or territorial law society may practise law. The law societies regulate lawyers and can investigate complaints against members, impose discipline and provide financial compensation to clients who are victims of negligence or misconduct.

- If you live in Canada and you want to hire a lawyer, call the law society of the province or territory in which you live for the names of lawyers. In many cases, you can consult a lawyer free of charge for half an hour before deciding if you want to hire him or her. However, in some cases, a fee may be charged for the consultation.

Immigration consultants

- Immigration consultants are not regulated by either the federal or provincial governments of Canada.

- Find out if the consultant (whether he or she is in Canada or overseas) belongs to a professional association in Canada and ask about his or her experience with immigration or citizenship matters.

- Call the Better Business Bureau (BBB) to find out if the consultant has a satisfactory rating. Business people who fail to respond to letters of complaint sent to the BBB receive an unsatisfactory rating.

Dealing with representatives

- CIC requires your written authorization in order to release information to your representative.

- You may give your own mailing address or the mailing address of your representative as a point of contact for CIC. If you choose to give your representative's address, all correspondence from CIC, including notices for interviews, requests for information, medical forms and visas, will be sent to the representative.

- If you change representatives or stop using their services, you must cancel your authorization in writing to CIC or CIC will continue dealing with them. If you hire a new representative, you will have to provide a new authorization to CIC.

- Make sure that the representative who helps you with your application is willing to be identified as your representative.

Information given to CIC must be truthful

- Submitting false or misleading information to CIC can lead to the refusal of your application, the cancellation of your visa, the revocation of your citizenship, your deportation from Canada, and criminal charges being laid against you.

- You are responsible for any documents you submit to CIC or that your representative submits on your behalf.

Where to go for help if things go wrong

CIC cannot help you if you have a dispute with your representative as it is a private matter between the two of you. However, you may write to the CIC office dealing with your case or to the following address to inform CIC of the situation:

> Citizenship and Immigration Canada
> Social Policy and Programs
> Selection Branch
> Jean Edmonds Tower North, 7th Floor
> 300 Slater Street
> Ottawa, Ontario KIA 1L1

Note: You should file a complaint with the proper authorities as soon as possible if you encounter serious difficulties with your representative as limitation periods may apply.

If your representative is a lawyer practising in Canada

- Address your complaint to the law society of the province or territory where your lawyer practises. Law societies impose a code of conduct on their members to try to protect the public interest. They have rules for disciplining lawyers and

128

compensating clients. You may be able to obtain financial compensation from the law society's insurance fund.

If your representative is a consultant practising in Canada

- If your consultant is a member of a professional association in Canada, file a complaint with that association.

- If your consultant is not a member of any association, you might ask the consumer protection office in your province or territory for advice. Some associations might offer to contact the consultant to seek a solution.

- You can report your problem to the Better Business Bureau in the province or territory where your representative works. The BBB might contact your representative to try to resolve the issue for you.

If your representative is either a lawyer or an immigration consultant practising in Canada

- If you believe your representative has committed an offense in the course of representing you, you should go to the local police or to the Royal Canadian Mounted Police.

- If you are in Canada and you wish to recover money you paid for services you did not get, you can file a lawsuit in small claims court. You do not need a lawyer to do so, but you will have to pay a small fee.

- Legal Aid services are available throughout Canada for people who cannot afford to pay for legal assistance. Contact them to see if you qualify for assistance.

If your representative's place of business is abroad

- If your representative is not a Canadian citizen or a permanent resident of Canada, you should present your complaint to the appropriate authorities overseas. The Canadian government cannot get involved in the dispute.

CIC Call Centre

In Montreal: (514) 496-1010

In Toronto: (416) 973-4444

In Vancouver: (604) 666-2171

For all other areas: 1-888-242-2100 (From Canada & U.S.A)

PERMANENT RESIDENT CARD

The Permanent Resident Card (also known as the Maple Leaf Card or the PR Card) is a new, wallet-sized, plastic card. People who have completed the Canadian immigration process and have obtained Permanent Resident status, but are not Canadian Citizens can apply for the card. The card replaces the IMM 1000 as the status document needed by Canadian Permanent Residents re-entering Canada on a commercial carrier (airplane, boat, train and bus) as of December 31, 2003.

Security features of the new PR Card will simplify the screening process of Permanent Residents when boarding a commercial carrier going to Canada. The card also increases Canada's border security and improves the integrity of Canada's immigration process.

Beginning on June 28, 2002, PR Cards will be mailed to new Permanent Residents of Canada as part of the landing process. People who are already in Canada as Permanent Residents can apply for the new PR Card beginning October 15, 2002.

About the Permanent Resident Card

Background

The Canadian government has understood the need for a Permanent Resident Card for quite some time. The events of September 11, 2001 raised the issue of border security and the safety of all Canadians to the forefront. This made the introduction of a PR Card a key government initiative.

Before June 28, 2002, a successful landing application process resulted in the issuing of an IMM 1000 form. This document showed the holder's Canadian entry history. It was a large, difficult-to-carry piece of paper with no photograph, few security features and little in the way of privacy for the Permanent Resident. Technological advancements have made it easy to change, copy or make fraudulent use of many documents, including the IMM 1000.

CIC was intent on finding a replacement for this form that would address convenience, safety, privacy and durability concerns. The new PR Card not only addresses these concerns, but also includes state-of-the-art security features, making it extremely resistant to forgery and alteration.

The new card is a wallet-sized, plastic card, which confirms the Permanent Resident status of the cardholder. It replaces the IMM 1000 Record of Landing Form for travel purposes.

Security Benefits

The new PR Card contains several security features that make it a safe proof of status document for the cardholder. As of December 31, 2003, the new card is a necessary document for every Permanent Resident re-entering Canada by commercial carrier (airplane, boat, train and bus) after international travel.

The card has a laser engraved photograph and signature, as well as a description of the physical characteristics (height, eye colour, gender) of the cardholder printed on the front.

The card's optical stripe will contain all the details from the cardholder's Confirmation of Permanent Resident form. This encrypted information will only be accessible to authorized official (such as immigration officers) as required to confirm the status of the cardholder. The card cannot be used to monitor the activities or track the movement of the cardholder; this will protect the cardholder's privacy.

The card's optical stripe is more advanced than a magnetic stripe (commonly used on bank cards) both in terms of information storage capacity and security of information. Much like a commercial compact disc (CD), it is impossible to change, erase or add to the information already encoded on the optical stripe.

New Immigrants

Beginning on June 28, 2002, all new Permanent Residents will automatically receive their PR Card in the mail following their arrival in Canada. At the point of entry in Canada, personal data will be confirmed as part of the landing process.

If you did not provide your mailing address to CIC at the point of entry, please do so as soon as possible. You can provide this information on-line at **http://www.cic.gc.ca/english/e-services/index.html** or you can contact the PR Card Call Centre at 1-800-255-4541. Please note that if CIC do not receive your address within 180 days of the date of your admission, you will need to re-apply for your PR Card and pay the applicable fee.

Please notify CIC of any change in your mailing address as soon as possible. You may send them your change of address by mail, or use the on-line Change of Address service.

If you do not receive your PR Card within 30 days after sending CIC your address, please contact CIC <u>Call Centre</u>.

You can obtain a PR Card Application kit from CIC website, or by contacting the PR Card Call Centre at 1-800-255-4541 (from Canada & USA).

Canadian Citizens

Permanent Resident Cards are not issued to Canadian Citizens. Citizens need a Canadian Passport for international travel.

New PR Card Fees

The PR Card costs $50.00 per applicant. Each person applying for Permanent Residence status in Canada will need a card (children included.) The Card is normally valid for five years. All Permanent Residents will need a valid PR Card for re-entry into Canada on a commercial carrier as of December 31, 2003. It will be the cardholder's responsibility to make sure their card will be valid at the time of their return to Canada. If a Permanent Resident with a PR Card has become a Canadian Citizen, the PR Card is automatically cancelled. This person would then need to obtain a Canadian passport for international travel purposes.

Apply for Canadian Citizenship

If you have been a Permanent Resident and have been living in Canada for three years or more, you are eligible to apply for Canadian Citizenship.

What does it mean to be a Canadian citizen?

Citizenship means working together with all other Canadians to build a stronger Canada, and making sure our values, dreams and goals are reflected in our institutions, laws and relations with one another.

After living in Canada for at least three years as a permanent resident, you have the right to apply for Canadian citizenship.

Canada is a country that:

- is free and democratic;
- is multicultural;
- has two official languages; and
- extends equal treatment to all its citizens.

What are the rights and responsibilities of a citizen?

The *Canadian Charter of Rights and Freedoms* sets out the democratic rights and fundamental freedoms of all Canadians. Some rights are essential for Canadian citizens:

- the right to vote or to be a candidate in federal and provincial elections;
- the right to enter, remain in or leave Canada;
- the right to earn a living and reside in any province or territory;

135

- minority language education rights (English or French); and
- the right to apply for a Canadian passport.

Canadian citizenship also implies the following responsibilities:

- to obey Canada's laws;
- to vote in the federal, provincial and municipal elections;
- to discourage discrimination and injustice;
- to respect the rights of others;
- to respect public and private property; and
- to support Canada's ideals in building the country we all share.

Who is entitled to apply for Canadian citizenship?

You can apply for Canadian citizenship if you:

- are at least 18 years of age;
- have been a legal permanent resident in Canada for three out of the previous four years;
- can communicate in English or French; and
- have knowledge of Canada, including the rights and responsibilities of citizenship.

Who cannot become a Canadian citizen?

You may not be eligible to become a Canadian citizen if you:

- are under a deportation order and are not currently allowed to be in Canada;
- are in prison, on parole or on probation; and
- have been charged or convicted of an indictable offence.

Could you be a Canadian citizen and not know it?

In most cases, you are a Canadian citizen if you were born:

- in Canada, or
- in another country, after February 15, 1977, and have one Canadian parent.

For more information, telephone the Call Centre.

How do you apply for Canadian citizenship?

If you meet the requirements for Canadian citizenship, you can get an "Application for Citizenship" form from the Call Centre, or download an application at http://www.cic.gc.ca.

Fill out the application form and follow the instructions provided. A non-refundable processing fee and a refundable Right of Citizenship fee must be paid at the time of the application. You must include the receipt of payment and necessary documents with your application form.

You will have to take a test to show that you meet the requirements for knowledge of Canada and of either English or French. Study the information in the booklet *A Look at Canada* which will be sent to you with the acknowledgment of your application.

If you meet the basic requirements for citizenship, you will be invited to a citizenship ceremony where you will take the oath and receive your citizenship certificate.

What is dual citizenship?

Dual or plural citizenship means holding citizenship in one or more countries in addition to Canada.

Canada has recognized dual citizenship since 1977. This means that, in some cases, you may become a Canadian citizen while remaining a citizen of another country.

Some countries will not allow their citizens to keep their citizenship if they become citizens of another country. You should check with the embassy or consulate of your country of origin to be sure of their rules and laws.

Where should you go for more information about Canadian citizenship?

If you are in Canada, telephone the Call Centre.

Outside Canada, contact a Canadian embassy or consulate.

HOW TO APPLY

Once you have decided that you want to bring your skills to Canada, make sure that you follow the correct steps to apply.

There are a number of steps to follow when you prepare your application as a Skilled Worker. It is important that you carefully read and follow the instructions for each step listed below to ensure that your application is complete and submitted correctly.

Before you start your application, you need the forms that are specific to the Visa Office in your country or region. You will need the forms from your Visa Office for some of the steps below. Look for the checklist in these documents. The checklist will help you make sure that you have completed your application.

Find the checklist and appendixes for the Canadian Visa Office in your country or region.

STEP 1. Gather Your Documents

Collect the documents you need to support your application. A full list of these documents is included in **Appendix A: Checklist** found in the Visa Office-specific instructions for your location. The Checklist will tell you how many copies of the application form you need, which documents must be originals and which should be photocopies, and whether a certified translation in English or French is required.

STEP 2. Prepare The Forms

If any of your family members are included in your application, you will need more than one copy of some forms. Photocopy the following forms, or download and print the appropriate number from www.cic.gc.ca/skilled:

Application for Permanent Residence in Canada (IMM 0008): Page two of the form asks for details of your family members. There is space for three family members on the form. If you have more than three family members, make enough copies for everyone.

Schedule 1: Background/Declaration and *Additional Family Information* (IMM 5406): You, your spouse or common-law partner and each dependent child aged 18 or over (whether accompanying you or not) must complete these forms. Make enough photocopies for everyone.

STEP 3. Complete The Forms

For specific instructions, see the **How to Complete the Forms**

STEP 4. Obtain Police Certificates

You need police certificates from every country in which you or your family members aged 18 years or over have lived for six months or longer since reaching the age of 18. You will find instructions in **Appendix B: Obtaining Police Certificates/Clearances**.

STEP 5. Calculate Your Fees

Use the instructions in the **Fees** section to calculate the fees you must send with your application. Pay the fees according to instructions in the Fee Payment section of **Appendix A: Checklist**. Do not mail cash.

STEP 6. Make Sure Your Application Is Complete

Use the **Checklist** to verify that you have all of the required documents. Note that we may request additional information at any time during the application process.

STEP 7. Submit Your Application

Submit your completed application to the address indicated in the Checklist. Print your name and address in the top left-hand corner of the envelope.

☻ **If you do not fully complete and sign the forms and pay all necessary fees, your application will be returned to you unprocessed.**

HOW TO COMPLETE THE FORMS

The following text does not contain instructions for all the boxes on the forms. Most questions are clear; instructions are provided only when necessary. Note the following:

- Print clearly with a black pen or use a typewriter.

- Attach a separate sheet of paper if you need more space and indicate the number of the question you are answering.

- You must answer all questions. If you leave any sections blank, your application will be returned to you and processing will be delayed. If any sections do not apply to you, answer "N/A" ("Not applicable").

- If your application is accepted and information you provide on the forms changes before you arrive in Canada, you must inform, in writing, the visa office to which you applied. You must do this even if your visa has already been issued.

WARNING! It is a serious offence to give false or misleading information on this form. We may check to verify your responses. Misrepresentation will result in a two-year ban from entering Canada.

Application for Permanent Residence in Canada (IMM 0008)

To be completed by:

- You, as the principal applicant

At the top of this form, you will find three boxes:

Box 1: Category under which you are applying.
Check the "Economic class" box.

Box 2: How many family members...
Write the total number of people included in your application, including yourself and any family members, whether they are accompanying you to Canada or not.

Family members include your:

- **Spouse:** A husband or wife of the opposite sex
- **Common-law partner:** A person of the opposite or same sex with whom you have lived in a conjugal relationship for at least one year
- **Dependent children:** Daughters and sons, including children adopted before the age of 18, who:
    - are under the age of 22 and do not have a spouse or common-law partner;
    - have been continuously enrolled as full-time students and financially supported by their parents since turning 22 (or from the date of becoming a spouse or common-law partner if this happened before the age of 22); or
    - have substantially depended on the financial support of their parents since before turning 22 and are

unable to support themselves due to a medical condition.

Box 3: Language you prefer for

Correspondence: Decide which of English or French you are more comfortable reading and writing, and check the appropriate box.

Interview: You may be selected for an interview. Interviews can be conducted in English or French. You may also be interviewed in another language of your choice; however, you will be responsible for the cost of hiring an interpreter.

Instructions for filling out the rest of the form are listed below:

1. Print your full **family name** (surname) as it appears on your passport or on the official documents that you will use to obtain your passport. Print all of your **given names** (first, second or more) as they appear on your passport or official documents. Do not use initials.

5. If you are a citizen of more than one country, give details on a separate page.

10. This section requires you to give details of your past marriages or common-law relationships. If you have never had a spouse or common-law partner other than your current one, check the "No" box and proceed to Question 11. If you have, check the "Yes" box and provide the details requested. If you have had more than two previous spouses or common-law partners, give details on a separate page.

12. Check the box that best describes the highest level of education you have completed. If you have not completed secondary school, check the "No secondary" box.

- **Secondary education:** the level of schooling after elementary and before college, university, or other formal training. Also called high school.

- **Trade/Apprenticeship:** completed training in an occupation, such as carpentry or auto mechanics.

- **Non-university certificate/diploma:** training in a profession that requires formal education but not at the university level (for example, dental technician or engineering technician).

- **Bachelor's degree:** An academic degree awarded by a college or university to those who complete the undergraduate curriculum; also called a baccalaureate. Examples include a Bachelor of Arts, Science or Education.

- **Master's degree:** An academic degree awarded by the graduate school of a college or university. Normally, you must have completed a Bachelor's degree before a Master's degree can be earned.

- **PhD:** the highest university degree, usually based on at least three years graduate study and a dissertation. Normally, you must have completed a Master's degree before a PhD can be earned.

14. This is the address we will use to mail correspondence regarding your application. Print your address in English and, if applicable, also in your own native script.

19. Identity cards issued by a foreign national, provincial, municipal or other government, as well as cards issued by a recognized international agency such as the Red Cross, can be used to identify yourself. If you have such a card, print the number in the space provided. Photocopy both sides of the card and attach the photocopy to your application. If you do not have an identity card, print "N/A".

Details of family members

There is space for three family members on this form. If you have more than three family members, photocopy this page before you start to fill it in so you have enough space for everyone.

Given name(s)

Print all of your family members' **given names** (first, second or more) as they appear on their passports or official documents. Do not use initials.

Country of citizenship

If your family member is a citizen of more than one country, give details on a separate page.

Relationship to you

Indicate whether the family member is your spouse, common-law partner, daughter or son.

Will accompany you to Canada

Tell us if your family member will come to Canada with you. He or she must immigrate before the visa expires, but may arrive in Canada after you.

Education

Indicate the level of education your family member has successfully completed. Use the categories listed in Question 12.

Photos

Ask a photographer to provide you with a set of photos of yourself and each of your family members included in your application, whether they will be accompanying you or not. The required number of photos for each individual is indicated in Appendix A, under **Photos**. (For information on printing the appendices, see **How to Apply to Immigrate to Canada**.)

Photos must comply with specifications given in Appendix C, Photo Specifications. Make sure you give a copy of these specifications to the photographer.

- On the back of one photo (and only one) in each set, write the name and date of birth of the person appearing in the photo as well as the date the photo was taken.

- Enclose each set of photos in separate envelopes. Write the family member's name, date of birth and relationship to you on the corresponding envelope and close the envelope with a paper clip.

- Photos must not be stapled, scratched, bent or bear any ink marks.

Background / Declaration (IMM 0008, Schedule 1)

To be completed by:

- You

- Your spouse or common-law partner (whether accompanying you to Canada or not)

- Your dependent children aged 18 or over (whether accompanying you to Canada or not)

1. Write all of your given names. Do not use initials.

6. Indicate your current status in the country where you now live (for example, citizen, permanent resident, visitor, refugee, no legal status, etc.).

10. Provide details of all secondary and post-secondary education. Begin with the most recent program completed.

11. You must account for every month since your 18th birthday. Under "Activity", print your occupation or job title if you were working. If you were not working, enter what you were doing (for example, unemployed, studying, travelling, etc.). Attach another sheet if necessary.

15. Give a complete address including the street, town or city, province or region, and country. If there was no street or street number, explain exactly the location of the house or building. You must account for every month during the past 10 years. Do not use post office (P.O.) box addresses.

Declaration

Read the statements carefully. Sign and date in the boxes provided. By signing, you certify that you fully understand the questions asked, and that the information you have provided is complete, truthful, and correct. If you do not sign, the application will be returned to you.

Economic Classes - Skilled Workers (IMM 0008, Schedule 3)

To be completed by:

- You, as the principal applicant

3. If you have an offer of employment that has been approved by Human Resources Development Canada, tick the "Yes" box and give the name of your potential employer. See Factor 5: Arranged Employment for more information.

5. Use the instructions under Factor 2: English and French Language Ability to help you determine your ability in English and French.

10. "Funds" refers to money in Canadian dollars, and includes the value of any property you own. It does not include jewellery, cars or other personal assets.

11. To Determine your National Occupational Code (NOC), refer to the instructions in the **Will You Qualify?** section of this guide.

Additional Family Information (IMM 5406)

To be completed by:

- You
- Your spouse or common-law partner (whether accompanying you to Canada or not)
- Your dependent children aged 18 or over (whether accompanying you to Canada or not)

It is very important that you list on this form any other children (even if they are already permanent residents or Canadian citizens) that you, your spouse or common-law partner or your dependent children might have who are not included in your Application for Permanent Residence. This includes

- married children
- adopted children
- step-children
- any of your children who have been adopted by others
- any of your children who are in the custody of an ex-spouse, common-law partner or other guardian

You must answer all questions. If any sections do not apply to you, answer "N/A".

Use of a Representative (IMM 5476)

Complete this form if you are appointing a representative.

If you have dependent children aged 18 years or older, they are required to complete their own copy of this form if a representative is also conducting business on their behalf.

A **representative** is someone who has your permission to conduct business on your behalf with Citizenship and Immigration Canada.

When you appoint a representative, you also authorize CIC to share information from your case file to this person.

You are not obliged to hire a representative. We treat everyone equally, whether they use the services of a representative or not. If you choose to hire a representative, your application will not be given special attention nor can you expect faster processing or a more favourable outcome.

The representative you appoint is authorized to represent you only on matters related to the application you submit with this form. You can appoint only **one** representative for each application you submit.

There are two types of representatives:

Unpaid representatives

- friends and family members who do not charge a fee for their advice and services

- organizations that do not charge a fee for providing immigration advice or assistance (such as a non-governmental or religious organization)

- consultants, lawyers and Québec notaries who do not, and will not, charge a fee to represent you

Paid representatives

If you want us to conduct business with a representative who is, or will be charging a fee to represent you, he or she must be authorized. Authorized representatives are:

- immigration consultants who are members in good standing of the Canadian Society of Immigration Consultants (CSIC)

- lawyers who are members in good standing of a Canadian provincial or territorial law society and students-at-law under their supervision

- notaries who are members in good standing of the *Chambre des notaires du Québec* and students-at-law under their supervision

If you appoint a paid representative who is not a member of one of these designated bodies, your application will be returned. For more information on using a representative, visit our Web site.

Section B.

5. Your representative's full name

If your representative is a member of CSIC, a law society or the *Chambre des notaires du Québec*, print his or her name as it appears on the organization's membership list.

8. Your representative's declaration

Your representative must sign to accept responsibility for conducting business on your behalf.

Section D.

10. Your declaration

By signing, you authorize us to complete your request for yourself and your dependent children under 18 years of age. If your spouse or common-law partner is included in this request, he or she must sign in the box provided.

Release of information to other individuals

To authorize CIC to release information from your case file to someone other than a representative, you will need to complete form *Authority to Release Personal Information to a Designated Individual* (IMM 5475) which is available on our Web site and from Canadian embassies, high commissions and consulates abroad.

The person you designate will be able to obtain information on your case file, such as the status of your application. However, he or she will **not** be able to conduct business on your behalf with CIC.

You must notify cic if your representative's contact information changes or if you cancel the appointment of a representative.

Visa Office Specific Forms

These forms are part of the Skilled Worker application for permanent resident status in Canada. This is **step four** in your application. Make sure you complete steps one, two and three. Determine which Canadian visa office is responsible for:

- the country in which you are residing, provided you have been lawfully admitted to that country for at least one year; or

- your country of nationality.

Check the list of countries and Visa Offices (http://www.cic.gc.ca/english/offices/apply-where.html) to find out where you must send your application. Print out the forms and instructions specific to this office. Read the instructions carefully. You will find:

- a checklist of the documents you need to include with your application

- information about the medical examination;

- information about getting police certificates or clearances; and

- instructions about where to send your application.

Note: Checklist and appendices are included in the application forms.

The Application Assessment Process

A Visa Office will process your application. The Visa Office may process your application differently depending on your application and the Visa Office. Some processing steps are common to all Visa Offices.

After you submit your application, a Citizenship and Immigration Canada (CIC) officer will check to see that you submitted everything with your application. The officer will make sure that you:

- Completed your application form correctly;
- paid your application fee correctly; and
- included all supporting documentation.

If your application is not complete, CIC will return it to you without starting to process it.

Your Visa Office will send you a letter when they receive your completed application. The letter will tell you what you need to do and what happens next.

Processing Time

The length of time it takes to process your application can be different in each mission or Visa Office. Visit the <u>mission Web site</u>

http://www.cic.gc.ca/english/offices/missions.html   (if   available) where you submitted your application for more information on how long it might take to process your application.

You may be able to speed up the process by:

- making sure all the necessary information is included with your application;
- notifying the Visa Office of any changes to the information on your application;
- avoiding unnecessary enquiries to the Visa Office;
- making sure the photocopies and documents you provide are clear and readable;
- providing certified English or French translations of documents, where indicated; and
- applying from a country where you are a citizen or permanent resident.

Your application will be delayed if the Visa Office has to take extra steps to assess your case. Your application will take longer if:

- there are criminal or security problems with your application;
- your family situation is not clear because of a situation such as a divorce or adoption that is not yet complete or child custody issues that have not been resolved; or
- the local Visa Office has to consult with other CIC offices in Canada or abroad.

The Decision on Your Application

The CIC officer will make a decision on your application based on the points you accumulate in the <u>six selection factors</u>. The officer will also evaluate your ability to meet the <u>Required Funds</u> amount for the size of your family.

The Visa Office will contact you if they need more documentation or if you have to come in for a personal interview.

Confirmation of Permanent Residence

You will be given a *Confirmation of Permanent Residence* (COPR) if your application is successful. The COPR will have identification information as well as a photo and your signature. You **must** bring the COPR to the Port of Entry with your visa when you enter Canada.

Checking the Status of Your Application

Once you have received notice from our office that your application has been received, you can check the status of your application online at http://www.cic.gc.ca/english/e-services/index.html

A Word For A Wise

You may feel that it is very difficult to prepare application for immigration by yourself but when you will go through the whole contents of the checklists, you will understand the exact requirements to prepare and submit your application. Start preparing your required documents one by one. You will observe that its very easy and simple. Just go through each and every item on checklist at least twice. Most of skilled workers prepare their immigration cases by themselves and save considerable amount of professional fee ranging from US$ 2000-4000

> *Note :* Before filing your application for immigration always visit CIC website to match-up with the current rules and regulations as those might be changed. Always update yourself.

What if I don't want to take IELTS Test

If you believe that you are proficient enough in English language and have a certificate or diploma in English language training from a reputable institution in your country or if your mother tongue is English by birth. If either is the case and you do not prefer to take IELTS test then you can try and submit following explanation. This is a specimen, you can re-write it according to your situation. Further, it is the sole discretion of visa officer to accept or reject your explanation to award the necessary points for your English language ability. Visa officer can instruct you to take official IELTS test and submit the results.

A Specimen of Explanation of English Language Proficiency and Experience

My Training in English Language

My training in English language starts from my 1st grade at school and I gradually refined and mastered it by the passage of time. English language was the medium of instruction throughout my academics.

How Commonly I use English

Being a professional and spending most of my time at work, English is the dominating language that I have to communicate in throughout the day. Following is my caliber with regards to my proficiency in English language.

Speaking

- I can communicate effectively in most daily practical and social situations, and in familiar routine work situations with my colleagues and my superiors

- I can participate in conversations with confidence

- I can speak on familiar topics at both concrete and abstract levels (20 to 30 minutes). As I often need to do presentations for foreign delegates about the deployment of I.T and new technologies in our organization.

- I can provide descriptions, opinions and explanations; can synthesize abstract complex ideas and can hypothesize.

- In social interaction, I demonstrate increased ability to respond appropriately to the formality level of the situation.

- I can use a variety of sentence structures, including embedded and report structures, and an expanded inventory of concrete, idiomatic and conceptual language in my routine progress meetings with staff and directors.

- My discourse is reasonably fluent. Grammar and pronunciation errors rarely impede my communication. I also use phone on less familiar and some non-routine matters.

Listening

- I can comprehend main points, details, speaker's purpose, attitudes, levels of formality and styles in oral discourse in moderately demanding contexts.

- I can follow most formal and informal conversations, and some technical work-related discourse in my field at a normal rate of speech.

- I can follow discourse about abstract and complex ideas on a familiar topic.

- I can comprehend an expanded range of concrete, abstract and conceptual language.

- I can determine mood, attitudes and feelings.
- I can understand sufficient vocabulary, idioms and colloquial expressions to follow detailed stories of general popular interest.
- I can follow clear and coherent extended instructional texts and directions.
- I can follow clear and coherent phone messages on unfamiliar and non-routine matters.

Reading

- I can follow main ideas, key words and important details in an authentic four to six page text on a familiar topic.
- I can read popular newspaper and international magazines (Time, Newsweek, Reader Digest). I can read general / technical articles and popular easy fiction as well as academic and business materials.
- I can extract relevant points, but sometime require clarification of idioms and of various cultural references.
- I can locate and integrate several specific pieces of information in visually complex texts (e.g., tables, directories) or across paragraphs or sections of text. That text can be on abstract, conceptual or technical topics, containing facts, attitudes and opinions.
- I also use a unilingual dictionary when reading for precision vocabulary building

Writing

- I have demonstrated fluent ability in performing moderately complex writing tasks like in my technology reports.
- I can link sentences and paragraphs (three or four) to form coherent texts to express ideas on familiar abstract topics, with some support for main ideas, and with an appropriate sense of audience.

- I can write routine business letters (e.g., letters of inquiry, cover letters for applications) and personal and formal social messages.

- I can write down a set of simple instructions, based on clear oral communication or simple written procedural text of greater length.

- I can fill out complex formatted documents.

- I can extract key information and relevant detail from a page-long text and write an outline or a one-paragraph summary.

- I have demonstrated good control over common sentence patterns, coordination and subordination, and spelling and mechanics. in my professional report writing.

Proof of English Language Training

Please find attached attested copy of my diploma in English language training from_____ in which I have **scored 85% marks** .

Sincerely

Susan Orlean

ASIAN CANADIAN HISTORIC TIMELINE.

1788
John Meare arrives on Nootka Sound on Canada's Pacific cost, with two ships carrying 50 Chinese carpenters and craftsmen. They build a two-storied fort and a schooner, but are captured by the Spanish and taken to Mexico.

1858
The first Chinese gold-miners migrate to Barkerville, British Columbia from San Francisco. Chinese miners join thousands of other prospectors in the trek northward along the Fraser River.

Many Chinese people who came to Canada in the nineteenth century are from Guangdong province in southern China. Their historical arrival marks the establishment of a continuous Chinese community in Canada.

1861
Won Alexander Cumyow is born in Victoria. He is the first Chinese baby to be born in Canada.

1863
The first Chinese community organization is formed. The Hong Shun Tang, in Barkerville. A booming little town with a large Chinatown, including 300 Chinese residents.

1872
The British Columbia Qualifications of Voters Act denies the Chinese the right to vote.

1877
Arrival of Manzo Nagano, the first Japanese person known to land and settle in Canada.

1878

A British Columbia law is passed making it illegal for Chinese people to be employed on construction projects paid for by the provincial government.

1880-1886

The construction of the western section of the Canadian Pacific Railway employs thousands of Chinese workers. More than 4,000 died in the effort.

1884

The federal government sets up a Royal Commission to review Chinese immigration.

1885

Following the Royal Commission, the federal government introduces the Act to Restrict and Regulate Chinese immigration into Canada, which requires that Chinese people entering Canada to pay a head tax of $50 per person.

1886

With the completion of the Canadian Pacific Railway, Chinese start small service-oriented businesses. Many move east to centers such as Calgary, Toronto and Montreal in search of job opportunities and less discrimination.

1895

The British Columbian government denies citizens of Asian heritage the right to vote.

1900

The federal government raises the Chinese immigration head tax to $100, to take effect in 1902. The Royal Commission on Chinese and Japanese immigration holds hearings and concludes limiting Chinese and Japanese immigration will not damage trade between China and Canada.

1902
The Royal Commission on Chinese and Japanese Immigration declared all Asians, "unfit for full citizenship .. obnoxious to a free community and dangerous to the state".

1903
The federal government raises the head tax to $500. With only eight Chinese entering Canada, the government's increase in head tax had a drastic effect on Chinese immigration.

The first South Asians settle in the southwest section of British Columbia. Most of them were Sikhs who worked in the lumber industry.

1907
Though immigration was severely limited early in the century, a poor economy in Vancouver continued to produce strong discriminatory feelings by the unemployed whites toward Asians. This frustration lead to the creation of The Asiatic Exclusion League in British Columbia.

September 8, 1907.
Several thousand league-organized marchers met in downtown Vancouver to spread anti-Asian sentiment. The crowd had grown to about 15,000 supporters. The mob eventually moved to Chinatown and little Tokyo where they looted, burned and destroyed Chinese and Japanese businesses. Because the South Asians lived in a different part of the city, their community was spared the violence of the riot. The federal government paid the Chinese community $26,990 and the Japanese community $9175 for damage to their property.

1908
With the Hayashi-Lemieux Gentlemen's Agreement, Japan voluntarily agreed to restrict the number of passports issued to male laborers and domestic servants to an annual maximum of 400.

January 8, 1908.

An immigration policy was passed that only allowed entry to those traveling by "continuous passage" from their country of origin to Canada. Without direct passage to Canada, South Asians were not able to enter Canada.

1914

Gurdit Singh attempted to challenge the "continuous passage" legislation. He hired a ship, the Komagata Maru, and planned a non-stop voyage to Vancouver with 376 East Indian immigrants. Canadian officials did not allow the men to disembark. Negotiations carried on for two months after which the federal government expelled the ship and escorted the ship and all of its 376 passengers back out to sea.

1916-1917

200 Japanese Canadians volunteer for service with Canadian army in France for World War I. 54 are killed and 92 are wounded.

1917

Employers in British Columbia, Alberta, and Saskatchewan propose importing Chinese workers to relieve the labor shortage caused by World War I.

1917-1918

Ontarian, Manitoba, Saskatchewan, and British Columbia pass laws making it illegal to hire white women in Chinese-owned restaurants and laundries. The Chinese community challenges the law in the courts, but the ruling favors the provinces.

1919

Japanese fishermen control nearly half of the fishing licenses (3,267). The Department of Fisheries responded by reducing the number of licenses issued to "other than white residents, British subjects, and Canadian Indians". By 1925 close to 1000 licenses were stripped from the Japanese.

1920
A dozen Chinese veterans who saved in the Canadian Army during World War I are given the right to vote.

1921
The School Board of Victoria puts all Chinese students in one separate school. Parents remove their children from the school, which eventually turns into a boycott. It lasts a year until the Victoria school board permits the Chinese students to return.

1923
The Chinese immigration Act (the Exclusion Act) prohibits Chinese immigrants from entering Canada, with few exceptions. Many wives and children in China are unable to join their husbands and fathers in Canada. All Chinese people already living in Canada, even the native born, have to register with the government to receive a certificate of registration.

1931
Surviving Japanese veterans of World War are given the right to vote.

First Filipino immigrant recorded to enter Canada.

Vietnamese flee their native country. Many leaving on boats destined for the United States and Canada.

1976
Jean Lumb, becomes the first Chinese-Canadian to receive the Order of Canada Award.

1977
To mark the hundredth anniversary of the settling in Canada of the first Japanese, a mountain in British Columbia was named after the first settler, Manzo Nagano.

1979

Chinese Canadians organize nationally to protest the racist depiction of Chinese Canadians in a story called "Campus Giveaway" on CTV's nationally televised current events program, W5. The protect results in the creation of the Chinese Canadian National Council.

1983

Thirty-seven organizations take part in the First Conference of Filipinos held in Ontario.

1987

The Vietnamese Canadian Centre is founded in Ottawa.

1988

Prime Minister Brian Mulroney announces the Canadian Government's formal apology for the wrongful incarceration, seizure of property and the disenfranchisement of thousands of Canadians of Japanese ancestry. A redress settlement was also announced which included individual compensation for all survivors.

1989

The Chinese communities across Canada organize and join the worldwide call for democracy and human rights in response to the Tianamen Square Massacre in China.

1990

Influx of skilled immigrants from India, Pakistan and Philippines are on rise.

1993

Raymond Chan and Gary Mar become federal and provincial members of parliament.

1994

Toronto holds its first annual Asian Heritage Month in May – Edmonton, Halifax, Montreal, and Vancouver also soon followed by adopting May as Asian Heritage Month as well.

100 Vietnamese and Canadian human rights advocates hold a workshop addressing the ongoing human rights violations in Vietnam.

1995

Japanese Canadian National Museum & Archives Society is incorporated and begins planning for museum and archives facility in National Nikkei heritage Center.

1997

In Toronto, an "all Chinese language" radio station is established, with numerous television, and print media outlets.

Premier Ralph Klein strengthens ties with Korea. Recognizing Alberta is home to over 5,000 Korean Canadians and that Korean studies are offered at Alberta universities and colleges.

June 30, 1997

Hong Kong reverts back to China, prompting a steady flow of Hong Kong Chinese entrepreneurs to Canada.

1999

British Columbia proclaims May as Asian Heritage Month. This proclamation marks the 50th anniversary of the first Asian Canadian participation in British Columbian and Canadian elections.

2002

Canada has become the 99th country to ratify the Kyoto Protocol on reducing greenhouse gas emissions

2005

As of Feb-01, 2005 same-sex couples can now marry in seven out of the ten provinces of Canada, and in one out of the three territories. A court case is expected in Alberta in early 2005. If that case authorizes SSM in the province, then only 3% of Canadians will live in a jurisdiction that still prohibits SSM.

On Feb 01, 2005, the federal government introduced a bill (C-38) to legalize SSM from sea onto sea. The main result of the bill will be that 13% of same-sex couples who wish to get married will be able to do it more conveniently -- without leaving their province or territory of residence

Bill C-38 came about because of court rulings that found the traditional definition of marriage violated the equality rights of gays and lesbians under the Charter of Rights and Freedoms.

Same-sex marriage is now the law in seven provinces and one territory. Bill C-38 would harmonize the definition of marriage across Canada.

Proportion of Foreign–born Highest in Ontario

- Data from the 2001 Census show that Ontario has the highest proportion of people born outside Canada, followed closely by British Columbia.

- In 2001, 3 million people or 26.8% of the population of Ontario were foreign-born, up from 23.7% ten years earlier. In 2001, British Columbia had one million people who were foreign-born, representing 26.1% of its total population.

- About one million of Ontario's foreign-born population arrived in the past 10 years, between 1991 and 2001. These individuals accounted for 9% of the Ontario population.

Immigrants to Ontario Increasingly from Asia

- Immigrants from Asia represented 58% of all immigrants to Ontario in the 1990s, and 45% in the 1980s. Before 1961, just 2.3% of immigrants who came to Ontario were Asian-born.

Proportion of Foreign-born (in per cent)

	1991	1996	2001
Newfoundland	1.5	1.6	1.6
Prince Edward Island	3.2	3.3	3.1
Nova Scotia	4.4	4.7	4.6
New Brunswick	3.3	3.3	3.1
Quebec	8.7	9.4	9.9
Ontario	**23.7**	**25.6**	**26.8**
Manitoba	12.8	12.4	12.1
Saskatchewan	5.9	5.4	5.0
Alberta	15.1	15.2	14.9
British Columbia	22.3	24.5	26.1
Yukon	10.7	10.4	10.6
Northwest Territories	6.6	6.6	6.4
Nunavut	1.9	1.9	1.7
Canada	**16.1**	**17.4**	**18.4**

Note: Foreign-born: the population who are, or have ever been, landed immigrants to Canada.

Source: Statistics Canada, *Census of Canada*, 2001

- In comparison, European immigrants accounted for the vast majority (92.7%) of the immigrants who came to Ontario before 1961. Since then, the proportion of European immigrants has declined steadily, falling to 20% in the 1990s.

- In the first 6 decades of the last century (prior to 1961), European nations, in particular the United Kingdom, Italy, Germany and the Netherlands, were the primary sources of immigrants to Ontario. Combined, these 4 European nations accounted for 64% of all immigrants to Ontario before 1961. However, in the 1990s, they accounted for just 3.1% of immigrants.

- Of the one million immigrants to Ontario who arrived between 1991 and 2001, 14.6% came from the Americas, up from 4.4% before 1961. In the 1990s, more than 80% of these came from Central America, the Caribbean or South America.

- Immigration from Africa also increased significantly in recent decades. People born in Africa made up 6.8% of immigrants to Ontario in the 1990s, up from 0.4% of immigrants who arrived prior to 1961.

China Leading Country of Birth for 1990s Immigrants

- China (and its Special Administrative Regions - Hong Kong and Macau) was the leading country of birth among people who immigrated to Ontario in the 1990s. It accounted for 16% of all immigrants who came to Ontario in the past decade.

Place of Birth, Immigrants to Ontario (in per cent)

	Before 1961 (in numbers)	1991-2001 (in numbers)	Before 1961 (in per cent)	1991-2001 (in per cent)
Asia	**11,365**	**593,740**	**2.3**	**58.1**
West Central Asia/Middle East	2,395	98,795	0.5	9.7
Eastern Asia	6,415	197,795	1.3	19.3
South-East Asia	950	92,875	0.2	9.1
Southern Asia	1,605	204,275	0.3	20.0
Europe	**465,995**	**206,565**	**92.7**	**20.2**
Western Europe	114,385	13,305	22.8	1.3
Eastern Europe	72,775	108,340	14.5	10.8
Northern Europe	140,815	22,525	28.0	2.2
Southern Europe	138,020	62,395	27.5	6.1
Americas	**22,165**	**149,720**	**4.4**	**14.6**
North America	14,930	23,765	3.0	2.3
Central America	475	22,830	0.1	2.2
Caribbean and Bermuda	4,365	57,845	0.9	5.7
South America	2,395	45,280	0.5	4.4
Africa	**1,795**	**69,035**	**0.4**	**6.8**
Western Africa	40	14,475	0.0	1.4
Eastern Africa	195	30,315	0.0	3.0
Northern	835	15,025	0.2	1.5

171

- India was the next leading country of birth of immigrants to Ontario. Between 1991 and 2001, Indian immigrants accounted for 9% of total immigrants to Ontario. The third leading country of birth of immigrants was the Philippines (6%), followed by Sri Lanka (5.2%) and Pakistan (4.5%).

- Among European immigrants who arrived in Ontario during the 1990s, the most frequent countries of origin were Poland (3.1%), Yugoslavia (2.1%) and Russia (2.1%).

- Of immigrants to Ontario from the Americas, Jamaica was the leading country of birth among those who arrived in the 1990s with 2.7% of all immigrants to Ontario, followed by the United States (2.3%), and Guyana (2.2%).

- Among African immigrants, Somalia was the leading birth country of immigrants to Ontario.

Toronto: One of Highest Proportion of Immigrants

- The Toronto Census Metropolitan Area** (CMA) had one of the highest proportions of foreign-born of all major urban centres in the world.

- About 44% of Toronto's population in 2001 was born outside Canada, higher than Miami (40%), Los Angeles (31%), and New York City (24%).

Northern Africa	835	15,025	0.2	1.5
Central Africa	30	3,120	0.0	0.3
Southern Africa	695	6,100	0.1	0.6
Oceania	1,015	2,930	0.2	0.3
Other	400	375	0.1	6.0
Total	**502,740**	**1,022,370**	**100.0**	**100.0**

Proportion of Foreign-born, Ontario CMAs

	Total Population	Foreign-born (in numbers)	Foreign-born (in per cent)
Greater Sudbury	153,895	10,775	7.0
Hamilton	655,055	154,660	23.6
Kingston	142,765	17,675	12.4
Kitchener	409,765	90,570	22.1
London	427,215	80,410	18.8
Oshawa	293,545	46,150	15.7
Ottawa-Gatineau (Ontario part)	795,255	168,125	21.1
St.Catharines-Niagara	371,400	66,045	17.8
Thunder Bay	120,370	13,320	11.1
Toronto	**4,647,955**	**2,032,960**	**43.7**
Windsor	304,955	67,880	22.3
Ontario	**11,285,550**	**3,030,075**	**26.8**

Note: Excludes non-permanent residents.

Source: Statistics Canada, *Census of Canada*, 2001

172

- Toronto CMA was home to 77.5% of Ontario's immigrants in the 1990s, compared to its 41% share of Ontario's population. Toronto CMA was home to 69% of the immigrants who came to Ontario in the 1970s.

- Vancouver was an even greater magnet for immigrants to British Columbia. About 325,000 or 87.6% of the 1990s immigrants to British Columbia settled in Vancouver compared to the CMA's 51% of the province's population in 2001.

* The Toronto CMA includes all of Toronto, Peel and York Census Divisions and parts of Durham and Halton.

Share of 1990s Foreign-born, Ontario CMAs

	Total Foreign-born	1990s Foreign-born (in numbers)	1990s Foreign-born (in per cent of Ontario)
Greater Sudbury	10,775	1,040	0.1
Hamilton	154,660	35,545	3.5
Kingston	17,675	3,425	0.3
Kitchener	90,570	26,120	2.6
London	80,410	19,475	1.9
Oshawa	46,150	6,900	0.7
Ottawa-Gatineau (Ontario part)	168,125	63,950	6.3
St.Catharines-Niagara	66,045	9,925	1.0
Thunder Bay	13,320	1,325	0.1
Toronto	2,032,960	792,035	77.5
Windsor	67,880	24,310	2.4
Ontario	3,030,075	1,022,370	100.0

Note: Excludes non-permanent residents.

Source: Statistics Canada, *Census of Canada*, 2001

173

PART-II

A **NEWCO**MER'S **INTROD**UCTION

TO

CANADA

FOREWORD

Congratulations! You are taking a big step. Moving to a new country offers exciting opportunities and new beginnings!

This information will help you get ready to leave your home country and make a new life in Canada. It tells you what documents you will need to bring, what to expect in the first few days and weeks, how to find a place to live, get a Social Insurance Number and a health-care card, and find a job. It also explains what services you can expect to receive from the immigrant-serving organizations across Canada. You will also find useful information about Canada's geography, history, government and way of life, and about how to become a Canadian citizen.

A Newcomer's Introduction to Canada was written to give you helpful information for planning ahead, but it is not a detailed guide. When you arrive in Canada, you will be given a book called'

Welcome to Canada: What You Should Know.
http://www.cic.gc.ca/english/newcomer/welcome/index.html.

It contains specific information on all the practical aspects of living in Canada.

A Newcomer's Introduction to Canada may not answer all of your questions, but it is a good place to start.

CONTENTS

GETTING READY -- BEFORE YOU LEAVE FOR CANADA

- Essential documents
- Important documents
- What you should know about health care
- What you can bring into Canada
- Getting ready to look for work
- Getting ready if you are a business immigrant
- Communities across Canada
- The Canadian climate: What to expect and what clothes to bring
- Schools and universities

THE DAY YOU ARRIVE IN CANADA

- Customs and immigration
- Reception services

IMMIGRANT-SERVING ORGANIZATIONS

- LINC (Language Instruction for Newcomers to Canada)
- Host Program

YOUR FIRST FEW DAYS IN CANADA

- Finding a place to live
  - To buy or to rent
  - Types of housing
  - How to find a place to live
  - What if you have a large family?
  - How much will it cost?
  - Signing a lease

- Applying for a health-insurance card
- Applying for a Social Insurance Number

FINDING A JOB, BUILDING A FUTURE

- International educational assessment services in Canada
- Provincial evaluation services
- Employment in regulated professions and trades
- Language skills
- Job opportunities
- Employment laws
- Discrimination
- Deductions and taxable benefits
    - Income tax
    - Canada Pension Plan
    - Employment Insurance
    - Taxable benefits
    - Union dues

GENERAL INFORMATION ABOUT CANADA

- Geography
- Distances
- Population
- Map of Canada
- The Francophone population
- History
- Economy
- Government
- Federal government
- Provincial governments
- Territorial governments
- Municipal governments

- Bilingualism
- Multiculturalism
- Protecting the environment -- Sustainable development

THE CANADIAN WAY OF LIFE

- o Family life and family law
- o Marriage, divorce and the law
- o Birth control and family planning
- o Youth and their parents
- o Youth and the law
- Standards and expectations
  - o Important social standards
- Some Canadian laws
- Interacting with officials
  - o People in authority
  - o Public officials
  - o Police officers

YOUR RIGHTS AND OBLIGATIONS

- Personal rights and freedoms
- Children's rights
- Women's rights
- Senior citizens' rights
- Becoming a Canadian citizen
- Responsible and active citizenship

AFTERWORD

GETTING READY -- BEFORE YOU LEAVE FOR CANADA

- **Essential documents**
- **Important documents**
- **What you should know about health care**
- **What you can bring into Canada**
- **Getting ready to look for work**
- **Getting ready if you are a business immigrant**
- **Communities across Canada**
- **The Canadian climate: What to expect and what clothes to bring**
- **Schools and universities**

Essential Documents

When you travel to Canada, you will need to have the following documents with you:

- a Canadian immigrant visa and Confirmation of Permanent Residence for each family member travelling with you;

- a valid passport or other travel document for each family member travelling with you;

- two copies of a detailed list of all the personal or household items you are bringing with you; and

- two copies of a list of items that are arriving later.

Note: The lists should state how much your personal and household items are worth.

- You must also bring with you enough money to cover living expenses such as rent, food, clothing and transportation for a six-month period. You may be asked to show proof of your funds.

Do not pack your documents in a suitcase. You will need to have them available to show to immigration and customs officials.

TIP ! Make two copies of these lists -- one for you to keep and one for the Canada Customs officer. You can get the Canada Customs and Revenue Agency form for this purpose from the Internet at www.ccra-adrc.gc.ca/E/pbg/cf/b4abq

Important documents

Depending on your personal situation, you should bring the following important documents with you to Canada:

- birth certificates or baptismal certificates;
- marriage certificates;
- adoption, separation or divorce papers;
- school records, diplomas or degrees for each family member travelling with you;
- trade or professional certificates and licences;
- letters of reference from former employers;
- a list of your educational and professional qualifications and job experience (this is also called a résumé);
- immunization, vaccination, dental and other health records for each family member;

- driver's licence, including an International Driver's Permit, and a reference from your insurance company;

- photocopies of all essential and important documents, in case the originals get lost (be sure to keep the photocopies in a separate place from the originals); and

- car registration documents (if you are importing a motor vehicle into Canada).

> **TIP** ! If possible, get all of your documents translated into English or French by a qualified translator before you leave for Canada.

What You Should Know About Health Care

Canada has a public health-care system known as "medicare." It provides insurance coverage for health-care services to all Canadian citizens and permanent residents. (You will be a "permanent resident.") The federal government sets health-care standards for the whole country, but the programs are run by the provincial ministries of health. More information on the health-care system can be found in *__Your first few days in Canada__.*

> **TIP** ! Apply for provincial health-care coverage as soon as possible after you arrive in the province where you plan to live.

Note: British Columbia, Ontario, Quebec and New Brunswick have a three-month waiting period before you become eligible for medicare coverage. If you are planning to settle in any of these provinces, you should buy private health insurance coverage for the first three months. Insurance companies are listed in the Yellow Pages of all Canadian telephone books, under "Insurance."

TIP ! Bring a supply of your medications with you to allow you time to find a family doctor in Canada from whom you will have to get new prescriptions. (getting insurance before you travel will cost you less)

What You Can Bring Into Canada

There are strict laws about what you can bring into Canada.

Cars must meet Canadian safety and pollution control standards. Many cars are not allowed into the country. Contact Transport Canada for more information before you ship your car.

Transport Canada, Vehicle Importation
330 Sparks Street, Tower C
Ottawa, Ontario K1A 0N5

Telephone: 1 (613) 998-8616
(when calling from outside Canada)

1 800 333-0371
(toll-free, from inside Canada)

Web site: **www.tc.gc.ca**

(follow the link to Vehicle Importation)

The following items cannot be brought into Canada:

- unauthorized firearms, explosives, fireworks and ammunition;

- narcotics, other than prescription drugs;

- meat, dairy products, fresh fruits and vegetables;

- plants, flowers and soil;

- endangered species of animals or products made from animal parts, such as the skin, feathers, fur, bones and ivory;

- cultural property, including antique and cultural objects considered to have historical significance in their country of origin (you may, however, bring family heirlooms);

- more than 200 cigarettes (you must pay tax on the excess amount) per person over 18 years of age if you are immigrating to Quebec, Alberta, Saskatchewan or Manitoba, or per person over 19 if you are immigrating to Ontario or any of the other provinces; and

- more than 1.5 litres of commercial alcohol (you must pay tax on the excess amount) per person over 19 years of age.

If you are not sure about an item, you can write to or telephone:

Canada Customs and Revenue Agency
Customs, Excise and Taxation
Information Services
2265 St. Laurent Boulevard
Ottawa, Ontario K1G 4K3

Telephone: 1 (506) 636-5064
(when calling from outside Canada)

1 800 461-9999
(toll-free, from inside Canada)

Web site: **www.ccra-adrc.gc.ca**

Getting Ready To Look For Work

If possible, have your documents translated into English or French before you leave for Canada. Essential documents for looking for work include:

- a résumé of your education, work and volunteer experience, and your skills and qualifications;
- diplomas, degrees, certificates and other qualifications;
- letters of recommendation; and
- school records or transcripts.

> **TIP !** Improving your English or French before coming to Canada would be extremely beneficial.

Research the labour market in the part of Canada where you plan to settle. The following federally funded Web sites will be helpful:

- **www.workinfonet.ca:** This is a national Web site for career and labour market information. It contains job information for each province and territory. It also contains information on self-employment, education and training.
- **www.workdestinations.org:** This Web site contains information on various jobs, working conditions, labour market trends, living conditions, and training and educational opportunities in different regions of Canada. It also lists regulated jobs in Canada. You can find out whether your job

is regulated and what you will need to do to get a licence to practise.

- **lmi-imt.hrdc-drhc.gc.ca:** This Web site offers labour market information, which can help you search for work and make general employment, training and career decisions.

- **workplace.hrdc-drhc.gc.ca/page2.asp?sect=1:** This Web site offers links to Canadian newspapers' on-line "Help Wanted" advertisements.

- **www.worksitecanada.com/news:** This Web site links to the employment section in the classified advertisements pages of Canada's daily newspapers to give you an idea of the jobs available now.

TIP ! Professionals in government-regulated occupations should contact the licensing body in their province of destination. See *Employment in regulated professions and trades. (Read Fact Sheet-2)*

TIP ! To be better prepared to look for work in Canada, have your credentials evaluated and compared with the Canadian education system to make it easier for employers to determine whether you meet their job requirements. See *International educational assessment services in Canada.*

Getting Ready If You Are A Business Immigrant

If you are coming to Canada as a business immigrant, use the Internet to find out about sources of financing, business opportunities, export and investment services, self-employment assistance and information for small businesses. There are many rules for starting a business in Canada. The following Government of Canada Web sites will help you get a head start in your planning:

- **www.cbsc.org:** The Canada Business Service Centre's Web site is your single point of contact for information on government services, programs and rules for business.

- **www.strategis.gc.ca:** This Industry Canada Web site has business information to help you find partners, do market research, find new technologies, and learn about financing opportunities and growth areas in the Canadian economy.

- **www.bdc.ca:** This is the Web site of the Business Development Bank of Canada. It provides financial and consulting services to Canadian small businesses, especially those in the technology and export sectors of the economy. It also offers information on how to start a business and make it succeed.

- **http://strategis.ic.gc.ca/sc_mangb/smallbus/engdoc/sbla.html:** This is the Web site of the Canada Small Business Financing Program. The program can help you finance your own business.

- **www.contractscanada.gc.ca:** This Web site has information on how and what the Government of Canada buys (both goods and services).

- **www.cic.gc.ca:** This is the Web site of Citizenship and Immigration Canada. It describes the Business Immigration Program. You will find many answers to your questions at this site.

> **TIP !** When you are deciding how much money to bring into Canada, it helps to research the cost of living in the part of Canada where you plan to live. This information can be found on the provincial and territorial Web sites at canada.gc.ca/othergov/prov_e.html.

Communities Across Canada

Most newcomers to Canada tend to settle in the three biggest cities - Toronto, Montréal and Vancouver. But many newcomers and many Canadians choose to live in the medium-sized cities, which they feel have as much to offer as the larger cities with a better quality of life.

Among the medium-sized cities are Halifax, Québec City, Ottawa, London, Windsor, Sudbury, Winnipeg, Saskatoon, Regina, Calgary and Edmonton.

All of the medium-sized cities have diverse, multi-ethnic populations ranging in size from approximately 100,000 to one million people, and all have the variety of public and private institutions and services found in the largest cities.

> **TIP !** To locate the medium-sized cities on a map of Canada, go to *Map of Canada*.

Some newcomers like the idea of living in smaller cities or towns like Moncton, Fredericton and Victoria, or prefer to live in a rural area. Depending on your skills or professional qualifications, some regions may have better job opportunities than others.

> **TIP !** Outside the larger cities, the costs of housing, higher education and services are often much lower.

If you use the Internet, visit the Web sites of each province and territory to see what each has to offer. To find these Web sites, visit **canada.gc.ca/othergov/prov_e.html**.

Each Web site has a list of government departments and agencies. In the bigger provinces, some government departments may have their own Web sites, with more detailed information. You may also find a directory of on-line services, a link to educational institutions, and a link to major cities and towns. Most of the Web sites also have a tourism section, where you can discover the special attractions of each province and territory.

As mentioned earlier in this chapter, the Web site **www.workdestinations.org** has links to information on the labour market and the housing market of communities across Canada. It also has useful tips and information about moving within Canada.

You can also visit a Web site called Canadian Government Information on the Internet at **www.cgii.gc.ca**. It is another useful link to federal, provincial and municipal government information.

> **TIP !** Research carefully the labour market trends or access to your profession in the province and city where you wish to live.

> **TIP !** Most Web sites have a search engine. When you click on the search button, you can look for specific information on immigration, multiculturalism, citizenship, education, training, employment, housing, labour, health, employment opportunities or jobs by typing in these key words.

The Canadian Climate: What To Expect And What Clothes To Bring

Most of Canada has four distinct seasons: spring, summer, autumn and winter. The temperatures and weather in each season can be different from one part of the country to another. Here is what you can expect:

Spring: Spring is a rainy season in most parts of Canada. Daytime temperatures rise steadily, but the nights remain cool. Average daytime temperatures are about 12°C in March, April and early May.

Summer: Summer officially begins on June 21, but July and August are summer for most Canadians. In summer, the weather is very warm in most parts of the country. In southern Canada, daytime temperatures are normally above 20°C and can sometimes rise above 30°C.

Autumn: The autumn season, or fall, as it's often called, begins in September. The weather cools and the leaves on many trees change colour and fall to the ground. It can also be very rainy at this time of year. In some parts of Canada, especially northern or mountain regions, snow may begin to fall by late October. Average daytime temperatures are about 10°C to 12°C in most of the country. The autumn months are September, October and November.

Winter: During the winter months (December, January and February), the temperature in most of the country usually stays below 0°C, day and night. Temperatures in some parts of the country periodically drop below -25°C, while along the West Coast, the temperature rarely drops below 0°C. In most of Canada, snow will be on the ground from mid-December to the middle of March. The higher in elevation and the farther north you go, the longer and colder winter becomes.

TIP ! You can find detailed weather information for each region of Canada on the Environment Canada Web site: weatheroffice.ec.gc.ca.

TIP ! If you arrive in Canada in the winter, you will need warm clothing such as insulated, waterproof boots; an overcoat; a scarf for your neck; a hat that covers your ears; and gloves or mittens. If you come from a warm climate, buy some winter clothes before you leave for Canada, if possible. Or, be ready to buy winter clothes soon after arriving (note also that winter clothes are more expensive than summer clothes). You may wish to contact an immigrant-serving organization in your new community for help.

Schools And Universities

There is no national school system in Canada. Schools and universities are run by the provinces; therefore, education varies somewhat from province to province. Most elementary and secondary schooling is public, meaning it is free and open to everyone.

Depending on the individual province, primary education starts at pre-kindergarten and continues to the end of grade 6 or 8. This is followed by secondary education or high school. In some provinces this may be divided into junior high (grades 7 to 9) and senior high (grades 10 to 12). Normally, students must complete the required academic courses in high school in order to be admitted to university or college.

The regular school year runs from late August or early September until mid- to late June. New students can usually be registered throughout the school year. Most schools are closed on national holidays. Also, all schools are closed between Christmas Eve and New Year's Day, and most are closed for a week in March for spring break. The longest school holiday occurs over the summer months of July and August.

Universities and community colleges hold their regular classes from late August or early September until April, although some courses are offered from January to April and a smaller number are available over the summer months. University and community college courses are not free and the costs vary among the provinces.

When you register your children at the local school or school board office, you must take with you:

- Canadian immigrant visa (Record of Landing);
- birth certificate or baptismal certificate;
- vaccination certificate;
- any previous school records.

> **TIP !** Education in Canada is available in English and French. Many Canadian parents, even if they do not speak French themselves, believe it is good for their children to be able to speak both English and French. Some put their children in a French immersion program, where children learn most of the regular subjects in French.

Your children's language and mathematical skills will be assessed, if necessary, and they will be placed in the program the school thinks is best for them.

> **TIP !** For information about the educational system in Canada, visit the provincial or territorial Web sites at canada.gc.ca/othergov/prov_e.html, or visit ceris.schoolnet.ca/e/, www.aucc.ca or www.accc.ca.

THE DAY YOU ARRIVE IN CANADA

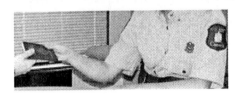

- **Customs and immigration**
- **Reception services**

Customs and immigration

You will probably find the entry procedure fairly straightforward because you have a passport and other <u>essential documents</u>.

You will be interviewed by a Canada Customs officer. You will need to give the officer a list of all the household and personal items that you will be bringing into Canada. You should also show the immigrant visa to the customs officer, who will refer you to an immigration officer.

The immigration officer will check your visa and travel documents and ask you questions similar to those on the Immigrant Application Form, to verify that you are of good character and in good health. At this time, you may also be asked to show proof of your funds. If there are no difficulties, the officer will authorize your entry to Canada as a permanent resident by signing your Record of Landing or Confirmation of Permanent Residence.

If you arrive at one of the major Canadian airports, you will get a booklet called *Welcome to Canada: What You Should Know*. It has information on most aspects of life in Canada. It also provides addresses and telephone numbers for:

- immigrant-serving organizations across Canada;
- language training assessment centres (which help eligible adult newcomers find free language classes);
- useful federal and provincial government offices.

Reception Services

If you arrive in Toronto, Montréal or Vancouver, you will find immigrant reception services in the airport. These services are run by immigrant-serving organizations. They help newcomers get the information and services they need, and this help is often available in several languages. In Montréal, the *Ministère des Relations avec les citoyens et de l'Immigration* runs this service.

TIP ! *Welcome to Canada: What You Should Know* and other useful information for newcomers can be found on the Internet at www.cic.gc.ca/english/newcomer, and at www.directioncanada.gc.ca

IMMIGRANT-SERVING ORGANIZATIONS

- **LINC (Language Instruction for Newcomers to Canada)**
- **Host Program**

There are hundreds of immigrant-serving organizations in Canada. Many are staffed by former newcomers to Canada, who understand the challenges that immigrants may face. They usually have people available who speak your language and can accompany you as interpreters. Citizenship and Immigration Canada supports many of these organizations financially, helping newcomers adapt to life in Canada.

Settling in will be much easier if you contact an immigrant-serving organization as soon as you arrive. The people who work for these organizations can help you find a place to live and can answer your questions about shopping, education for your children, transportation, language training and other important matters.

Immigrant-serving organizations can help you:

- find a place to live;
- get your Social Insurance Number and health-care card;
- enroll your children in school;
- get language training;

- find a family doctor;
- find out about government and community services for newcomers;
- look for a job;
- develop a realistic budget; and
- get emergency food aid, if it is needed.

Note: In Quebec, the *Ministère des Relations avec les citoyens et de l'Immigration* is organized into different regions. Each region has a local office, called a *Carrefour d'intégration,* which works with the immigrant-serving organizations to help newcomers adapt to life in Quebec.

Most immigrant-serving organizations offer, or can provide information on, the following Government of Canada programs:

LINC (Language Instruction for Newcomers to Canada)

LINC is a federal government program for all eligible adult immigrants. It offers:

- free language training for adult newcomers who want or need basic English or French;
- language classes given by school boards, colleges and local organizations;
- the choice of studying part time, full time, evenings or weekends, depending on your needs and your schedule; and
- transportation and child-minding, if necessary.

> **TIP !** Your local immigrant-serving organization can direct you to a LINC Assessment Centre, which will then refer you to organizations offering LINC classes. You can also refer to the book *Welcome to Canada: What You Should Know* to find a LINC Assessment Centre in your area.

Host Program

The Host Program is a federally funded program that matches newcomers with a Canadian family or individual. Host volunteers help you:

- overcome the stress of moving to a new country;
- learn about available services and how to use them;
- practise English or French;
- prepare to look for a job; and
- participate in community activities.

> **TIP !** Your local immigrant-serving organization can direct you to a Host Program organization in your community.

Immigrant-serving organizations are prepared to help newcomers as soon as they arrive in Canada. These organizations can:

- refer you to economic, social, health, cultural, educational and recreational services;
- give you tips on banking, shopping, managing a household and other everyday tasks;
- provide interpreters or translators, if you need them;
- provide non-therapeutic counselling; and
- help you prepare a professional-looking résumé and learn job-searching skills.

200

The Immigrant Settlement and Adaptation Program (ISAP), a federal government program, pays for these services.

A list of immigrant-serving organizations across Canada can be found on the Internet at
www.cic.gc.ca/english/newcomer/welcome/wel-20e.html

> **TIP !** Manitoba, British Columbia and Quebec have programs similar to LINC, the Host Program and ISAP, but they may have slightly different names.

YOUR FIRST FEW DAYS IN CANADA

- **Finding a place to live**
    - ○ **To buy or to rent**
    - ○ **Types of housing**
    - ○ **How to find a place to live**
    - ○ **What if you have a large family?**
    - ○ **How much will it cost?**
    - ○ **Signing a lease**
- **Applying for a health-insurance card**
- **Applying for a Social Insurance Number**

Finding A Place To Live
To Buy or To Rent

When you first arrive in Canada, you will probably be living in a temporary home. You will soon be looking for a more permanent place to live. Canada has many different types of housing and a wide range of prices. Finding the right place will take some time and effort. Your first decision will be whether to rent a house or an apartment, or to buy a house.

Whether you rent or buy will depend on your personal finances and whether you already have a job in Canada. Most newcomers decide they should first rent a house or apartment. This gives them more time to save money to buy a house and to decide where they want to live.

If you want to buy a house, unless you can pay the full price, you will need to get a long-term loan called a mortgage. Mortgage loans are provided by banks and other financial institutions. They decide whether the borrower has enough income, more assets than debts, and a good credit rating. Most will ask you to pay at least 10 percent of the cost of the house from your own money.

Types of housing

- **Furnished or unfurnished:** Furnished housing should include beds, tables, chairs, lamps, curtains, a stove and a refrigerator. Unfurnished housing may include a stove and a refrigerator, but not always.

- **Room for rent:** This is usually in a house or an apartment that is owned or rented by other people. Everyone shares the kitchen and bathrooms.

- **Bachelor or studio apartment:** These are small apartments designed mainly for one person. They have one large room with a kitchen and a sleeping area, plus a separate bathroom.

- **Other apartments:** Most other apartments have from one to three bedrooms. All will have a separate kitchen, a living room and a bathroom.

- **Duplex:** This is a house divided into two separate apartments. It may be bought or rented.

- **Townhouse:** This is a small house joined to other houses. It may be bought or rented.

- **Condominium:** This is an apartment or townhouse that is individually owned, while "common areas" are jointly owned. As well as the mortgage payment and property taxes, each owner pays a monthly fee for maintenance, such as snow removal, grass cutting and repairs.

How To Find A Place To Live

Here's how to look for the right home for you:

- search the classified advertisements in local newspapers;
- become familiar with the public transportation available;
- ask an immigrant-serving organization in your area for advice;
- ask friends and family already living in the area for advice;
- look for "Vacancy" or "For Rent" signs on houses and apartment buildings;
- check bulletin boards in grocery stores, Laundromats, health clinics and community centres; and
- ask for advice at your place of worship.

What if you have a large family?

If you have three or more children, or you have older relatives living with you, you will probably not be able to find a big enough apartment. In that case, you may need to think about renting a house.

How much will it cost?

You could expect to pay between $350 a month for a room, and $2,000 a month for a luxury apartment or a large house. Rental costs vary greatly across cities and across Canada. Housing is more reasonable outside the large cities. An immigrant-serving organization in the area where you plan to settle can help you find affordable housing.

Signing a lease

Once you agree to rent an apartment or a house, you may be asked to sign a one-year lease. This legal document of one or two pages describes the rental property, the utilities included and the options, such as parking and storage. It may also state whether pets or more people are allowed. Most apartments are leased by the year, although some are rented monthly.

You will probably need to pay the first and last month's rent when you sign the lease.

If your apartment requires a lease, your landlord will give you the lease form to sign. Read it over carefully before you sign it. Pay special attention to the parts that state exceptions and additions. You should know which utilities you will pay for and which ones will be paid for by the landlord. Be sure you know what the monthly rent payment includes. For example, is the electricity included? the water included? the parking included?

> **TIP !** As people in Canada tend to move in the spring and summer months, these are the best times to look for a home; there will be more choices available.

Also find out whether you have to pay a fee if you leave before the lease term is over. You cannot usually break a lease agreement. It is also likely you will be asked to provide a Canadian reference or to have a co-signer sign the lease to guarantee your financial commitment.

If you don't understand some of the legal terms used in the lease document, contact one of the groups that help immigrants, or someone you know and trust who can help you. Once you sign the lease, it is a legal document.

> **TIP !** Plan on spending 35 to 50 percent of your income on housing. This should include the cost of electricity, heating, telephone service and water. To find out more before you arrive in Canada, visit the Web site www.cic.gc.ca or www.cmhc-schl.gc.ca/en/bureho/reho

Applying For A Health Insurance Card

One of the most important things you need to do as soon as you arrive in Canada is to apply for a health insurance card. All members of your family, even newborn babies, must have their own card. You can get an application form from the provincial ministry of health office, any doctor's office, a hospital or a pharmacy. If necessary, the immigrant-serving organization in your area can help you fill out the form. To apply for a health card, you will need your birth certificate, Record of Landing (IMM 1000) or Confirmation of Permanent Residence (IMM 5292) or PR Card and passport. The Permanent Residence card may also be presented. In most provinces, you will receive coverage as soon as you apply.

> **TIP !** In Ontario, British Columbia, New Brunswick and Quebec, there is a three-month waiting period before you become eligible for medicare coverage. If you are immigrating to any of these provinces, you should get private, short-term health-care insurance for the first three months. Insurance companies are listed in the Yellow Pages of all Canadian telephone books, under "Insurance."

Health-care services covered by medicare include:

- examination and treatment by family doctors;

- many types of surgery;

- most treatment by specialists;

- hospital care;

206

- X-rays;
- many laboratory tests; and
- most immunizations.

Health-care services not covered by medicare, and for which you will have to pay, include:

- ambulance services;
- prescription drugs;
- dental care; and
- glasses and contact lenses.

These services are sometimes covered by workplace benefit packages.

Your health insurance card is mainly for use in the province where you live. If you are visiting another province and have a medical emergency, you can use your card. However, if you move to another province, you will need to apply for a new card.

Applying For A Social Insurance Number

To work in Canada, you must have a Social Insurance Number. This is a nine-digit number that you will need to look for a job and to receive government benefits. Sometimes, you will hear people call it the SIN number. You can get a SIN application form through the Human Resources Development Canada Centre near you. These centres are run by the federal government. You can also get a form through your local immigrant-serving organization or from the post office, or you can download one from the Internet at **www.hrdc-drhc.gc.ca/sin-nas.** The SIN card will be sent to you in the mail. There is a small fee for processing the application.

> **TIP !** To find the nearest Human Resources Centre, look in the Blue Pages of any telephone book under "Government of Canada -- Employment," or go on the Internet at www.hrdc-drhc.gc.ca/menu/profile-search.shtml#100

FINDING A JOB, BUILDING A FUTURE

- **International educational assessment services in Canada**
- **Provincial evaluation services**
- **Employment in regulated professions and trades**
- **Language skills**
- **Job opportunities**
- **Employment laws**
- **Discrimination**
- **Deductions and taxable benefits**
  - **Income tax**
  - **Canada Pension Plan**
  - **Employment Insurance**
  - **Taxable benefits**
  - **Union dues**

In Canada, full-time jobs are common. However, a growing number of people have part-time or short-term jobs. Women make up a large portion of the work force and many have important, senior positions.

Canadians may change jobs and careers several times. This is often a personal choice. Sometimes people must change jobs because the economy changes. For these, and other reasons, getting a job is not easy. Many people are looking for work.

Newcomers to Canada rarely enter the job market quickly and often must start with jobs below the skill level they worked at in their home country. Once they have Canadian job experience and their ability in English or French improves, so do their job prospects.

International educational assessment services in Canada

Even if you have many years of experience, you do not automatically have the right to practise your trade or profession in Canada. In most cases, you will need to have your credentials assessed to see whether you need more training, education or Canadian work experience before being qualified to practise. You may wish to get your credentials evaluated before you leave for Canada. The following organizations can tell you how to get your credentials assessed:

The Canadian Information Centre for International Credentials Web site (www.cicic.ca) has information on academic and occupational credentials for all of Canada and lists nearly 100 professions and trades, in alphabetical order. When you click on your profession or trade, you will find a link to the address and telephone number of the professional or trade association, the addresses and telephone numbers of provincial evaluation services and regulatory agencies, and labour market information (for example, whether there is a demand for people with your particular trade or profession). You will also be able to find out whether your profession or trade is regulated.

The Centre does not grant equivalencies or assess credentials. It gives advice and refers newcomers to sources of help. To contact the Centre by mail, write to:

Canadian Information Centre for International Credentials

95 St. Clair Avenue West, Suite 1106
Toronto, Ontario M4V 1N6
Telephone: 1 (416) 962-9725
Fax: 1 (416) 962-2800
E-mail: info@cicic.ca
URL: **www.cicic.ca**

Provincial evaluation services

World Education Services assesses academic credentials for a fee. Its assessment will tell you how your education compares with educational standards in the province where you are planning to settle. You can give your assessment to any employer in Canada. It may help you in your job search. To contact World Education Services, write to:

World Education Services Academic
Credential Assessment Service
45 Charles Street East, Suite 700
Toronto, Ontario
M4Y 1S2 Canada
Telephone: 1 (416) 972-0070
Toll-free: 1 866 343-0070 (within Canada)
Fax: 1 (416) 972-9004
E-mail: ontario@wes.org
URL: **www.wes.org/ca**

Education Credentials Evaluation
(Service des équivalences d'études)
Ministère des Relations avec les citoyens
et de l'Immigration
Suite 200
800, De Maisonneuve Boulevard East
Montréal, Quebec
H2L 4L8 Canada
Telephone: 1 (514) 864-9191
Toll-free: 1 877 264-6164 (within Canada)
Fax: 1 (514) 873-8701
E-mail: equivalences@mrci.gouv.qc.ca
URL: **www.immq.gouv.qc.ca/equivalences**

International Qualifications
Assessment Service
Ministry of Learning
Government of Alberta
4th Floor, Sterling Place
9940-106 Street
Edmonton, Alberta
T5K 2N2 Canada
Telephone: 1 (780) 427-2655
Fax: 1 (780) 422-9734
E-mail: iqas@gov.ab.ca
URL: **www.learning.gov.ab.ca/iqas/iqas.asp**

International Credential Evaluation Service
4355 Mathissi Place
Burnaby, British Columbia
V5G 4S8 Canada
Telephone: 1 (604) 431-3402
Fax: 1 (604) 431-3382
E-mail: icesinfo@ola.bc.ca
URL: **www.ola.bc.ca/ices**

**Manitoba Credentials
Recognition Program**
Manitoba Culture, Heritage and Citizenship
Settlement and Labour Market
Services Branch
5th Floor, 213 Notre Dame Avenue
Winnipeg, Manitoba
R3B 1N3 Canada
Telephone: 1 (204) 945-6300 or
1 (204) 945-3162
Fax: 1 (204) 948-2256
E-mail: immigratemanitoba@gov.mb.ca
URL: *www.gov.mb.ca/labour/immigrate/newcomerservices/7c.html*

Employment in Regulated Professions and Trades

In Canada, about 20 percent of jobs are regulated by the government to protect public health and safety. For example, nurses, doctors, engineers, teachers and electricians all work in regulated professions. People who want to work in regulated jobs need to get a licence from the regulatory body in the province in which they live. If you want to know more about how to enter a particular profession or trade in a particular province, you should contact the provincial regulatory body for that job. The professions are self-regulating and they administer the provincial laws that apply to their profession. Rules for entering professions also differ from province to province. (For more information, visit **www.cicic.ca**.)

> **TIP !** Regulated occupations in Canada usually require many years of education, training and practical experience, and the successful completion of a technical examination. Technical examinations to enter a trade or profession can be very expensive.

Language Skills

It is important to learn English or French as quickly as possible. Many newcomers begin life in Canada by looking for a job that will allow them to learn or improve their English or French. The

Language Instruction for Newcomers to Canada (LINC) program gives eligible adult immigrants the chance to take basic English or French classes at no charge.

People with foreign credentials need a Test of English as a Foreign Language (TOEFL) score to enter Canadian colleges and universities. Colleges and universities offering courses in French use various French language tests.

> **TIP !** Look into taking English classes through the LINC Program.

Job Opportunities

- **Human Resources Development Canada Centres:** Counsellors at these centres can give you free advice and information about job and language training and work creation programs for newcomers. They can help you plan an effective job search and prepare a résumé of your education and experience. Each centre also has listings of available jobs on computer or on bulletin boards.

- **Classified advertisements:** Every daily newspaper in Canada has a classified advertisements section where you will find a variety of jobs listed. In many areas, there are also weekly or monthly employment papers that advertise jobs.

- **Local help:** To help newcomers prepare to enter the Canadian work force or to gain access to their profession or trade in Canada, immigrant-serving organizations have a variety of programs. Some give workshops on job search skills, where participants get an overview of the job market where they live. Participants learn, among other things, how to write a good résumé and how to behave in an interview. In some areas, there are job-finding clubs, mentoring programs, programs to help you get volunteer work experience, and wage subsidy programs.

- **Your personal "network":** One of the best ways to learn about jobs is to talk to people. They can be people you know well, or people you have just met. Even if they cannot lead you directly to a job, they can provide you with information, ideas and names of other people who might be able to help and encourage you.

- **The Internet:** Many Web sites have information on job opportunities. You can search for a job on-line in any part of Canada. Some sites also give practical advice on how to plan your job search. Others allow you to apply for a job directly on the Internet, or to post your résumé (in English or French). When you do this, your résumé goes into a database that can be searched by employers. Try visiting the following Web sites, run by the federal government:

- **www.hrdc-drhc.gc.ca:** This is the national Web site of Human Resources Development Canada, a federal department. It is also the gateway to many of the sites mentioned below.

- **ele-spe.hrdc-drhc.gc.ca:** This is an on-line database of jobs and work or business opportunities across Canada. It matches work to people and people to work. You can click on the province where you plan to settle and submit a list of your skills to the database to find work opportunities that match your profile.

- **worksearch.gc.ca:** This site will take you through all the steps needed to choose a career and to carry out an effective work search.

- **www.workinfonet.ca:** This is a national site for career and labour market information. It will link you to job information for each province and territory. It also includes information on self-employment, education and training.

- **jb-ge.hrdc-drhc.gc.ca:** This is the "Job Bank" Web site. It contains an on-line database of thousands of job vacancies across Canada.

- **lmi-imt.hrdc-drhc.gc.ca:** This site will link you to detailed labour market information for every city in Canada.

- **www.SkillNet.ca:** This is a large network of job and career information Web sites. It can link you to full-time and part-time job opportunities.

- **www.canadait.com:** This site is a gateway to job opportunities in the information technology and communications sector. It has links to company directories and associations that will help you find potential employers.

- **www.jobs.gc.ca:** This site posts federal government jobs available across the country and accepts on-line applications.

- **www.integration-net.cic.gc.ca:** This site is run by Citizenship and Immigration Canada. It includes links to many different types of jobs and other useful information for newcomers.

TIP | When you arrive in Canada, refer to the pamphlet called "Finding Help in Your Community" in the booklet *Welcome to Canada: What You Should Know* for a list of the immigrant-serving organizations across Canada. Contact an agency in your area and ask about job search programs for newcomers.

Employment laws

Federal and provincial laws protect workers and employers by setting minimum wage levels, health and safety standards, and hours of work. They provide for maternity leave, annual paid vacation and protection of children who are working. There are also human rights laws that protect employees from unfair treatment by employers based on sex, age, race, religion or disability.

216

Discrimination

There are laws to protect workers from discrimination. For example, an employer must hire employees on the basis of their qualifications. Employers cannot refuse to hire you because they don't like your skin colour or your religion. This is discrimination. It is also discrimination if you are refused a job because of your age, sex, marital status, disability or sexual orientation.

Deductions And Taxable Benefits

Whether you are a Canadian citizen or a permanent resident, when you are hired, your employer will deduct money from your pay cheque to pay for the following:

Income tax

All Canadian residents who are old enough to work must file an income tax return each year, whether they earned any money or not. That is the law. If you are working for an employer, a percentage of your pay cheque will be deducted and sent to the federal government to cover the income tax that you owe. If too much is deducted, you will get a refund. If you paid too little, you will have to pay more. This money helps pay the cost of government services.

Canada Pension Plan

A small part of your pay cheque goes into this plan. When you retire, you will receive a monthly pension from the federal government. The amount will vary according to how many years you worked in Canada before retiring and what your salary was. Residents of Quebec pay into the Quebec Pension Plan, which works the same way as the federal plan. These plans also include survivor's pensions for the spouses of deceased pensioners, disability pensions and death benefits.

Employment Insurance

When you are working, a small percentage of your pay cheque will be deducted each month to go into the Employment Insurance Account. Your employer contributes to the account as well. Employment Insurance gives money to eligible, unemployed Canadian residents for a short time, while they look for a new job or take some training to learn new skills.

Taxable benefits

Your employer may provide some benefits (for example, life insurance, special medical care, a dental plan or a private pension plan) that are taxable.

Union dues

If you are in a union, and the union has an agreement with your employer, some money will be deducted to pay for the union dues.

GENERAL INFORMATIONABOUT CANADA

- **Geography**
- **Distances**
- **Population**
- **Map of Canada**
- **The Francophone population**
- **History**
- **Economy**
- **Government**
- **Federal government**
- **Provincial governments**
- **Territorial governments**
- **Municipal governments**
- **Bilingualism**
- **Multiculturalism**
- **Protecting the environment -- Sustainable development**

Geography

Canada consists of 10 provinces and three territories in five main regions: the Atlantic region, Central Canada, the Prairies, the West Coast and the North. The culture and population are different in each region.

The **Atlantic** region consists of the provinces of Nova Scotia, New Brunswick, Prince Edward Island, and Newfoundland and Labrador. Activities such as fishing, farming, forestry, tourism and mining are important to the Atlantic economy.

Central Canada consists of the provinces of Ontario and Quebec. This is the most populated region of the country. Together, Ontario and Quebec produce more than three-quarters of all Canadian manufactured goods.

The **Prairies** include the provinces of Manitoba, Saskatchewan and Alberta. Much of the land is flat and fertile, excellent for farming and rich in energy resources. In western Alberta, the Prairies end and the Rocky Mountains begin. The Canadian Rockies include some of the largest peaks in North America.

On the **West Coast,** the province of British Columbia is famous for its mountain ranges and forests. Natural resources such as lumber and fish are important to the economy. Fruit farming is also a major industry, as is tourism.

The **North** consists of Canada's three territories: Yukon, the Northwest Territories and Nunavut. Together, they make up over one-third of Canada's land mass. Northern resources include oil, natural gas, gold, lead and zinc.

Distances

Distances in Canada are measured in kilometres. Canada is over 7,000 kilometres from east to west. You would need seven days to drive from Halifax, Nova Scotia, to Vancouver, British Columbia. By airplane, the same trip would take about seven hours.

Population

Canada has about 32 million people. More than 80 percent of all the people in Canada live in towns and cities within 250 kilometres of the United States border. Ottawa is Canada's capital city, with a population of nearly one million. It is located in the province of Ontario. Canada's largest cities are Toronto, Ontario (5.2 million people); Montréal, Quebec (3.6 million); and Vancouver, British Columbia (2.1 million).

Map of Canada

Region	Province/Territory	Capital
Atlantic Region	Newfoundland and Labrador	St. John's
	Prince Edward Island	Charlottetown
	Nova Scotia	Halifax
	New Brunswick	Fredericton
Central Canada	Quebec	Québec
	Ontario	Toronto
Prairie Provinces	Manitoba	Winnipeg
	Saskatchewan	Regina
	Alberta	Edmonton
West Coast	British Columbia	Victoria
North	Nunavut	Iqaluit
	Northwest Territories	Yellowknife
	Yukon	Whitehorse

Note: *You can view a full size coloured North American map by visiting following link.*
http://www.lonelyplanet.com/mapshells/north_america/canada/canada.htm

The Francophone Population

French is the mother tongue of 6.6 million Canadians. Most Francophones live in Quebec, but almost one million Francophones live in Canada's other provinces and territories. About 76 percent of Francophones living outside Quebec live in Ontario and New Brunswick. Manitoba, Alberta and British Columbia each have approximately 50,000 Francophones, while Nova Scotia has 35,000 and Saskatchewan has fewer than 20,000. The areas with the smallest French-speaking populations are Prince Edward Island, Newfoundland and Labrador, and the three territories.

TIP ! For information on Francophone communities outside Quebec, visit the following Web sites: franco.ca/atlas/ or www.ocol-clo.gc.ca/7e_2.htm

History

Canada is a land of many cultures and many peoples. Aboriginal peoples have occupied the territory now called Canada for several thousands of years. Everybody else, either by birth or by descent, has been an immigrant -- we have all come from somewhere else. It has been said that Canada is a "nation of immigrants."

There are three main groups of Aboriginal peoples in Canada: the First Nations, the Inuit and the Métis. There are more than 50 different languages spoken by Canada's Aboriginal peoples, most of which are spoken only in Canada. In fact, the name "Canada" may have come from the word "Kanata," which means a settlement in the language of the Huron-Iroquois **First Nations peoples.**

As a country, Canada came into being on July 1, 1867. This event is known as "Confederation." Before 1867, the French arrived first, then the British. Each brought their own language, system of government, laws and culture. In 1763, after a long war between the British and the French, all of Canada came under British rule and was known as "British North America."

In the late 18th and into the 19th century, during and after the time of the American Revolution, many African-Americans and United Empire Loyalists fled the United States for Canada, where British ties remained and slavery had been abolished.

During the mid- to late 19th and early 20th century, waves of immigrants arrived from Europe, attracted by the opportunity of a new and better life in Canada. Some settled in towns and cities; others worked in factories, mines and lumber camps. Many were farmers who turned the Prairie region into wheat fields. Asian immigrants from China, Japan and India settled mainly in the western provinces during this time. Many immigrants helped build Canada's national railways, which joined the east and west coasts and opened up the interior for settlement.

After both world wars, thousands of Europeans came to Canada as immigrants and refugees and helped build Canada's post-war economy. Canada's experience during and after the Second World War raised awareness of the needs of refugees and the desire of families to be together.

Over the last 50 years, people from all over the globe have sought a better life or have sought refuge in Canada, fleeing civil wars, political unrest and natural disasters.

Canada still needs the skills, talents and enthusiasm of newcomers to build our country, together with those who have come before them. All of this has been reflected in Canada's immigration and refugee policies. Today, Canada is home to immigrants from more than 240 countries. Most newcomers decide to become citizens of Canada, after they are settled and have met the requirements of Canadian citizenship.

Economy

Canada has a diversified economy. Natural resources industries, such as forestry, mining, oil and gas extraction, farming and fishing, are important sources of jobs and export earnings. Canada is also a world leader in the fields of telecommunications, biotechnology, aerospace technologies and pharmaceuticals. More and more jobs involve work in service industries or in information technology. Along with the United States and Mexico, Canada is a partner in the North American Free Trade Agreement.

Canada has a decimal system of currency. The Canadian dollar is the basic unit of money. The most common paper bills are the $5, $10 and $20, but $50 and $100 bills are also used. Canadian coins include the penny (one cent), nickel (five cents), dime (10 cents), quarter (25 cents), loonie ($1) and toonie ($2).

Government

Canada is a federation, with a parliamentary system of government. Being a federation means that powers and responsibilities are divided between the federal government and the 10 provincial governments. Canada also has three territorial jurisdictions. Canada has three levels of government: federal, provincial and municipal (cities and towns). These governments are elected by the citizens of Canada.

Federal government (Government of Canada)

The federal government is responsible for:

- defence;
- foreign policy and foreign relations;
- banking;
- the postal service;
- criminal law;
- immigration; and
- citizenship.

Provincial governments

Provincial governments are responsible for:

- education; and
- municipal institutions.

They also share responsibility with the federal government for:

- health services;
- farming;
- social assistance;
- transportation; and
- the environment.

Territorial Governments

The Northwest Territories, Yukon and Nunavut are not sovereign units. They get their powers from the federal parliament, but they have elected assemblies that follow many of the same practices as the provincial governments.

Municipal Governments

Municipal governments have functions delegated to them by other levels of government. They are responsible for local matters and services. These include:

- police and fire protection;
- water and sewer services;
- recreation; and
- local public transportation.

If you are interested, the Web site **canada.gc.ca/howgoc/glance_e.html** has more information about how Canadians govern themselves.

Bilingualism

Under the *Official Languages Act,* Canada is an officially bilingual country. This means that Canadians have the right to get federal government services in English or French, no matter what part of Canada they are living in.

New Brunswick is the only province that is officially bilingual. New Brunswick residents receive services in both official languages from all of their provincial government departments and agencies.

In Quebec, French is the official language and in most cases, provincial and municipal services are provided in French.

In the other provinces and territories, English is the official language, and the availability of provincial services in both official languages varies.

At the municipal level, the availability of services in both official languages varies greatly.

Multiculturalism

Canada is populated by people who have come from every part of the world. Through the *Canadian Multiculturalism Act,* the government encourages Canadians to take pride in their language, religion and heritage and to keep their customs and traditions, as long as they don't break Canadian laws.

Protecting the environment --Sustainable development

Canada has a beautiful natural environment. Because we have lots of land and a small population, most of our country is wild and unspoiled. However, it is becoming harder to preserve our environment as our population and cities grow. Pollution helps cause large-scale environmental problems, such as acid rain. And as more people use and live in natural areas, threats to the environment increase.

Canadians are very concerned about environmental issues. They know that damage to the environment can be hard to fix.

Canadians know that economic growth is crucial for the future prosperity of Canada. But growth must be managed carefully so that it does not harm the environment. The Canadian government is committed to "sustainable development," which is economic growth that does not hurt the environment and helps people.

A healthy environment is important to quality of life. Everyone living in Canada should act in a responsible way, both toward the environment and within their community. This way, future Canadians have the opportunity to live in a country that is clean and prosperous. Both individuals and groups can help Canada develop in a sustainable way.

Here are a few things you can do to help protect quality of life:

- throw waste paper and other garbage in public garbage cans;
- compost, recycle and re-use as many products as possible, such as paper, glass and cans;
- conserve energy and water by turning off lights and taps when you are not using them;

- walk, join a car pool, or use a bicycle or public transit whenever possible;

- use products that are environmentally friendly;

- plant trees or grow a garden, but avoid using chemicals;

- never pour paint, oil or other harmful chemicals down sinks or toilets, into sewers or onto the ground (telephone your local government to find out where you can throw out these hazardous materials);

- volunteer with a local organization; and

- educate yourself and your children about environmental issues.

For further information, contact:

Environment Canada
Enquiry Centre
351 St. Joseph Boulevard
Hull, Quebec K1A 0H3

Telephone: 1 (819) 997-2800
1 800 668-6767 (toll-free, within Canada)

Fax: 1 (819) 953-2225
E-mail: enviroinfo@ec.gc.ca
Web site: **www.ec.gc.ca**

TIP ! Contact your local government to find out about the services and bylaws that protect the environment (for example, garbage disposal schedules, water management and recycling programs). You can find local government telephone numbers in the Blue Pages of the telephone book.

THE CANADIAN WAY OF LIFE

- **Family life and family law**
- **Marriage, divorce and the law**
- **Birth control and family planning**
- **Youth and their parents**
- **Youth and the law**
- **Standards and expectations**
  - **Important social standards**
- **Some Canadian laws**
- **Interacting with officials**
  - **People in authority**
  - **Public officials**
  - **Police officers**

Family Life And Family Law

Many people in Canada find that it takes two incomes to raise a family, even though parents are having fewer children. Most mothers have a job outside the home, and in many families, both parents share the work of shopping, cooking, cleaning the house and looking after the children. Because divorce has become more common, there are many one-parent families in Canada. Most single parents who raise their children on a full-time basis are women. There are also same-sex couples with children.

Marriage, divorce and the law

Canadian law views marriage as a legal agreement or contract between a man and a woman. Married people are considered equal partners. Marriage laws apply to all Canadian citizens and permanent residents. Many unmarried couples live together. In most provinces, unmarried heterosexual couples who have lived together for a certain period of time have legal status as "common-law" couples. They may call each other "husband" and "wife," or they may simply say "my partner."

Either the wife or the husband can ask for a divorce. This request will normally be approved by the courts if both people have agreed to end the marriage. Divorce will also be approved if one partner has been harmed through cruelty, adultery or a similar injustice.

Birth control and family planning

Many people use birth control. It is a matter of personal choice. Women can get a prescription for birth control pills from a doctor. Family planning information is available from government departments of health and public health offices, as well as from local health clinics. Abortion is legal but is only available from a doctor.

Youth and their parents

When children arrive in Canada, they usually learn about Canadian life quickly through schools, television, movies and music. If they need to learn English or French, they often learn it quite quickly.

Parents find out about Canadian life differently, as they search for housing and work. They too may need to learn English or French, but often need more time than their children to do so.

If you have children, you will know that you see the world somewhat differently than they do, because you are older and have more life experience. After immigrating to Canada, however, you may find that these differences increase, because you are having different experiences of Canadian life. These differences affect the behaviour of all family members and can lead to tension in the family between parents and their children.

Discussing concerns with teachers, doctors, public health workers, social workers, settlement workers, and friends and relatives who have already settled in Canada will help you and your children understand your experiences and make good choices about your future.

Youth and the law

Youth in Canada who commit a crime are held accountable for their actions. However they are not dealt with in the same way as adult offenders. This is because they may not have an adult's understanding of their crime. They are also more likely than adult offenders to be reformed and become law-abiding citizens. The law for young offenders is called the *Youth Criminal Justice Act.*

STANDARDS AND EXPECTATIONS

Some of Canada's standards for public behaviour may be more conservative than you are used to, while others may seem more liberal. For example, Canadians may seem impersonal and cold to some newcomers; to others, we may seem overly friendly.

Important social standards

Social practices -- not laws -- govern many types of behaviour in Canada. Some traditions are well established and are politely but firmly enforced. For example:

- **Lining up, or queuing:** People normally line up or queue according to the principle of "first-come, first-served." They will be angry if you push ahead in a line-up instead of waiting your turn.

- **Not smoking in private homes:** Most Canadians do not smoke. When you are in people's homes, you should always ask their permission to smoke. If they do not smoke themselves, they may ask you to go outside to smoke.

- **Being on time:** You should always arrive on time -- at school, at work and for any meeting. People who are often late may be fired from their jobs or suspended from school. Many Canadians will not wait more than 10 or 15 minutes for someone who has a business meeting. For social events, people expect that you will arrive within half an hour of the stated time.

- **Respect for the environment:** Canadians respect the natural environment and expect people to avoid littering (dropping waste paper and other garbage on the street or throwing it out of your car). They will expect you to carry your garbage until you can find a proper garbage can.

- **Bargaining:** Bargaining for a better price is not common in Canada, but there are some exceptions. For example, almost everyone bargains for a better price when buying a car or a house, or other expensive items such as furniture. People who sell things privately may also bargain.

- **Smart shopping:** Stores compete with one another to attract customers, so it is wise to check and compare prices at different stores before you buy.

- **Note:** The price marked on goods in stores does not usually include the federal and provincial sales taxes, which add from 7 percent to 15 percent to the cost of an item, depending on the province in which you buy it.

TIP ! If you have questions about social standards or customs, you can ask the local immigrant-serving organization for advice. If you have been matched with a Canadian family under the Host Program, the family members can help answer your questions as well.

SOME CANADIAN LAWS

Some laws you should be aware of

- It is illegal to drive without a driver's licence, registration and insurance.

- It is illegal to drive if you have been drinking alcohol.

- The driver and all passengers must wear seat belts at all times when driving in Canada.

- Babies and children who are too small to wear seat belts must be placed in properly installed infant or child car seats, appropriate to the age and weight of the child.

- Children under 12 years of age cannot be left at home alone, or to care for younger children.

- All children aged six to 16 must attend school.

- Smoking is not permitted in federal buildings, in elevators, on Canadian airlines, on buses and on other public transportation, nor in many banks, shops, restaurants and other public places (some municipalities have banned smoking in all public buildings).

- Depending on which part of Canada you live in, you must be either 18 or 19 years old to buy or drink alcohol in any form.

- It is against the law to hit your spouse or children, either in the home or in public.

- It is illegal to use, buy or sell marijuana, heroin, cocaine and other addictive drugs.

- It is illegal to make any kind of sexual remarks or advances if the other person does not like them.

Interacting With Officials

Knowing how to behave and what to expect can be very useful when you are dealing with public officials and people in authority. Usually, there is no need to worry about making mistakes. Except for matters of law, most Canadians do not insist on strict formality. Officials who know that you are a newcomer will make allowances for your inexperience with Canadian ways.

People in authority

In Canada, a person's authority is related to his or her position and responsibility. Women hold the same kinds of positions as men and have the same kinds of authority. People do not have authority just because of their name, status, social class or sex.

Public officials

Public officials will normally treat you in a polite but impersonal way. Public officials follow set procedures. They do not make the rules. They may not want to or be able to become involved with your situation. Do not respond to them in a personal or emotional way. Never try to bribe a public official. Bribery and other forms of corruption are illegal and will offend most Canadians.

Police Officers

The police are part of the community and are accountable to the public. They may be either men or women. They are trained to serve and protect the public, including you. Police operate within strict regulations and follow established procedures. Canadians expect honesty and fairness from the police.

Calling the police: Most cities and towns have an emergency number for the police. Call this number if you or someone else is hurt or in danger, or if you see a crime taking place. In most parts of Canada, the emergency number is 911. Emergency numbers are always printed inside the front cover of the telephone book.

What if you are questioned by a police officer?

- Call the police officer "officer."
- Accept the police officer's authority; do not try to argue.
- Be ready to show identification if a police officer asks you for it. If you are stopped by the police while driving a car, the officer will probably ask you for your driver's licence, proof of insurance and car registration.
- Tell the officer the facts about what has happened. Do not offer your own opinion.
- Never try to give money to a police officer. Canadians do not bribe police officers. It is a serious crime to do this.

What if you are arrested by a police officer?

- Police officers must tell you who they are and show you their badge number.

- They must explain why they are arresting you and tell you what your rights are.

- They must allow you to call a lawyer right away. If you don't have a lawyer, they must give you the Legal Aid telephone number and let you call.

- You do not have to give any information, other than your name and address, until you have talked to a lawyer.

YOUR RIGHTS AND OBLIGATIONS

- **Personal rights and freedoms**
- **Children's rights**
- **Women's rights**
- **Senior citizens' rights**
- **Becoming a Canadian citizen**
- **Responsible and active citizenship**

As a newcomer, you should be aware of your rights and obligations. Having the right to participate in Canadian society also means that you have a responsibility to respect the rights and freedoms of others and to obey Canada's laws.

Personal rights and freedoms

The *Canadian Charter of Rights and Freedoms* describes the basic principles and values by which Canadians live. The Charter is part of Canada's Constitution. The Charter protects you from the moment you arrive on Canadian soil. It gives everyone in Canada the following fundamental rights and freedoms:

- the right to life, liberty and personal security;
- freedom of conscience and religion;

- freedom of thought, belief, opinion and expression, including freedom of the press and other media of communication;

- freedom to hold peaceful meetings;

- freedom to join groups;

- the right to live and work anywhere in Canada;

- protection from unreasonable search or seizure and arbitrary detainment and imprisonment;

- the right to be presumed innocent until proven guilty;

- the right to have a lawyer;

- the right to a fair trial, through due process of law; and

- the right to equal protection and benefit under the law, without discrimination.

Children's Rights

In Canada, you are required by law to properly care for your children. Police, doctors, teachers and children's aid officials will act when children are being abused. This includes any form of harm and abuse -- physical, psychological or sexual. All forms of child abuse are serious crimes. In serious cases of abuse, children can be taken away from their parents.

Physical abuse is any intentional physical contact that causes injury. For example, spanking a child long enough or hard enough to cause bruises, or spanking with anything other than an open hand, is a form of abuse. Some cultural practices, such as female circumcision, are also considered physical abuse and are against the law.

Psychological abuse includes terror and humiliation.

Sexual abuse includes any form of sexual contact between an adult and a child.

Neglect is also a form of child abuse. Parents who fail to protect and provide for their children are guilty of neglect. By law, children **under 12 cannot be left alone to look after themselves or younger siblings.**

Kids' "help-lines" are available for children who need someone to help them or just need someone to talk to.

Women's rights

In Canada, women have the same legal status, rights and opportunities as men. Most Canadian men respect women as equals -- socially, in the workplace and in the home. Violence against women is against the law. Women who are abused can seek help for themselves and their children in local shelters. They are also entitled to legal protection to keep them safe.

Senior citizens' rights

A senior citizen is someone 65 years of age or older. It is common in Canadian society for healthy senior citizens to live on their own, instead of living with their children. Older people who need special care often move to a retirement or nursing home that provides trained staff and health-care workers. However, many Canadians still care for older family members in their own home.

Old Age Security: The Old Age Security (OAS) program ensures a basic income to all people in Canada 65 years of age or over who meet the residence requirements. Usually, OAS is paid after a person has lived in Canada at least 10 years, although people who have lived or worked in countries with which Canada has an agreement may qualify after as little as one year. Low-income people who get OAS may also qualify for the Guaranteed Income Supplement (GIS) and their spouses (or widows) may also qualify for the Spouse's Allowance if they are between 60 and 64 years of age.

The Canada Pension Plan pays benefits to contributors in the event of retirement or disability, as well as benefits to surviving spouses and orphans in the event of death of a contributor. All workers in Canada contribute to the plan.

> **TIP !** You may also be eligible for old age security benefits from your former country.

Becoming A Canadian Citizen

Once you have been in Canada for at least three years, you may apply to become a Canadian citizen. Immigrants who become citizens have the same rights as citizens who were born in Canada. As a citizen you can:

- vote and be a candidate for political office in federal, provincial and territorial elections;
- apply for a Canadian passport;
- enter and leave Canada freely;
- enjoy full economic rights, including the right to own any type of property; and
- be eligible for some pension benefits.

An adult applying for Canadian citizenship must:

- be at least 18 years old;
- be a permanent resident of Canada who entered the country legally;
- have lived in Canada for three of the four years before applying for citizenship;
- speak either English or French;
- know something about Canada's history, geography, system of government and voting;
- know the rights and responsibilities of citizenship;
- apply for citizenship and pass the citizenship test; and

245

- take the oath of citizenship.

You cannot become a Canadian citizen if you:

- are considered a risk to Canada's security;
- are under a deportation order;
- are in prison, on parole from prison or on probation; or
- have been found guilty of a serious crime within the past three years.

Responsible and active citizenship

For many Canadians, being a good citizen means getting involved in their community. Regardless of your interests, contributing to your society is rewarding and is appreciated by others who, like you, are proud to make Canada their home.

> **TIP !** Getting involved in volunteer activities is also an excellent way to meet new people, make friends, practise English or French, and learn about Canadian customs.

AFTERWORD

We hope this information has answered some of your questions about Canada, about adapting to life in Canada and about the Canadian way of life. As you prepare to leave for Canada, refer again to the tips and checklists provided here.

One last checklist:

- Have you gathered all of your essential and important documents? Have you had them translated into English or French?

- Have you considered buying health insurance for the time you are traveling and for the short period before you become eligible for Canada's Medicare system?

- Do you know what you can and cannot bring into Canada?

- Have you prepared yourself for finding work in Canada?

- Have you researched Canada's labour market in general and in each of the five regions? Have you used the Internet to learn about finding work in Canada?

- Have you considered living in one of Canada's smaller or medium-sized cities, or in a rural community? Have you used the Internet to learn about these choices?

- Have you considered the season and climate you will find when you arrive, and the clothing that you will need?

- Have you considered contacting an immigrant-serving organization soon after you arrive in Canada?

- Have you considered taking English or French lessons through the LINC (Language Instruction for Newcomers to Canada) program?

247

The best way to adjust to your new home will be to get involved! Try to speak English or French as much as possible, even if you make mistakes. Ask questions when you need help. Most people are pleased to help and will understand your needs. With time, you will feel more and more at home. Canada and Canadians will welcome you and your family into the larger Canadian family. Good luck on your journey!

Welcome to Canada -- your new home

UNDERSTANDING CULTURAL SHOCK

1.   WHAT IS CULTURE SHOCK?

It happens when a person is placed in a different social setting. The accepted social rules are not immediately clear and one does not know what is expected, or how to get things done. Move from one country to another or one culture to another is a perfect example; however, culture shock also occurs to people within their own country. For example:

- Moving from the countryside to a large city,
- Moving from one region to another,
- Joining the military and experiencing "boot camp",
- Changing schools or jobs;

You can, no doubt, think of others.

What do you do in such situations? Observe, seek advice from others, begin to follow the leads of others, build your confidence and then begin to participate fully. There are well designed set of actions which you can use to minimize culture shock and make a successful transition to your new or overseas situation.

Whenever a person enters a strange culture, many of the familiar cues which have been a part of his everyday experiences are removed. He may feel like a fish out of water. He has come face to face with a problem we call "culture shock". Oberg, a prominent social scientist, states that "culture shock is precipitated by the anxiety that results from losing all familiar sings and symbols of social intercourse. These signs or cues include the thousand and one ways in which people orientate themselves to the situation of daily life". The term culture shock describes how our mind tells us to act when we are in a new and different environment.

Culture shock affects everyone – it will affect you. Some people are affected slightly and quickly adjust, whilst others receive a severe shock and never really enjoy their overseas experiences. Basically, culture shock is a mental attitude problem which affects people soon after arrival in the foreign environment.

Culture shock seems to affect wives more than husbands. Usually, the husband has his profession and job-related activities to occupy his time, but the wife is the one who must cope with the rigors of the new environment. The strain on her is the greatest. She must adapt her methods and activities to provide a stabilizing influence for her entire family.

The chart included in this article depict the various phases of culture shock. As can be seen, shortly after the family has arrived in the foreign environment, the "honeymoon" is over and realization sets in. Some people develop a mild culture shock and adjust easily to the environment, while others remain in a depressed state for their entire overseas tour. This crisis phase is very real for many people and may easily prevail for several months. An adjustment and recovery phase follows this crisis phase as the individual adjusts to his new environment. Five or six months after arrival, most individuals have adjusted adequately and are actively pursuing their own interests and activities.

2.   HOW TO OVERCOME CULTURE SHOCK

Realizing that you will experience culture shock is half the battle of overcoming it. Accept the fact that the adjustment and transition into the new environment is difficult, but remember that the situation is temporary and will pass as you learn the language, mannerisms and local customs. When you find yourself getting angry, 'uptight' and condemning everyone around you, realize that you are under an emotional strain and that you will be adjusting to the unfamiliar situation. Culture shock seems to build up until it overpowers you. It results from a series of little things which are hard to put your finger on.

The following suggestions are offered to help in overcoming culture shock:

A.   Make a conscious effort to get to know the people of the host country. Learn as much as you can about the language, history and the culture.

B.   Recognize that your negative attitude and reactions are caused by culture shock.

C.   Consciously look for logical reasons behind the customs and activities you identify as being different from your own. Accentuate the positive and look for the good traits and characteristics of the foreign environment.

D.   Identify a host country national or some other person to whom you would enjoy talking about your feelings and situation. That means a friend.

E.   Keep a diary of your thoughts and feelings. Every few weeks review what you have written and reflect back on your thoughts and feelings.

F.   Develop some useful hobbies and outside interests to occupy some of your spare time. Don't sit around complaining about how miserable you are.

G.   Be flexible, curious and self-reliant. Make the most out of a seemingly unhappy situation.

H.   Remember, you are not alone. Others are having the same problems, although they might not be willing to admit it.

After you adjustment phase is completed, you will undoubtedly associate with others who are going through the trials of culture shock. Remember how you felt in your crisis phase. Be patient, understanding and sympathetic. Soon, time which is the great healer, will set things right.

3.   CULTURE SHOCK VICTIMS – WHO ARE THEY?

Probably every person relocating to a new culture suffers varying degrees of this psychological malady. Do not think this problem applies to only Eastern going to Western countries, it even happens to others nationals going to Eastern countries. Having culture shock does not indicate a psychological weakness or the inability to adjust to your new environment. Experiencing culture shock is probably a necessary phase of making a successful transition. The keys to overcoming culture shock are:

- Knowing that you may encounter it;
- Understanding that it is normal and part of your adjustment;
- Recognizing the symptoms, if they occur;
- Taking a logical and practical approach to conquering it.

4. ORIGIN AND DEVELOPMENT

Culture shock is a psychological malady that has been responsible for much of the personnel turnover experienced by Immigrants arriving in Canada. It occurs when people suddenly find themselves in an unfamiliar environment. The origin of the shock is in the anxiety resulting from the absence of familiar signs and symbols of one's basic culture. Each person's peace of mind, emotional balance and efficiency depend on hundreds of cues instilled in the mind whilst growing up in a specific culture. In response to these cues we form habits that are learned whilst confronting situations of daily life. These include when to smile, laugh, shake hands and courtesies such as ladies first, queuing up and many more expressions that reveal how we think, how we feel and what we believe.

When a person enters a different culture environment, all or most of his life patterns are absent. He can become like the proverbial "fish out of water".

5. COMMON CULTURE SHOCK SYMPTOMS

Each person may exhibit different symptoms and varying degrees of culture shock and may possibly exhibit some of the following:

- A verbal rejection of the new country.
- Unwarranted criticism of the culture and the people.
- Constant complaints about the climate.
- Utopian ideas concerning one's native culture.

- A viewpoint that all things from the past are suddenly wonderful.
- Making light of, or forgetting serious past misfortunes and problems.
- Excessive washing of the hands.
- Continuous concern over the purity of the drinking water.
- Unreasonable concern about the food to be eaten.
- Fear of touching or physical contact with the local people.
- Inappropriate anger over slight delays and frustrations.
- Refusal to learn the new language.
- Indifference about meeting the local people.
- Pre-occupation with returning home.
- Pre-occupation with the fear of being robbed, cheated or molested.
- Pressing desire to talk with people who really make sense.
- Misconception of the local's attitude towards a foreigner.
- Expression of other non-valid criticism.

6.   POST CULTURE SHOCK

Even the individual who remains in the country and adapts his lifestyle to the local donations of everyday life, will continually encounter the need to adjust to such factors as:

- Social custom
- Language
- Job search
- Domestic help
- Housing
- Shopping
- Traffic
- Climate
- Unfamiliar sights and sounds.

The locals will try to help, but they do not always seem to understand the newcomer's great concern over these insignificant

253

frustrations, many of which they have grown up with. Consequently, they may be perceived as being insensitive and indifferent.

If the person suffering from culture shock is upset and shows anger, the locals may sense this hostility and will probably either avoid him or respond in a similar manner, consequently compounding the problem.

7.   CULTURE SHOCK RESULTS

The end result, whether positive or negative, depends entirely upon how you handle the situation. The Immigrants who adjusts and adapts to the new environment becomes a happier and more productive thus settles in considerably short period of time.

The immigrants who becomes discontented and directs their displeasures towards others, causing friction within the community, is usually decide to go back to home country and may retain a bitter attitude towards all foreign countries and their nationals.

GENERAL STAGES OF CULTURE SHOCK

	PRE–DEPARTURE	FIRST MONTH (Exploratory or Honeymoon)	2ND & 3RD MONTH (Crisis)	4TH & 5TH MONTH (Adjustments)	SIXTH MONTH (Recovery & Equilibrium)
GENERAL ATTITUDES	Excitement & pleasure	Fascination Spirit of Adventure	Disenchanted Restless and Impatient	Gradual Recovery and Adjustment	Normal
SIGNIFICANT EVENTS	Planning, Packing, Processing, Partying, Parting	Red Carpet Welcome, New Office, New friends, Colleagues and Living Quarters (Others stand as buffers between the new family and the problems)	**Varied** - Fully Duty Responsibilities - Shipment delayed - Smells, Foods, and Local travel. Complications	**Varied** Acceptable Duty performance	Normal Duty Performance
EMOTIONAL RESPONSE TO EVENTS	Excitement and Enthusiasm. - Some concern about leaving friends, family and the familiar environment.	Tourist Enthusiasm.	Insecure and Irritable. - Home sickness. - Mental fatigue	Sparking Interest. - Lessening of tension. - Return of a sense of humour - Empathy for others.	Emotional Equilibrium . - Enjoyment.
ATTITUTINAL RESPONSE TO EVENTS	Anticipation	Curiosity and enthusiasm. - Job enthusiasm. - High expectations	Frustration, Withdrawn and antagonistic. - Skepticism and uncertainly. - Questions the values of people, self and job -	Emerging. - Constructive attitude. - Understanding of own feelings and cultural patterns.	Equilibrium .
PHYSICAL RESPONSES TO EVENTS	Weary, but normal health	Minor insomnia, slight headaches.	Minor illness	Normal health	Normal health.

255

PART-III

WORKING IN **CAN**ADA

WORKING IN CANADA

Finding employment in Canada requires planning. You should learn as much as possible before you apply to immigrate. Be aware that there is no guarantee that you will find a job and be able to work in your preferred occupation.

Regulated and Non-Regulated Occupations

Some professions and trades are regulated in Canada to protect public health and safety. Twenty percent of people working in Canada, such as nurses, engineers, electricians and teachers, work in regulated occupations.

Provincial and territorial organizations are responsible for:

- setting entry requirements for people in individual occupations;
- recognizing credentials, training or experience; and
- issuing licences required to work in regulated occupations.

The way to have your qualifications recognized is different in each province and territory, and for each occupation. In most cases, you can only apply to have your qualifications recognized once you are in Canada. You may be asked to:

- provide documentation of qualifications;
- take a language test;
- complete a technical exam (with applicable fee); and
- do supervised work.

Non-regulated Occupations

If your occupation is **not** regulated, you do not need a licence. Your employer will decide what requirements you must meet and if you need to register with a professional association.

For more information on regulated and non-regulated occupations in Canada:

- Canadian Information Centre for International Credentials
- Work Destinations at Human Resources Development Canada.
- Workopolis

Information For Foreign-Trained Medical Doctors

Information on requirements to practise

Those who practise this profession use one of the following titles: doctor, medical doctor, physician, family physician, general practitioner, or resident-in-training for one of these roles. Entry into the professions is **regulated** in Canada. This means that the requirements to practise are set by each provincial and territorial medical association. Once you know where you will settle and work in Canada, contact the appropriate provincial/territorial medical association (see list below) to obtain further information.

Information for Graduates of Foreign Medical Schools

If you immigrate to Canada through the Family Class or Refugee categories without regard to occupation, you must sign a statement that you have been fully informed of the difficulties you will encounter in obtaining a licence to practise medicine.

Before your application for immigration can be approved, your basic medical knowledge must be evaluated. In most cases, this means that you must pass the Medical Council of Canada's Evaluating Examination (MCCEE). This examination evaluates your general medical knowledge compared to that of graduates of Canadian medical schools. It tests your understanding of the principal fields of medicine - including internal medicine, obstetrics and gynecology, pediatrics, psychiatry, preventive medicine and community health, and surgery. Most of the questions are intended to evaluate clinical knowledge, but there are some questions on basic medical sciences.

The examination is held twice yearly, usually in March and September, in various centres in Canada and abroad. It is given in English and in French. Before you are eligible to write the Evaluating Examination, you must complete all the requirements to obtain qualification of Doctor of Medicine, or equivalent, from the university that granted your medical degree.

To obtain an application to write the examination or to receive a list of examination centres, contact the Executive Director at:

Medical Council of Canada (MCC)
P.O. Box 8234, Station T
Ottawa, Ontario K1G 3H7
Canada

Tel.: (613) 521-6012
Fax: (613) 521-9417
http://www.mcc.ca/

Some provinces have pre-residency training for permanent residents of the province who are graduates of foreign medical schools. The contents and length of the program varies in these provinces. For specific details, contact the provincial/territorial licensing authority.

In 2001, only 15.5 per cent of graduates of foreign medical schools who applied to CaRMS were successful in obtaining a postgraduate medical position. Of the 1219 postgraduate training positions in the 2001 match, only 60, or 5 per cent, of the positions were matched to graduates of foreign medical schools.

Information on assessment of qualifications

Contact the <u>Medical Council of Canada</u> for assessment of your qualifications **prior to arrival in Canada**.

Information For Foreign-Trained Engineering Technologists And Technicians

Information on requirements to practise

In Canada, the different occupations in technology are **not regulated**. In Quebec, the use of the title "technologue professionnel" (professional technologist) is controlled. You do not require certification in order to work as a technician or technologist in the other provinces and the territories. However, certification is available but voluntary in all provinces through the Canadian Council of Technicians and Technologists (CCTT), a federation of the professional associations and societies of technicians and technologists in many applied science and engineering disciplines (see list of disciplines and sub-disciplines at <u>http://www.cctt.ca/dlist.htm</u>).

The provincial associations of CCTT (<u>see list below</u>) handle the certification procedures according to national standards. Once certified as a full member of a provincial association, **technologists** are known either as Certified Engineering Technologists (C.E.T.), Applied Science Technologists (A.Sc.T.), or Registered Engineering Technologists (R.E.T.), depending on the province in which they receive certification and entitlement to the designation. **Technicians** are known as Certified Technicians (C. Tech). In Canada, it is illegal to use these designations without being certified as a full member of an association. In Quebec, membership in the regulatory body is

262

required to use the title of **technologue professionnel/ Professional Technologist**, which is a "profession à titre réservé."

The Canadian Technology Accreditation Board (CTAB) evaluates college-level and private programs of study in applied science and engineering technology. The Board includes representatives from the provincial associations and societies, the Department of National Defence (DND), the Canadian Technology Human Resource Board (CTHRB), the Canadian Society for Chemical Technology (CSCT), and the National Council of Deans of Technology (NCDOT). Additional technology educators participate as observers.

Information on assessment of qualifications

For immigration purposes only, the CCTT works with Citizenship and Immigration Canada (CIC) in assessing the qualifications of people applying for permanent residence in Canada who intend to work as technicians or technologists. In this regard, CCTT has prepared an information note entitled Informal Assessment of Foreign Qualifications for Applied Science and Engineering Technicians and Technologists. Note that CCTT charges a fee for this service, and that its assessments do not guarantee recognition of your credentials for purposes of employment or certification in Canada. You may also contact the CCTT for further general information:

Canadian Council of Technicians and Technologists (CCTT)
285 McLeod Street
Ottawa, Ontario K2P 1A1
Canada

Tel.: (613) 238-8123
Fax: (613) 238-8822

Email: ctabadm@magma.ca
http://www.cctt.ca/

The purpose of the CCTT assessment is to evaluate the likelihood of acceptance into the provincial technology association's examination program. As regulatory bodies, the provincial associations are not bound in any way by the candidate's results on the initial immigration assessment. They will conduct their own assessment of certification applicants, for which fees are also charged.

You may also contact an <u>evaluation service</u>, and consult the <u>Fact Sheet No. 2</u>, "Assessment and recognition of credentials for the purpose of employment in Canada." Although the evaluation services offer expert advice on how qualifications obtained abroad compare with credentials obtained in a Canadian province or territory, the evaluation is **advisory only and does not guarantee recognition** of your qualifications for employment or certification purposes in Canada. Please note that they charge a fee for their services.

Information For Foreign-Trained Accountants And Auditors

Information on requirements to practise

The occupations of financial auditors and accountants are **regulated** by legislation **in most jurisdictions**. Requirements to practise vary, but membership in a professional accounting association is usually required. The three major national accounting organizations are identified below, and each has its own professional designation: Chartered Accountant (CA), Certified General Accountant (CGA), and Certified Management Accountant (CMA). The related provincial/territorial bodies are listed at the end. Therefore, once you know where you will settle and work in Canada, you should contact the appropriate association for details on licensing procedures.

264

Canadian Institute of Chartered Accountants (CICA)
227 Wellington Street West
Toronto, Ontario M5V 3H2
Canada

Tel.: (416) 977-3222
Fax: (416) 977-8585

Email: qualification.reform@cica.ca
http://www.cica.ca/

Certified General Accountants Association of Canada (CGA-Canada)
1188 West Georgia Street, Suite 700
Vancouver, British Columbia V6E 4A2
Canada

Tel.: (604) 669-3555 or 1-800-663-1529
Fax: (604) 689-5845

Email: public@cga-canada.org
http://www.cga-canada.org/

Society of Management Accountants of Canada (CMA-Canada)
One Robert Speck Parkway, Suite 1400 P.O. Box 176
Mississauga, Ontario L4Z 3M3
Canada
Tel.: (905) 949-4200 or 1-800-263-7622
Fax: (905) 949-0038

Email: info@cma-canada.org
http://www.cma-canada.org/

Public Accountants

For professional accountants who expect to perform **public accounting services**, particularly as an **auditor** of the financial statements of companies listed on stock exchanges, the requirements for licensure are regulated by legislation as follows:

- **Licences** to practise **public accounting** are **required** by legislation in **Newfoundland, Nova Scotia, Ontario, and Prince Edward Island**. With few exceptions, only CAs are licensed to practise public accounting in Nova Scotia and Ontario. Only CAs may be licensed in Prince Edward Island. Newfoundland legislation provides for the licensing of CAs, CMAs, and CGAs.

- In **Quebec**, the performance of statutory **audits** for publicly listed companies is limited by legislation to CAs. However, CAs, CGAs, and CMAs are able to perform certain other audits in Quebec.

- In **Alberta**, only CAs, CMAs, and CGAs are permitted to engage in **public accounting** if they hold a certificate of practice from one of the three accounting bodies. In British Columbia the right to perform statutory **audits** is restricted to CAs, CGAs, and persons approved by the provincial Auditor Certification Board.

- There is no licensing or certification required by legislation to practise **public accounting** in Manitoba, Saskatchewan, New Brunswick, Northwest Territories, Nunavut, or the Yukon. However, the securities commissions in some of these jurisdictions require that professional accountants performing **audit or review services** for publicly listed companies be CAs, CGAs, or CMAs.

Information For Foreign-Trained Engineers

Information on requirements to practise

The profession of engineer is **regulated** in Canada. It is illegal to practise the profession of engineer or to use the title "engineer" without being licensed as a full member in a provincial or territorial association. **However, individuals can do engineering work under the direct supervision of licensed engineers.**

Provincial and territorial associations of professional engineers are responsible for setting the standards for entry into the profession and for issuing licences to those who meet established standards of qualifications and practice.

Therefore, once you know where you will settle and work in Canada, you should contact the appropriate provincial or territorial association for details on licensure procedures. Below is a list of addresses of the national, provincial, and territorial associations of professional engineers.

List Of Associations of Professional Engineers

Alberta

Association of Professional Engineers, Geologists and Geophysicists of Alberta (APEGGA)
10060 Jasper Avenue 1500 Scotia One
Edmonton AB T5J 4A2
Canada

Tel.: (780) 426-3990 or 1-800-661-7020
Fax: (780) 425-1722
http://www.apegga.org/

British Columbia

Association of Professional Engineers and Geoscientists of British Columbia (APEGBC)
200-4010 Regent Street
Burnaby BC V5C 6N2
Canada

Tel.: (604) 430-8035 or 1-888-430-8035
Fax: (604) 430-8085
http://www.apeg.bc.ca/

Manitoba

Association of Professional Engineers and Geoscientists of Manitoba (APEGM)
850A Pembina Highway
Winnipeg MB R3M 2M7
Canada

Tel.: (204) 474-2736
Fax: (204) 474-5960
http://www.apegm.mb.ca/

New Brunswick

Association of Professional Engineers and Geoscientists of New Brunswick (APEGNB)
535 Beaverbrook Court, Suite 105
Fredericton NB E3B 1X6
Canada
Tel.: (506) 458-8083
Fax: (506) 451-9629
http://ctca.unb.ca/apenb/

Newfoundland and Labrador

Association of Professional Engineers and Geoscientists of Newfoundland (APEGN)
10 Fort William Place, Suite 203, P.O. Box 21207
St. John's NF A1A 5B2
Canada

Tel.: (709) 753-7714
Fax: (709) 753-6131
http://www.apegn.nf.ca/

Northwest Territories

Association of Professional Engineers, Geologists and Geophysicists of the Northwest Territories (NAPEGG)
201, 4817-49th Street
Yellowknife NT X1A 3S7
Canada

Tel.: (867) 920-4055
Fax: (867) 873-4058
http://www.napegg.nt.ca/

Nova Scotia

Association of Professional Engineers of Nova Scotia (APENS)
1355 Barrington Street, P.O. Box 129
Halifax NS B3J 2M4
Canada

Tel.: (902) 429-2250 or 1-888-802-7367
Fax: (902) 423-9769
http://www.apens.ns.ca/

Ontario

Professional Engineers of Ontario (PEO)
25 Sheppard Avenue West, Suite 1000
Toronto ON M2N 6S9
Canada

Tel.: (416) 224-1100 or 1-800-339-3716
Fax: (416) 224-8168 or 1-800-268-0496
http://www.peo.on.ca/

Prince Edward Island

Association of Professional Engineers of Prince Edward Island (APEPEI)
549 North River Road
Charlottetown PE C1E 1J6
Canada

Tel.: (902) 566-1268
Fax: (902) 566-5551
http://www.apepei.com/

Québec

Ordre des ingénieurs du Québec (OIQ)
2020, rue University, 18e étage
Montréal QC H3A 2A5
Canada

Tel.: (514) 845-6141 or 1-800-461-6141
Fax: (514) 845-1833
http://www.oiq.qc.ca/

Saskatchewan

Association of Professional Engineers and Geoscientists of Saskatchewan (APEGS)
2255-13th Avenue, Suite 104
Regina SK S4P 0V6
Canada

Tel.: (306) 525-9547 or 1-800-500-9547
Fax: (306) 525-0851
http://www.apegs.sk.ca/

Yukon

Association of Professional Engineers of Yukon (APEY)
3106 Third Avenue, Suite 404, P.O. Box 4125
Whitehorse YT Y1A 5G1
Canada

Tel.: (867) 667-6727
Fax: (867) 668-2142
http://www.apey.yk.ca/

NOTE: Not all engineering graduates in Ontario are professional engineers. A professional engineer must have satisfied the requirements set by PEO to earn a licence. However, you can work in engineering without a licence, if a professional engineer supervises and takes responsibility for your work. You cannot use the title "professional engineer", the abbreviation "P.Eng.", or any similar title that may lead to the belief that you are qualified to practise professional engineering unless you are a licensed professional engineer.

Information on Assessment of Qualifications

For immigration purposes only, to any province or territory except Quebec, you can obtain an assessment of your engineering qualifications prior to your arrival from the Canadian Council of Professional Engineers (CCPE). You may consult online the information prepared by the Canadian Council of Professional Engineers in this regard.

Canadian Council of Professional Engineers (CCPE)
180 Elgin Street, Suite 1100
Ottawa, Ontario K2P 2K3
Canada

Tel.: (613) 232-2474
Fax: (613) 236-5759

Email: ia@ccpe.ca
http://www.ccpe.ca/

For immigration to Quebec, you should contact the Ordre des ingénieurs du Québec (OIQ):

Ordre des ingénieurs du Québec (OIQ)
> 2020, rue University, 18e étage
> Montréal, Québec H3A 2A5
> Canada

> Tel.: (514) 845-6141 or 1-800-461-6141
> Fax: (514) 845-1833

> Email: admission@oiq.qc.ca
> http://www.oiq.qc.ca/

Please note that both OIQ and CCPE charge a fee for their services, and that their assessments **do NOT guarantee** recognition of your credentials for purposes of employment or licensure/certification in Canada.

You may also consult <u>Fact Sheet No. 2</u>, which has been compiled to help individuals learn more about how to obtain an assessment of their qualifications for employment purposes in Canada.

Information For Foreign-Trained Registered Nurses And Psychiatric Nurses

Nurses may be employed in many settings such as hospitals and doctors' offices; in community health agencies, health centres, and clinics; in nursing homes and extended-care facilities; in rehabilitation centres and mental health centres; in schools, governments, businesses, and industries; and in private homes; or they may be self-employed. But all nursing professions are regulated in Canada. In some provinces, anyone using the title "nurse," even a self-employed nurse, must be a registered member of one of the nursing regulatory bodies in that jurisdiction. When you know where you will settle and work in Canada, you should contact the appropriate provincial/territorial regulatory body (see list below) for more specific information.

In order to obtain the designation Registered Nurse (RN), candidates must apply for registration, have their credentials assessed, and pass the Canadian Registered Nurse Examination or for Quebec, l'examen professionnel de l'Ordre des infirmières et infirmiers du Québec. The provincial/territorial regulatory bodies register the applicants in their jurisdiction who meet their professional criteria and standards of practice. These regulatory bodies, with the exception of the College of Nurses in Ontario and the Ordre des infirmières et infirmiers du Québec, are member bodies of the Canadian Nurses Association (CNA).

The CNA, in collaboration with specialist nursing associations, offers certification in 14 nursing specialties: neuroscience, occupational health, nephrology, emergency, critical care, critical care pediatrics, psychiatric/mental health, perioperative care, oncology, hospice palliative care, gerontology, gastroenterology, perinatal care, and cardiovascular nursing. Each of these nursing specialties has its own national professional association.

For more information on membership, specialization, and certification, you can contact the CNA at

Canadian Nurses Association (CNA)
50 Driveway
Ottawa ON K2P 1E2 Canada
Tel.: (613) 237-2133 or 1-800-361-8404
Fax: (613) 237-3520
Email: cna@cna-aiic.ca
http://www.cna-aiic.ca/

Psychiatric/Mental Health Nurses

There are separate provincial regulatory bodies (see list below) in British Columbia, Alberta, Saskatchewan, and Manitoba to register nurses specifically qualified in the area of psychiatric/mental health nursing. In the other provinces/territories, there may be a special interest group for Psychiatric/Mental Health Nurses within existing professional bodies. The Canadian Federation of Mental Health Nurses can also provide more information on the field of mental health nursing in Canada. The federation can be contacted at

Canadian Federation of Mental Health Nurses (CFMHN)
50 Driveway
Ottawa ON K2P 1E2 Canada
Tel.: (613) 237-2133 or 1-800-450-5206
Fax: (613) 237-3520
http://cfmhn.org/

Information on assessment of qualifications:

The regulatory body for nursing in each province and territory handles the assessment of qualifications for foreign-trained nurses and the scheduling of nurses to write the Canadian Registered Nurse Examination. With special permission, candidates may write the Canadian Registered Nurse Examination in a Canadian province or territory other than the one in which they reside. However, candidates cannot write the exam outside Canada. Consult the CNA document Information for foreign-trained registered nurses about nursing in Canada for further information.

You may also contact an evaluation service to evaluate your credentials. Consult our Fact Sheet No. 2, "Assessment and recognition of credentials for the purpose of employment in Canada." Although the evaluation services offer expert advice on how qualifications obtained abroad compare with credentials obtained in a Canadian province or territory, the evaluation is advisory only and does not guarantee recognition of your qualifications for employment or registration purposes in Canada. Please note that evaluation services charge a fee for their services. To become registered as a nurse in Canada, you will still need to have your credentials assessed by the provincial/territorial nursing regulatory body.

Other relevant information

The Canadian Association of Schools of Nursing (CASN) accredits university and college nursing programs in Canada. CASN represents degree-level nursing education and nursing research across Canada. CASN member schools and its regional associations work collaboratively with provincial and territorial regulatory colleges/associations of nursing to ensure that standards of education meet entry to practice requirements. For more information on member schools, standards, and the accreditation program, you can contact the association through inquire@casn.ca.

LIST OF PROVINCIAL/TERRITORIAL REGULATORY BODIES

Alberta
Alberta Association of Registered Nurses (AARN)
11620 - 168 Street
Edmonton AB T5M 4A6 Canada
Tel.: (780) 451-0043 or 1-800-252-9392
Fax: (780) 452-3276
Email: aarn@nurses.ab.ca
http://www.nurses.ab.ca/

Registered Psychiatric Nurses Association of Alberta (RPNAA)
9711 - 45 Avenue, Suite 201
Edmonton AB T6E 5V8 Canada
Tel.: (780) 434-7666 or 1-877-234-7666
Fax: (780) 436-4165
Email: rpnaa@rpnaa.ab.ca
http://www.rpnaa.ab.ca/

British Columbia
College of Registered Psychiatric Nurses of British Columbia (CRPNBC)
307 - 2502 St. Johns Street
Port Moody BC V3H 2B4 Canada
Tel.: (604) 931-5200 or 1-800-565-2505
Fax: (604) 931-5277
Email: info@crpnbc.ca
http://www.crpnbc.ca/

Registered Nurses Association of British Columbia (RNABC)
2855 Arbutus Street
Vancouver BC V6J 3Y8 Canada
Tel.: (604) 736-7331
Fax: (604) 738-2272
Email: info@rnabc.bc.ca
http://www.rnabc.bc.ca/

Manitoba
College of Registered Nurses of Manitoba (CRNM)
647 Broadway Ave.
Winnipeg MB R3C 0X2 Canada
Tel.: (204) 774-3477
Fax: (204) 775-6052
Email: info@crnm.mb.ca
http://www.crnm.mb.ca/

College of Registered Psychiatric Nurses of Manitoba (CRPNM)
1854 Portage Avenue
Winnipeg MB R3J 0G9 Canada
Tel.: (204) 888-4841
Fax: (204) 888-8638
Email: crpnm@crpnm.mb.ca
http://www.crpnm.mb.ca/

New Brunswick
Nurses Association of New Brunswick (NANB)
165 Regent Street
Fredericton NB E3B 3W5 Canada
Tel.: (506) 458-8731
Fax: (506) 459-2838
Email: nanb@nanb.nb.ca
http://www.nanb.nb.ca/

Newfoundland and Labrador
Association of Registered Nurses of Newfoundland and Labrador (ARNN)
55 Military Road, P.O. Box 6116
St. John's NL A1C 5X8 Canada
Tel.: (709) 753-6040 or 1-800-563-3200
Fax: (709) 753-4940
Email: info@arnn.nf.ca
http://www.arnn.nf.ca/

Northwest Territories
Registered Nurses Association of the Northwest Territories and Nunavut (RNANT/NU)
Box 2757
Yellowknife NT X1A 2R1 Canada
Tel.: (867) 873-2745
Fax: (867) 873-2336
Email: admin@rnantnu.ca
http://www.rnantnu.ca/

Nova Scotia
College of Registered Nurses of Nova Scotia (CRNNS)
Suite 600, Barrington Tower, 1894 Barrington Street
Halifax NS B3J 2A8 Canada
Tel.: (902) 491-9744
Fax: (902) 491-9510
Email: info@crnns.ca
http://www.crnns.ca/

Ontario
College of Nurses of Ontario (CNO)
101 Davenport Road
Toronto ON M5R 3P1 Canada
Tel.: (416) 928-0900 or 1-800-387-5526
Fax: (416) 928-6507
Email: cno@cnomail.org
http://www.cno.org/

PEI
Prince Edward Island Registered Nurses Association of Ontario (RNAO)
438 University Avenue, Suite 1600
Toronto ON M5G 2K8 Canada
Tel.: (416) 599-1925 or 1-800-268-7199
Fax: (416) 599-1926
Email: info@rnao.org
http://www.rnao.org/

Association of Nurses of Prince Edward Island (ANPEI)
137 Queen Street, Suite 303
Charlottetown PE C1A 4B3 Canada
Tel.: (902) 368-3764
Fax: (902) 628-1430
Email: anpei@pei.sympatico.ca
http://www.anpei.ca/

Quebec
Ordre des infirmières et infirmiers du Québec (OIIQ)
4200, boul. Dorchester Ouest
Montréal QC H3Z 1V4 Canada
Tel.: (514) 935-2501 or 1-800-363-6048
Fax: (514) 935-1799
Email: inf@oiiq.org
http://www.oiiq.org/

Saskatchewan
Registered Psychiatric Nurses Association of Saskatchewan (RPNAS)
2055 Lorne Street
Regina SK S4P 2M4 Canada
Tel.: (306) 586-4617
Fax: (306) 586-6000
Email: rpnas@rpnas.com
http://www.rpnas.com/

Saskatchewan Registered Nurses' Association (SRNA)
2066 Retallack Street
Regina SK S4T 7X5 Canada
Tel.: (306) 359-4200 or 1-800-667-9945
Fax: (306) 525-0849
Email: info@srna.org
http://www.srna.org/

Yukon
Yukon Registered Nurses Association (YRNA)
204-4133-4th Avenue
Whitehorse YT Y1A 3T3 Canada
Tel.: (867) 667-4062
Fax: (867) 668-5123
Email: yrna@yknet.ca

Information Resources For Foreign-Trained School Teachers

LIST OF REGULATING AGENCIES

Alberta
Alberta Learning, Teacher Certification and Development
10155-102 Street, 7th Floor
Mail: 11160 Jasper Ave.
Edmonton AB T5J 4L5 Canada
Tel.: (780) 427-7219
Fax: (780) 422-1263
Email: comm.contact@learning.gov.ab.ca
http://www.learning.gov.ab.ca/k_12/teaching/certification/

British Columbia
British Columbia College of Teachers (BCCT)
400-2025 West Broadway
Vancouver BC V6J 1Z6 Canada
Tel.: (604) 731-8170
Fax: (604) 731-9142
http://www.bcct.ca/certification/default.aspx

Manitoba
Department of Education, Training and Youth, Professional Certification
Box 700
Russell MB R0J 1W0 Canada
Tel.: (204) 773-2998 or 1-800-667-2378
Fax: (204) 773-2411
http://www.edu.gov.mb.ca/metks4/profdev/profcert/index.html

New Brunswick
Department of Education, Office of Teacher Certification
P.O. Box 6000
Fredericton NB E3B 5H1 Canada
Tel.: (506) 453-2785
Fax: (506) 444-4761
Email: yves.king@gnb.ca
http://www.gnb.ca/0000/index-e.asp

Newfoundland and Labrador
Department of Education, Registrar of Teacher Certification
Confederation Building, P.O. Box 8700
St. John's NL A1B 4J6 Canada
Tel.: (709) 729-3020
Fax: (709) 729-5826
Email: rparsons@edu.gov.nf.ca
http://www.nlta.nf.ca/HTML_files/html_pages/archives/certftn.html

Northwest Territories
Department of Education, Culture and Employment, (School) Board Operations
P.O. Box 1320
Yellowknife NT X1A 2L9 Canada
Tel.: (867) 873-7392
Fax: (867) 873-0338
Email: joyce_mclean@ece.learnnet.nt.ca
http://www.newteachersnwt.ca/

Nova Scotia
Department of Education, Teacher Certification
2021 Brunswick Street, P.O. Box 578
Halifax NS B3J 2S9 Canada
Tel.: (902) 424-6620
Fax: (902) 424-3814
Email: certification@EDnet.ns.ca
http://certification.ednet.ns.ca/

Nunavut
Nunavut Educators' Certification Service, Department of Education
P.O. Box 390
Arviat NU X0C 0E0 Canada
Tel.: (867) 857-3081
Fax: (867) 857-3090
Email: dlefebvre@gov.nu.ca
http://www.ecss.nu.ca/necs/

Ontario
Ontario College of Teachers (OCT)
121 Bloor Street East, 6th Floor
Toronto ON M4W 3M5 Canada
Tel.: (416) 961-8800 or 1-888-534-2222
Fax: (416) 961-8822
Email: info@oct.ca
http://www.oct.ca/

Prince Edward Island
Department of Education, Registrar's Office
P.O. Box 2000
16 Fitzroy Street
Charlottetown PE C1A 7N8 Canada
Tel.: (902) 368-4650
Fax: (902) 368-4663
http://www.gov.pe.ca/educ/index.php3?number=78284&lang=E

Quebec
Québec - Ministère de l'Éducation, Direction de la formation et de la titularisation du personnel scolaire
1035, rue De La Chevrotière, 28e étage
Québec QC G1R 5A5 Canada
Tel.: (418) 646-6581
Fax: (418) 643-2149
Email: louise.beaudoin@meq.gouv.qc.ca
http://www.meq.gouv.qc.ca/dftps/

Saskatchewan
Saskatchewan Education, Student and Teacher Services
4635 Wascana Parkway
Regina SK S4P 3V7 Canada
Tel.: (306) 787-6085
Fax: (306) 787-1003
Email: diane.neill@sasked.gov.sk.ca
http://www.sasked.gov.sk.ca/branches/prov_exams/teacher_services/teachcert.sht ml

Yukon
Teacher Certification, Department of Education, Yukon
1000 Lewes Boulevard, P.O. Box 2703
Whitehorse YT Y1A 2C6 Canada
Tel.: (867) 667-8631 or 1-800-661-0408
Fax: (867) 393-6339
Email: peggy.dorosz@gov.yk.ca
http://www.education.gov.yk.ca/employment/certification.html

Information Resources For Foreign-Trained Pharmacists

Pharmacy Examining Board of Canada (PEBC)
415 Yonge Street, Suite 601
Toronto ON M5B 2E7 Canada
Tel.: (416) 979-2431
Fax: (416) 599-9244
Email: pebccdn@attglobal.net
http://www.pebc.ca/

Alberta
Alberta College of Pharmacists (ACP)
Suite 1200, 10303-Jasper Avenue
Edmonton AB T5J 3N6 Canada
Tel.: (780) 990-0321 or 1-877-227-3838
Fax: (780) 990-0328
Email: acpinfo@altapharm.org
http://www.altapharm.org/

British Columbia
College of Pharmacists of British Columbia (COPBC)
200-1765 West 8th Avenue
Vancouver BC V6J 1V8 Canada
Tel.: (604) 733-2440 or 1-800-663-1940
Fax: (604) 733-2493 or 1-800-377-8129
Email: info@bcpharmacists.org
http://www.collpharmbc.org/

Manitoba
Manitoba Pharmaceutical Association (MPhA)
187 St. Mary's Road
Winnipeg MB R2H 1J2 Canada
Tel.: (204) 233-1411
Fax: (204) 237-3468
Email: info@mpha.mb.ca
http://www.napra.org/docs/0/203/204.asp

New Brunswick
New Brunswick Pharmaceutical Society (NBPhS)
101-30 Gordon Street, Burbank Complex
Moncton NB E1C 1L8 Canada
Tel.: (506) 857-8957
Fax: (506) 857-8838
Email: nbphs@nbnet.nb.ca
http://www.napra.org/docs/0/203/227.asp

Newfoundland and Labrador
Newfoundland Pharmaceutical Association (NPhA)
Apothecary Hall
488 Water St.
St. John's NL A1E 1B3 Canada
Tel.: (709) 753-5877
Fax: (709) 753-8615
Email: npha@npha.nf.ca
http://www.npha.nf.ca/

Northwest Territories
Registrar, Health Professional Licensing, Northwest Territories
Eight Floor, Centre Square Tower
P.O. Box 1320
Yellowknife NT X1A 2L9 Canada
Tel.: (867) 920-8058
Fax: (867) 873-0484

Nova Scotia
Nova Scotia College of Pharmacists
1464 Dresden Row
Halifax NS B3J 3T5 Canada
Tel.: (902) 422-8528
Fax: (902) 422-0885
Email: nsps@ns.sympatico.ca
http://www.napra.org/docs/0/203/245.asp

Ontario
Ontario College of Pharmacists (OCP)
483 Huron Street
Toronto ON M5R 2R4 Canada
Tel.: (416) 962-4861
Fax: (416) 703-3108
Email: vduczek@ocpinfo.com
http://www.ocpinfo.com/

Prince Edward Island
Prince Edward Island Pharmacy Board (PEIPB)
South Shore Professional Building
Trans Canada Highway
Crapaud PE C0A 1J0 Canada
Tel.: (902) 658-2780
Fax: (902) 658-2198
Email: peipharm@auracom.com
http://www.napra.org/docs/0/203/260.asp

Quebec
Ordre des pharmaciens du Québec (OPQ)
266, rue Notre-Dame Ouest, Bureau 301
Montréal QC H2Y 1T6 Canada
Tel.: (514) 284-9588 or 1-800-363-0324
Fax: (514 284-3420
Email: ordrepharm@opq.org
http://www.opq.org/eng/default.htm

Saskatchewan
Saskatchewan Pharmaceutical Association (SPhA)
4010 Pasqua Street, Suite 700
Regina SK S4S 7B9 Canada
Tel.: (306) 584-2292
Fax: (306) 584-9695
Email: saskpharm@sasktel.net
http://www.napra.org/docs/0/203/262/266.asp

Yukon
Registrar for Licensed Practical Nurses Justice Services Division
Justice Services Division
Department of Community Services
P.O. Box 2703
Whitehorse YT Y1A 2C6 Canada
Tel.: (867) 667-5257
Fax: (867) 667-3609
Email: consumer@gov.yk.ca
http://www.gov.yk.ca/depts/community/consumer/csleg.html

FACT SHEET No. 2

Assessment and recognition of credentials for the purpose of employment in Canada

Most individuals who plan to come to Canada to settle permanently and who wish to enter the labour force will need to know the value of the education, training, and experience they have acquired outside Canada. This fact sheet answers the most frequently asked questions about the process so that it may help individuals learn more about how to obtain assessment and recognition of their qualifications. Individuals intending to continue their education in Canada can learn more about the process by consulting **CICIC's** **Fact Sheet No. 1**, *Information for students educated abroad applying for admission to Canadian universities and colleges*. Both fact sheets are available in French and may be obtained by contacting CICIC directly or through its Web site http://www.cicic.ca/indexe.stm

1. *How can I get my qualifications obtained abroad recognized in Canada?*

   The procedures for evaluating and recognizing qualifications earned outside Canada **will depend on** whether you wish to **enter an occupation** or **pursue further studies**, whether your chosen occupation is **regulated or non-regulated**, and the **province/territory** in which you intend to settle. For the purpose of this document, occupations will refer to both professions and trades. As a general rule, if your chosen occupation is regulated, the recognition of qualifications will be determined by the appropriate provincial or territorial regulatory body, while for a non-regulated occupation, recognition is normally at the discretion of the employer.

2. *What is the difference between a regulated and a non-regulated occupation?*

A **"regulated" occupation** is one that is controlled by provincial and territorial (and sometimes federal) law and governed by a professional organization or regulatory body. The **regulatory body** governing the profession/trade has the **authority** to set entry requirements and standards of practice, to assess applicants' qualifications and credentials, to certify, register, or license qualified applicants, and to discipline members of the profession/trade. Requirements for entry, which may **vary from one province to another**, usually consist of such components as examinations, a specified period of supervised work experience, language competency, etc. If you want to work in a regulated occupation and use a regulated title, **you MUST have a licence or certificate or be registered** with the regulatory body for your occupation. Some occupations are regulated in certain provinces and territories and are not regulated in others.

About 20 per cent of Canadians work in regulated occupations such as veterinarian, electrician, plumber, physiotherapist, medical doctor, engineer, etc. The system of regulation is intended to protect the health and safety of Canadians by ensuring that professionals meet the required standards of practice and competence.

A **"non-regulated" occupation** is a profession/trade for which there is **no legal requirement or restriction** on practice with regard to licences, certificates, or registration. **The vast majority of occupations** in Canada fall into this category. For some non-regulated occupations, certification/registration with a professional body is available to applicants on a voluntary basis, whereas for other non-regulated occupations there is no certification/registration available at all.

In general, applicants for non-regulated occupations will have to demonstrate to their potential employers that they possess the experience and training required for the job. Even when an occupation is not regulated, employers can still require that an applicant for a job be registered, licensed, or certified with the relevant professional association.

3. *If I want to work in a regulated occupation, what can I do to get my qualifications assessed and recognized?*

Each regulated occupation sets its own requirements for assessment and recognition, usually through the **provincial or territorial professional association or regulatory body.** (In some cases, there are federal requirements for recognition.) In order to qualify for practice in Canada, you may be required to undergo professional and language examinations, submit to a review of your qualifications, and undertake a period of supervised work experience. You can find out more about the specific requirements for recognition of your qualifications in your profession/trade by doing the following:

1. Contact the professional association governing your occupation in **your own country** to find out if there are any links with similar associations in Canada. Consult the publication entitled National Occupational Classification at the closest Canadian diplomatic mission to find out more about employment requirements for your occupation.

2. Find out the name and address of the professional regulatory body governing your profession/trade in the province or territory where you intend to settle by enquiring with CICIC.

3. Write to the regulatory body and ask about the specific requirements and costs for licensing, certification, or registration, as well as the recommended procedure for an assessment. The regulatory body will advise you concerning the required documentation and the fees for assessment.

You should be aware that the recognition process is different in each province and territory and for each profession/trade. It can be a costly and time-consuming process; so it is important that you obtain all the information you need to know about the process and specific requirements before undertaking an assessment.

4. *If I want to work in a non-regulated occupation, what can I do to get my qualifications assessed and recognized?*

For a **non-regulated occupation**, requirements for employment can vary from very specific to very general. You may be expected to demonstrate a certain level of skill and competence, to have completed a certain number of years of education, and even to have personal characteristics suitable for the job. Since these requirements are **not regulated by provincial or territorial law**, it is up to the **employer to decide** whether your qualifications earned outside Canada are equivalent to Canadian credentials required for the occupation. Because registration and certification may be available for certain non-regulated occupations, some employers will require, as a condition for employment, that applicants be registered or certified by the relevant professional association.

There is no single process in place for the assessment of qualifications for purposes of entry into non-regulated occupations. However, there are several ways an applicant can try to facilitate the process for a potential employer.

o Get in touch with the association or organization relevant to your occupation in your home country and in Canada. Find out about the procedures recommended for an assessment of your qualifications. CICIC can direct you to the relevant organization in Canada, if one exists.

o Contact employers in your area of work experience to find out what the general expectations are for employment in Canada. Consult the publication entitled National Occupational Classification. A copy is available at the nearest Canadian diplomatic mission. Verify if there is voluntary certification or registration available and what the requirements are for the province or territory where you intend to work. To determine if there is a provincial agency providing certification in your particular occupation, visit the relevant page listed on http://www.cicic.ca/professions/indexe.stm

o If there are no provincial agencies, then contact one of the evaluation services listed below for an assessment of your credentials. Although these services offer **expert advice** on how qualifications obtained abroad compare with credentials obtained in a Canadian province or territory, the evaluation is advisory only and **does not guarantee** recognition of your qualifications for employment or certification purposes in Canada. However, it will assist employers, post-secondary institutions, and professional bodies in understanding your academic background. Please note that these agencies charge a fee for their services.

PROVINCIALLY-MANDATED EVALUATION SERVICES

Alberta
International Qualifications Assessment Service
Alberta Learning
4th Floor, Sterling Place
9940 - 106 Street
Edmonton, Alberta   T5K 2V1   Canada

Tel: (780) 427-2655; Fax: (780) 422-9734
E-mail: iqas@gov.ab.ca
http://www.learning.gov.ab.ca/iqas/iqas.asp

British Columbia
International Credential Evaluation Service
4355 Mathissi Place
Burnaby, British Columbia   V5G 4S8   Canada

Tel: (604) 431-3402; Fax: (604) 431-3382
E-mail: ICES@ola.bc.ca
http://www.ola.bc.ca/ices/

Manitoba
Academic Credentials Assessment Service - Manitoba (ACAS)

Manitoba Labour and Immigration
Settlement & Labour Market Services Branch
5th Floor, 213 Notre Dame Avenue
Winnipeg, Manitoba, Canada R3B 1N3

Tel: (204) 945 - 6300 or (204) 945 - 5432
Fax: (204) 948 - 2148

E-mail: glloyd@gov.mb.ca
http://www.immigratemanitoba.com

Ontario
World Education Services-Canada

45 Charles Street East, Suite 700
Toronto, Ontario M4Y 1S2   Canada

Tel.: (416) 972-0070
Fax : (416) 972-9004
Toll-free: (866) 343-0070 (from outside the 416 area code)

Email: ontario@wes.org
http://www.wes.org/ca/

Quebec
Service des équivalences (SDE)

Ministère des Relations avec les citoyens et de l'Immigration
800, boulevard de Maisonneuve Est, 2e étage
Montréal (Québec)   H2L 4L8   Canada

Tél : (514) 864-9191 ou (877) 264-6164; Fax : (514) 873-8701
Email: equivalences@mrci.gouv.qc.ca
http://www.immq.gouv.qc.ca/equivalences

OTHER EVALUATION SERVICES

Academic Credentials Evaluation Service

Office of Admissions, Room 150, Atkinson College
York University
4700 Keele Street
Toronto, Ontario M3J 1P3   Canada

Tel.: (416) 736-5787; Fax: (416) 736-5536
E-mail: dstadnic@yorku.ca
http://www.yorku.ca/admissio/aces.asp

Comparative Education Service

University of Toronto
315 Bloor Street West,
Toronto, Ontario M5S 1A3   Canada
Tel: (416) 978-2185; Fax: (416) 978-7022
http://www.adm.utoronto.ca/ces/

International Credential Assessment Service of Canada

147 Wyndham Street North, Suite 409
Guelph, ON
Canada   N1H 4E9

Tel: (519) 763-7282
Toll-free: (800) 321-6021
Fax : (519) 763-6964

Email: icas@sympatico.ca
http://www.icascanada.ca/

Evaluation services have an appeal process in place for individuals who wish to challenge the assessment of their credential.

1. *If I am applying for an immigration visa and need to know the value of my credentials, how can I get my credentials assessed prior to immigration?*

Although regulatory bodies will provide information on what is required to practise a profession or a trade, most regulatory bodies are not set up to assess foreign credentials prior to your arrival in Canada. Assessments are conducted by examinations and interviews, which means that you **MUST already be in Canada**. With very few exceptions, it is virtually impossible to obtain an assessment of credentials that would lead to eventual licensure, certification, or registration in the relevant occupation before you immigrate to Canada. Some regulated professions offer an initial assessment prior to immigration. Information can be obtained concerning this service by communicating directly with the regulatory body.

When a pre-immigration assessment is not available because the regulatory body does not offer it, or because your occupation is non-regulated, you can consult one of the credentials evaluation services listed under question 4. Although an assessment by one of these services does not guarantee recognition of your credentials for purposes of employment, licensure/certification, immigration, or further studies in Canada, it does provide an expert comparison of your qualifications with credentials obtained in a Canadian province or territory.

You should be aware that even if you meet the occupational requirements for immigration and are admitted to Canada, this, in itself, does not constitute a guarantee of employment. Acceptance for employment is a decision that rests solely with the employer.

2. *Where can I obtain a translation of my qualifications into English or French?*

If documents need to be translated, the evaluation service or regulatory body will advise you as to the requirements for translation and authentification of official documents.

3. *Is the university where I studied in my country recognized in Canada?*

Recognition of universities is the responsibility of the educational authorities of the country in which such institutions are located. Canadian evaluation services consult specialized tools such as the World Higher Education Database and the World Directory of National Information Centre for Academic Recognition and Mobility to determine if an institution is recognized. Recognition does not automatically mean that a given credential is automatically recognized in Canada. Other factors, such as national or provincial/territorial legislation and other specific requirements are considered in the evaluation of credentials and the licensing of professionals.

4. *What is a trade, and what is a <u>Red Seal</u> Trade?*

A trade is an occupation generally regarded as requiring one to three years of post-secondary education at a community college or university, two to four years of apprenticeship training, two to three years of on-the-job training, or a combination of these requirements. Some trades are regulated which means that a licence/certificate is required to practise in such cases.

Some trades are referred to as **<u>Red Seal</u> Trades.** A <u>Red Seal</u> Trade is a trade for which all the provinces and territories have agreed on standards for entry into the occupation allowing for the portability of qualifications across Canada. Red Seal Trades are designated by the Interprovincial Standards Program under the authority of the Canadian Council of Directors of Apprenticeship, the body that is also responsible for setting standards in the designated trades. The Red Seal is a passport that allows the holder to work anywhere in Canada without having to write further examinations.

In some provinces, certification is voluntary, meaning that neither a formal certificate nor a formal apprenticeship is required to practise the trade. However, the Red Seal Certificate would indicate that the holder has reached a certain level of expertise, and it may be required by some employers as a condition of employment. For a list of designated Red Seal Trades and the addresses of the Provincial Apprenticeship Directors, please contact CICIC.

5. *If I want an assessment of my credentials for my own information, how can I proceed?*

The best way to get an assessment of your credentials for information purposes is to consult one of the credentials evaluation services listed under question 4 or, for licensing purposes, to contact the appropriate professional regulatory body.

Credential evaluation services offer expert advice about how your qualifications compare with credentials obtained in a Canadian province or territory; their evaluations are advisory only and **do not guarantee** recognition of your qualifications for immigration, further studies, employment, or licensure/certification purposes. However, this advice will assist employers, post-secondary institutions, and professional bodies in understanding your academic background. Please note that these agencies charge a fee for their services.

6. *Where can I learn more about employment opportunities in Canada?*

There is no central source of information about employment opportunities. **Please note that CICIC does not have information about employment opportunities. Once in Canada**, you can learn more about opportunities by contacting the **relevant professional associations**, reading the professional newsletters and bulletins, if available, and consulting the classified advertising section of the **local newspapers**. A number of **community and settlement organizations** also provide employment advice to newly arrived immigrants. In addition, many private employment agencies will help to place individuals. Some may charge a fee for this service.

Visit the various websites for job search like www.workopolis.ca

Labour market information

Job Futures: http://www.jobfutures.ca/

Work Destinations: http://www.workdestinations.ca/

Work*info*NET: http://www.workinfonet.ca/

WorkSearch: http://www.worksearch.gc.ca/

National Occupational Classification
http://cnp2001noc.worklogic.com/

7. *If I want to pursue further education in Canada, how do I get an assessment of my credentials?*

If you are thinking of studying in a Canadian college or university, contact the **office of admissions** of the institution in which you are interested and ask about the procedure required for an assessment of your credentials. The university or college has the sole authority to make decisions about recognition of credentials for purposes of admission. Individuals intending to continue their education in Canada can learn more about the process by consulting CICIC's Fact Sheet No. 1, *Information for students educated abroad applying for admission to Canadian universities and colleges.*

8. *What other sources of information are available?*

Immigration: general information and advice
to Canada : http://www.cic.gc.ca/

to Québec:
http://www.immq.gouv.qc.ca/anglais/index.html

Post-secondary education in Canada
List of recognized institutions:
http://www.cicic.ca/postsec/indexe.stm

Company, business, and industry information
http://strategis.ic.gc.ca/

Reference Publications
Guide to Canadian terminology usage in the field of credential assessment and recognition
http://www.cicic.ca/pubs/guidtofb_en.stm

9. *What can CICIC do for me?*

The Canadian Information Centre for International Credentials (CICIC) assists persons who want to know how to obtain an assessment of their educational, professional, and occupational credentials by referring them to the appropriate bodies. **CICIC does not itself grant equivalencies or assess credentials, nor does it intervene on behalf of individuals or in appeals**. While colleges, universities, and licensing bodies have the sole authority to recognize foreign programs and degrees, CICIC fosters the dissemination of information about recognition procedures, promotes good and consistent practice in credentials assessment, and serves as a link for Canadian academic and professional bodies to international organizations and to similar institutions around the world.

CICIC collects data about procedures for recognizing academic and occupational credentials in different Canadian jurisdictions. This information is stored in a regularly updated database covering more than 800 professional, educational, and community agencies.

You are welcome to contact CICIC regarding qualifications assessment and recognition procedures by e-mail, telephone, fax, or post. Be sure to state in your enquiry the purpose for which you are seeking information on assessment, your intended occupation, and the province or territory where you plan to work.

Further information about post-secondary education and about other relevant organizations in Canada can be obtained by visiting the CICIC Web site: http://www.cicic.ca/

If you need further details, please contact at the following address:

Canadian Information Centre for International Credentials

95 St. Clair Avenue West, Suite 1106
Toronto, Ontario M4V 1N6   Canada

Phone: (416) 962-9725
Fax: (416) 962-2800
Email: info@cicic.ca

LABOUR MARKET INFORMATION BY PROVINCE AND TERRITORY

Canada is a large and diverse country. Job opportunities and labour market conditions are different in each region. It is important to obtain labour market information about the area where you want to live. Most provinces and territories provide information on their labour markets.

Alberta
Alberta Learning
7th Floor, Commerce Place
10155 102 Street
Edmonton, Alberta T5J 4L5

Telephone: 780-427-7219
Toll-free access, first dial 310-0000.
Fax: 780-422-1263

E-mail: comm.contact@learning.gov.ab.ca
URL: www.learning.gov.ab.ca/welcome/English/pdf/Employment.pdf

British Columbia
Aboriginal, Multiculturalism and Immigration Programs
PO Box 9214
Stn Prov Govt
Victoria, British Columbia V8W 9J1

Telephone: 250 952-6434
Fax: 250 356-5316
URL: www.gov.bc.ca/mi/popt/movingtobc.htm

Manitoba
Immigration and Multiculturalism Division
5th floor - 213 Notre Dame Avenue
Winnipeg, Manitoba R3B 1N3

Telephone: (204) 945-3162
Facsimile: (204) 948-2256

Email: immigratemanitoba@gov.mb.ca
URL: www.gov.mb.ca/labour/immigrate/newcomerservices/8.html

New Brunswick
Investment and Immigration,
Department of Business New Brunswick
P O Box 6000
Fredericton, New Brunswick E3B 5H1

Telephone: (506) 444-4640
Facsimile: (506) 444-4277

E-mail:immigration@gnb.ca
URL: www.gnb.ca/immigration/english/work/work.htm

Ontario
Access to Professions and Trades Unit
Ministry of Training, Colleges and Universities
12th Floor, 900 Bay Street, Mowat Block
Toronto, Ontario M7A 1L2

Telephone: (416) 326-9714
Facsimile: (416) 326-6265

E-mail: aptinfo@edu.gov.on.ca
URL: www.equalopportunity.on.ca/eng_g/apt/index.asp

Prince Edward Island
Immigration and Investment,
Development and Technology
94 Euston Street 2nd Floor
Charlottetown, PEI C1A 1W4

Telephone: (902) 894-0351
Facsimile: (902) 368-5886
URL: www.gov.pe.ca/infopei/Employment/index.php3

Quebec
Ministère des Relations avec les citoyens
et de l'Immigration (MRCI)

How to reach :
www.immigration-quebec.gouv.qc.ca/anglais/ reach.html
Email: Renseignements.DRM@mrci.gouv.qc.ca
URL: www.immigration-quebec.gouv.qc.ca/anglais/services/insertion_en.html

Saskatchewan
Saskatchewan Government Relations and Aboriginal Affairs
8th Floor, 1919 Saskatchewan Drive
Regina, Saskatchewan S4P 3V7

Email: immigration@iaa.gov.sk.ca

URL: www.iaa.gov.sk.ca/iga/immigration/Immigration.htm

(Accreditation and Services sites under development)

Yukon
Labour Market Program and Services -
Department of Education
Advanced Education Branch
Box 2703Whitehorse, Yukon Y1A 2C6

Telephone: (867) 667-5141 or
Toll Free: 800-661-0408
Facsimile: (867) 667-8555

AN URGENT ISSUE AND A CHALLENGE

Canada is one of the world's leading immigrant-receiving countries. Both our country, and the newcomers themselves, benefit greatly when newly arrived immigrants and refugees are able to integrate smoothly into Canadian society.

Statistics indicates that many immigrants and refugees who arrived to Canada during the 1990s are experiencing greater settlement difficulties (eg. poverty, housing duress, social difficulties) than earlier waves of newcomers

The barriers to the recognition of the credentials and experience of immigrant professionals and trades-people by regulatory bodies and employers and the dramatic under-utilization of their skills and experience has become an increasingly urgent issue. While Canada's immigration policy encourages and invites immigrants with professional qualifications and experience, Canada continue to be disturbingly ineffective in integrating these highly-skilled and educated newcomers.

Canada's future prosperity and social cohesion depends on maximizing the talents of visible minorities, the fastest-growing segment of the labour force. Yet, despite substantial investment of time and resources in workplace diversity, too few Canadian organizations successfully attract, develop and promote visible minorities.

The impact of having thousands of underemployed immigrant professionals and trades-people is felt in families and in communities in the form of lost dreams and opportunities, social and economic distress. It is felt across Canadian society and at all levels of government in the form of lost tax dollars and increased social assistance and social service costs. One recent study has examined the inequalities between immigrants and non-immigrants on measures such as average earnings, occupation and hours of work. *Using a respected economic model, the study projects that if these inequalities were completely eliminated, an additional $64.5 billion could be expected to be added to Canada's GDP by 2036. (Harvey: 2001).*

The issue is a complex one involving a multitude of stakeholders in both the public and private sectors. While immigration and human resource policy are within federal jurisdiction, occupational regulation falls within provincial jurisdiction and, in most professions, responsibility for regulating and administering the licensing of practitioners has been devolved to self-regulating professional bodies. The relationship of licensing and employment is equally complex, often involving a "chicken-egg" conundrum in which practitioners need a licence to get a job, but need Canadian experience to get a licence. In order to be effective, policy and program approaches to the issue, public and private organizations at federal and provincial levels are trying their best to address the issue on urgent basis. But it will certainly take few years to achieve the desired results and acceptable statistics. For more detailed information about these issues and challenges, please visit following links and read the research reports:

Formal Occupational Barriers –Human Resources and Skill development Canada
http://www11.hrsdc.gc.ca/en/cs/sp/hrsdc/lmp/publications/2001-002653/SP-588-04-04E.pdf

Access to Experience:
http://www.peo.on.ca/publications/DIMENSIONS/marapr2004/AccesstoExperience.pdf

Immigrant Skill Utlization in the Canadian Labour Market- Implications of Human Capital Research
http://www.utoronto.ca/ethnicstudies/Reitz_Skill.pdf

The Colour of Poverty: A study of the poverty of ethnic and immigrant groups in canada -Authors: Kazemipur A.; Halli S.S.

Color My World –Krishna Pendakur –
http://www.sfu.ca/~pendakur/colour_cpp.pdf

The Color of Money: earning differentials among ethnic groups in Canada - Krishna Pendakur -
http://www.sfu.ca/~pendakur/colour.pdf

Tip: ***Business Critical: Maximizing the Talents of Visible Minorities—An Employer's Guide***, the culmination of a Conference Board of Canada project involving 30 public and private sector partners, will help Canadian organizations take the steps needed to fully embrace diversity. The Employers Guide brings together policies, practices, tools and initiatives that can lead to more inclusive workplaces. It draws on case studies of 12 Canadian and international organizations that illustrate what leading organizations do to excel at diversity management. For details please visit http://www.conferenceboard.ca

LETS FIND A JOB

The very first activity on your line of action towards finding a job in Canada is to create a North American style resume (C.V). Visit various recruiters or job search websites listed at the end of this book. You will find help to create your resume from these sites. Tailor your resume according to each job title and description that you decide to apply for. It is worthwhile to spend few minutes to review and edit your resume every time when you apply for a new job. If the employer wants apples and oranges in the job description or experience of the candidate then you should incorporate both in your resume otherwise you may not get an interview call. So avoid mailing generic resume that may lead you to frustration. Following is an example of North American style resume.

NORTH AMERICAN STYLE RESUME

Robert Lyfareff

101-1465 Lawrence Avenue E., Toronto, ON Z1R 2P8 ☎ (416) 798-1543 ✒
Robert_lyfareff@hotmail.com

OBJECTIVE: Project Engineer / Project Supervisor (Mechanical)

SUMMARY OF QUALIFICATIONS

10+ years of international experience in the Electro-Mechanical Construction and Engineering industry especially in Oil/Gas sector. Broad knowledge base in engineering and project management. Competent in office management and accounting. **Well-groomed in EPCM environment** with problem solving abilities.

RELEVANT SKILLS AND EXPERIENCE

- Extensive experience and knowledge of ASME Codes.
- Proven management skills and record of accomplishment as per schedules.
- Management talent for "seeing the whole picture"
- Confident and decisive under stressful conditions,
- Effective in budgeting (managed up to $ 200,000) and cost control.
- Extensive experience in report writing and proposals
- Enthusiastic, committed, resourceful team player with exceptional communication & interpersonal skills.
- Self-motivated, Adaptable, Quick Learner.

SUMMARY OF COMPETENCIES

- Project Design & Management
- Engineering Management
- Estimating, Budgeting and P&L
- Resource Planning & Managemer
- Field Installation Management
- Client Presentations & Negotiations
- Cross-Functional Team Leadership
- Vendor Selection & Negotiation
- Material Selection & Management
- Product and Technology R&D

Excellent in client relationship management and cross-cultural communications. PC proficient with Microsoft Office Suit, MS Project, Autocad Rel. 14/2000 and familiar with Primavera P3.

EDUCATION & PROFESSIONAL LISCENSE

- B.Sc Mechanical Engineering - 1991
- Professional Engineer **(P.Eng) – Ontario**

EMPLOYMENT HISTORY

Project Engineer - Alfa Constructions Inc.   Toronto - 1995 to the present

Supervised a staff of 25+ professional and support personnel and completed various multi-million $ projects in oil/gas/energy sector.

Supervisor – Sonic Engineering -   Alberta   1992 to 1994

Supervised a staff of 30+ professional and support personnel and participated in a $4Billion underground fuel oil storage facility. Completed 20-25 Kilometer of ½"-20" various services pressure piping   installation and testing as per ASME Codes

---

Note: *One page resume has always been considered the best to get an interview call because* the average time spent by HR generalists in Canada to shortlist resume is 10-15 seconds.

TOP INTERVIEW QUESTIONS ASKED BY CANADIAN EMPLOYERS

1. Tell me about yourself?
2. Tell me about any of your weakness?
3. What are some of your strengths?
4. Where do you see yourself in 5 years?
5. What work experience have you had that prepares you for this position?
6. Why should we hire you?
7. Do you consider yourself a creative problem solver? Give me an example.
8. Why did you leave your last position?
9. Your resume shows you have moved around a lot. How can I be sure you will stay at this company?
10. What did you think of your last supervisor/manager?
11. Describe your ideal position.
12. What did you like about your last job?
13. What did you dislike about your last job?
14. Describe how you work under pressure.
15. Describe your ideal boss.
16. What do you have to offer this company that others may not?
17. What kind of salary are you looking for?
18. What was your annual salary at your last position?
19. What have you gained from working at your last job?
20. What were your responsibilities and duties?
21. What motivates you?
22. Do you consider yourself successful?
23. What traits or qualities do you most admire in someone?
24. What are your hobbies?
25. Are you willing to relocate?
26. Tell me about your proudest accomplishment?
27. What has been your most meaningful educational experience?
28. Can you tell me something about our company.
29. Describe how you perform in a high stress position?
30. How do you feel about routine work?
31. What steps are you taking to improve yourself?

32. Do you have a personal goal that you still want to achieve?
33. Tell me about what you would do to get organized for a project.
34. Have you ever been responsible for financial management?
35. There is a period of time on your resume when you were not employed. Can you tell me what you did in that time period?
36. Would it be appropriate to contact your most recent employer?
37. What do you think will be the most difficult aspect of this job?
38. What special skills / talents do you have?
39. Do you have any questions for me? (usually at the end of interview)

Note: When you will visit your nearest Human Resource Centre or an HRDC sponsored agency in Canada, you will find many books on interview questions with their answers and some with professions specific answers. You will also find many books on resume writing.

INTERVIEW QUESTIONS BY DIFFERENT GROUPS

Your Past

1. Why did you leave your last job?
2. What aspects of your responsibilities did you consider most critical?
3. What type of management did you have in your last job?
4. Which job, of all the ones you have had, did you like the best? Why?
5. Which job did you like the least? Why?
6. What did you accomplish which benefited the company? The job?
7. Where does this job fit in to your overall career plan?
8. How do you organize for major projects?

What You Learned

1. What special aspects of your education/training have prepared you for this job?
2. In what area would you most like additional training if you do get this job?

Why you Learned

1. What are your career goals?
2. What kid of job do you see yourself holding in five years time? Why?
3. What would you most like to accomplish if you get this job?
4. What do you consider your biggest career success to date?

Type of Jobs & Your Style

1. Tell me about one of your favourite work experiences. What did you like best about it.
2. How do you know when you have done a good job.

3. How did your past supervisor evaluate your performance? What areas of improvement were suggested?
4. Why do you feel that you are qualified for this position?

Stress Management

1. Tell me about a work situation that gave you difficulty?
2. Define co-operation.

Strengths

1. What key factors have accounted for your career success to date?
2. In what areas have others been particularly complimentary about your abilities?

Weakness

1. What do you think your co-workers would view as your greatest weakness?

Interpersonal Skills.

1. What sorts of people do you have difficulty working with?
2. With which of your past work groups did you most enjoy working?
3. What factors most influenced your positive feelings.
4. With which of your past work groups did you least enjoy working? What accounted for that, what did you do about it and what was the outcome?
5. What aspects of your interpersonal skills would you like most to improve?
6. Tell me about a confrontational situation at work. How did you handle it?

Type of Work you Like

1. What type of work do you find most stimulating and rewarding? Why? Least stimulating? Why?
2. In which of your last positions were you most motivated and productive?
3. What has your experience taught you about the type of work you least enjoy?
4. What factors contributed the most to your job dissatisfaction?

Your Preferred work Environment

1. In which of your past work environments (team, independent) were you the happiest? Why?
2. In which of your past work environments did you feel you had the greatest amount of influence and impact?
3. How would you describe the ideal work environment? Which things would be present? Which things would be absent?

Traits and Characteristics

1. What word best describes your personal style?
2. Which of your personal traits has been most helpful in your career?
3. If 3 of your close associates were here, what would they say about you?

Business Philosophy

1. How do you think successful businesses manage their employees.

Your Operating Style

1. How would you categorize your operating style (the way you go about your business/work?)
2. What are the basic work principles by which you operate?

Overcoming Rejections & Objections

1. You're overqualified!
2. We're looking for someone a little younger/older!
3. All hiring is done by personnel/we're supposed to go through personnel with these things!
4. We're cutting back right now. Why don't you call in three months/we're actually laying people off right now!
5. I'd love to see you, but I'm tied up in a meeting!

INTERVIEW PRACTICE – AN EXAMPLE

Practicing for the interview means practicing several behaviours – not just answering questions. You must dress well, watch your body language and posture, practice your manners and eye contact, as well as practice answering questions correctly, smoothly and with confidence.

The practice questions below, in one form or another, account for a large percentage of interview questions. With each question, you are given a series of choices as to how you might answer the question. When you select an answer, you will learn to whether your answer is correct or not - and why. Answering these questions will help you polish your interviewing techniques. The questions and answers in this exercise are generic and in many cases, must be tailored to your individual situation. Still, the logic behind the answer remains essentially the same.

1.   Why are you the best person for the job?

(a)   "I've held a lot of positions like this one and that experience will help me here."

(b)   "Because I am good at what I do."

(c)   "Our discussion here leads me to believe this is a good place to work."

(d)   "You need someone who can produce results and my background and experience are proof of my ability. For example..."

2.   If asked a point blank question such as : Are you creative? Are you analytical? Can you work under pressure? Etc. what is the best way to answer?

(a)   Answer yes or no.

(b)   Answer yes and give a specific example.

(c)   Answer yes and give an explanation.

3.   Describe yourself.

(a)   Outline personal data, hobbies and interests.

(b)   Give an overview of your personality and work habits.

(c)   Give three specific examples of your personality traits and accomplishments.

4.   Why are you in the job market?

(a)   "I have invested a great deal of time with my company and become disenchanted with the ways things are done".

(b)   "I have a solid plan for my career. Within that plan I am looking for additional responsibility and more room for growth."

(c)   "I have been passed over for promotions when I know I am capable of doing

more. I want to move on to a company that will not stunt my growth."

5.   What are you looking for in a position?

(a)   "I'm looking for an opportunity to apply my skills and contribute to the growth of the company while helping create some advancement opportunities for myself ".

(b)   *"I'm looking for an organization that will appreciate my contributions and reward my efforts."*

(c)   "I'm looking for a position that will allow me to make enough money to support my lifestyle. I am a hard worker and will give a concerted effort to earn the money I need."

6.   What do you know about our organization?

(a)   "I've done a little homework and here is what I know about your organization... (cite examples)."

(b)   "Everything I've seen and heard makes me want to be a part of this organization. I understand your industry is _____ and your primary customer is _____. A particularly exciting part of your business appears to be_____

(c)   "I know enough to know this is an exciting place to work. It appears to be fit for my career goals."

7. **What are your strengths?**

(a) "I am good at giving constructive criticism to my co-workers. This honesty is something I'm very proud of and have found essential to having open working relationships."

(b) "I consider myself to be very consistent. I have proven myself to be someone who can be counted upon to do what is expected."

(c) "I would have to choose between two skills. I am very proud of my determination and ability to get things done. At the same time I am very proud of my analytical abilities and problem solving skills These skills combine to give me a unique ability to solve problems and then implement the solutions."

8. **Why haven't you taken a job yet?**

(a) "I've talked to a number of people, but it is very difficult to find an organization that is the right fit."

(b) "I've come across a few attractive opportunities but, so far. I haven't found a position that pays what I feel I am worth."

(c) "I have done some careful planning because this decision is very important to me. I have been offered positions but, to date, I have not been able to find a position that meets my criteria and this is important because the match must be good for me as well as the company. The position we are discussing today appears to be a good fit."

9. **Where do you see yourself in five years?**

(a) "In five years, I will have either been promoted to your job or have started my own business."

(b) "This is a very volatile market. I find it difficult to project out five years."

(c)   "That really depends on the firm I join. I would like to take a position with some responsibility and room for growth. The key is with the right challenge, I intend to continually contribute and grow with the firm."

10.   Before we go any further, what kind of money do you need to make?

(a)   "I was making 50K at my last job and I feel I am worth at least 10 % more."

(b)   "The current job market shows a salary range of $____ to $____ for this type of position. However, my salary requirements are negotiable. Your firm has a reputation of compensating employees fairly and I trust you would do the same in my case. I am very interested in finding the right opportunity and will be open to any fair offer when I do so."

(c)   "Money is not very important to me. I need to be able to pay the bills, but the work environment is far more important to me."

Questions To Ask From Hiring Managers

- What is the organization structure of your department?
- How would you describe your company culture?
- What is your vision for your department over the next two to three years?
- What major challenges are you currently facing as a manager?
- What is your competitive advantage in the marketplace?
- What makes your company better than your competitors?
- What are the areas where your competitors are better than your company?
- What would you consider to be exceptional performance from someone performing in this position in the first 90 days?
- What is the internal perception of pursuing further education, such as a Master's degree?
- What is your management style?
- What is your preferred method of communicating with your team?
- How are you measured as a manager?
- What can I do to make you successful?
- How long have you been with the organization?
- What has been your career path within the organization?
- What will be the measurements of my success in this position?
- What are the organizational goals?
- What are the metrics used to measure whether or not you are achieving your goals?
- How far out into the future is the organization planning?
- How are new strategic initiatives communicated to the organization?
- Do you have control over your own budget? How is the initial budget amount determined?
- What is your approach with regard to the use of technology?
- What is the next step in the interviewing process?

TIPS FOR YOUR INTERVIEW

Some "Dos" and "Don't"

1. Do plan to arrive on time or a few minutes early. Late arrival for a job interview is never excusable.

2. If presented with an application, do fill it out neatly and completely. Don't rely on your application or resume to do the selling for you. Interviewers will want you to speak for yourself.

3. Do greet the interviewer by last name if you are sure of the pronunciation. If not, ask the employer to repeat it. Give the appearance of energy as you walk. Smile! Shake hands firmly. Be genuinely glad to meet the interviewer.

4. Do wait until you are offered a chair before sitting. Sit upright, look alert and interested at all times. Be a good listener as well as a good communicator.

5. Do look a prospective employer in the eye while speaking.

6. Do follow the interviewer's leads, but try to get the interviewer to describe the position and the duties to you early in the interview so that you can apply your background, skills and accomplishments to the position.

7. Do make sure that your good points come across to the interviewer in a factual, sincere manner. Stress achievements. For example: sales records, processes developed, savings achieved, systems installed, etc.

8. Do always conduct yourself as if you are determined to get the job you are discussing. Never close the door on opportunity.

9. Do show enthusiasm. If you are interested in the opportunity, enthusiastic feedback can enhance your chances of being further

considered. If you are not interested, your responsiveness will still demonstrate your professionalism.

10. Don't forget to bring a copy of your resume! Keep several copies in your briefcase if you are afraid you will forget.

11. Don't smoke, even if the interviewer does and offers you a cigarette. Do not chew gum.

12. Don't answer with a simple "yes" or "no." Explain whenever possible. Describe those things about yourself which relate to the situation.

13. Don't lie. Answer questions truthfully, frankly and succinctly.

14. Don't make unnecessary derogatory remarks about your present or former employers. Obviously, there were issues or else you would not have left a prior company or be looking to leave a present employer. However, when explaining your reasons for leaving, limit your comments to those necessary to adequately communicate your rationale.

15. Don't over-answer questions. And if the interviewer steers the conversation into politics or controversial issues, try to do more listening than speaking since this could be a sensitive situation.

16. Don't inquire about salary, vacations, bonuses, retirement, etc., on the initial interview unless you are sure the employer is interested in hiring you. If the interviewer asks what salary you want, indicate what you've earned but that you're more interested in opportunity than in a specific salary.

Negative Factors Evaluated by An Interviewer

Personal appearance which is less than professional.

Overbearing, overaggressive or egotistical behavior.

No positive purpose.

Lack of interest and enthusiasm -- passive and indifferent.

Lack of confidence and poise; nervousness.

Overemphasis on compensation.

Evasiveness; making excuses for unfavorable factors in work history.

Lack of tact, maturity and courtesy.

Condemnation of past employers, managers, projects or technologies.

Inability to maintain a conversation.

Lack of commitment to fill the position at hand.

Failure to ask questions about the position.

Persistent attitude of "What can you do for me?"

Lack of preparation for interview -- failure to get information about the company, resulting in inability to ask intelligent questions.

Closing the Interview

1.   If you are interested in the position, let the interviewer know. If you feel the position is attractive and you want it, be a good salesperson and say something like: "I'm very impressed with what I've seen here today; your company, its products and the people I've met. I am confident I could do an excellent job in the position you've described to me." The interviewer will be impressed with your enthusiasm.

2.   Don't be too discouraged if no immediate commitment is made. The interviewer will probably want to communicate with other people in the company or possibly interview more candidates before making a decision.

3.   If you get the impression that the interview is not going well and that you have already been rejected, don't let your discouragement show. Once in a while an interviewer who is genuinely interested in you may seem to discourage you as a way of testing your reaction.

4.   Thank the interviewer for his or her time and consideration. If you have answered the two questions-- "Why are you interested in this position?" and "What can you offer?"-- you have done all you can.

DO YOU HAVE INTERNATIONAL EXPERIENCE?

Do you have International Experience? That is the question employers should be asking candidates. However more realistically the question many job seekers are hearing is - do you have Canadian Experience?

International experience is an asset. This means companies can tap into different cultural groups, understand cultural differences and employ people that can communicate effectively with other groups of people. You can bring new and innovative ideas to the table – things that worked in your country. Also international experience gives companies that competitive edge globally.

So, when you are asked if you have Canadian Experience – How do you answer that question? Do you simply say 'no' and believe that all employers are looking for Canadian Experience. Or do you tell employers how your experience can benefit that company. Researching companies and looking at their websites will give you an idea about how your experience can benefit the company.

I know that it's hard to keep hope when you have been rejected so many times. However hope and staying positive is the key to being successful. If you assume you will be rejected when you meet with an employer, you probably will be rejected.

I met one individual last week that was so negative about everything. She had lost hope – for her everything was impossible. When you have so much negativity it is hard to see the possibilities out there – and they are out there, trust me!

A survival job is one you can take to pay the bills, which is not in your field of interest. Take a survival job, but don't get too comfortable in that position. An interesting fact is if you stay in your survival job for over 2 years you will never leave. When I am doing jobs that are not challenging me or of interest, this affects my entire attitude and self-esteem. You are professionals and for some of you have many years experience in your field from another country. Don't loose that experience. Don't stop job searching and trying to find a job that will make you happy. Coming to a new country might be a difficult ride and you may have to do jobs that you don't want to. However when you finally do get a job in your field, everything that you experienced will be worthwhile and you will be a stronger person.

A long time ago, one of my clients shocked me. He knew that the terminology in his profession was different in Canada then in his native country. Every time I saw him he reported that he had done tons of research and was learning everything about his profession in Canada.

Some occupations in Canada require you to have a license in order to practice your profession. For example engineering is a regulated profession and you need a license. However you can still work in an engineering related position, as long as your work under a licensed engineer. The first step is to find out if your field is regulated. If so what steps do you need to take to work in your profession. There is a great website that will give you all this information: – http://www.equalopportunity.on.ca/eng_g/apt/index.asp

It is also important to have your education assessed in Canada to see if it matches the Canadian standards. Employers are sometimes not sure of the quality of education people received. So if you write on your resume that your education equals a Masters degree in Canada, employers will be more willing to call you for an interview. To get your education assessed goto: www.wes.org

Once again I will say that it is a struggle to settle in a new country and find work in your field. There are a lot of non-profit agencies that provide employment services for free. Many of these agencies will give you the tools to be successful in your job search. Take advantage of these resources.

Good luck and remember nothing is impossible, unless you think it is.

TOP 10 WAYS TO GET CANADIAN EXPERIENCE

Are you Internationally Educated? If so you should congratulate yourself, you are brave and courageous. It' takes a very special person who can leave their country and start over in Canada. The following are the top ten ways to find work in Canada:

1. A good way to learn about your occupation in Canada is to have information interviews with people who are working in your field, associations and licensing bodies. An information interview is when you meet with someone and ask them questions about what they like about their job, dislike and the future potential to name a few. This will help you become better informed about the industry. There are other ways to find out about your field such as: websites and printed reports. However talking to an expert or someone already employed will give you a greater insight.

2. Certain terminology in your occupation may be different in Canada. You may want to go to the library and the Internet to learn the language your industry uses.

3. Start to reform at your resume to a Canadian style. Information that may have been relevant in your own country may not be relevant in Canada. In some other countries it's normal to write your marital status, age and religion. In Canada we have the Ontario Human Rights Code, which protects us against discrimination. Also have someone look over your resume before you send it out. You can go to a non-profit employment service and have your resume critiqued for free.

4. 80% of the jobs are unadvertised and in the 'Hidden Job Market'. Tapping into the 'Hidden Job Market' involves a lot of networking and making cold calls. These two methods may seem a little intimidating but they are worth trying.

20% of the job market consists of jobs that are advertised on the Internet, Newspapers and Trade Magazine. I recommend using these methods a little bit during your job search. However focus on the 'Hidden Job Market', there's less competition.

5. In your own country you probably had a big network of contacts, however in Canada your network may be small. I have a challenge for you it's time to re-build your network in Canada. Socialize with people, attend job search workshops offered by your community, volunteer, attend job fairs and join associations. Talk to everyone! Your family doctor may be able to help connect you to people, your children's teacher or a priest. Remember that people like to help other people.

6. Unfortunately you may not be able to have the same job in Canada right away. Try to find a job that's related to your field of expertise. If you are an engineer find a job as a technician or technologist. Research the positions that are related to your occupation and apply to them. Getting your foot in the door of a company is a great start, once in you will probably be able to apply to internal openings.

7. Through volunteering, co-op, on-the-job programs and job trials you will be able to prove your skills and abilities to a Canadian employer, learn about the Canadian workplace culture, gain 'Canadian Experience' and build your network. I would use my availability to volunteer as a marketing strategy. For example if an employer doesn't have current openings say "I understand that you do not have current openings, I would love to volunteer for you company."

8. When asked 'Do you have Canadian Experience?' don't just say no and feel that you have been rejected and that all employers are looking for this so called 'Canadian Experience'. Tell the employer how your skills are similar to the skills that they are looking for. Also tell them how

your international experience will help to benefit the company.

9. In an interview prepare yourself by researching the company, position and yourself. Sell your skills to the employer by telling them stories of your accomplishments and achievements. You are a small company selling your most valuable product yourself.

10. Stay positive, be persistent, proactive, follow-up with all contacts and maintain your motivation level. You will do it and you can do it. Good Luck.

MANAGE YOUR IMPRESSION

How Stereotypical Associations Form Your Future in Canada

How to manage your impression in Canada? I'm going to provide you an alternate strategy that really works most of the time to minimize the negative impact of your foreign credentials, international experience or fit for an employment in Canadian labour market.. This information can help you to smoothly integrate into Canadian society and to secure a job in your field within a shorter period of time if you cannot afford to upgrade your education with a Canadian college or university. In fact this alternate strategy is just the universal principles of managing your impressions.

Canadians are highly productive nation. With only 32 million of population and being the world's largest country in size, in 2003–04, Canada's federal government has collected about $186 billion in taxes (http://www.fin.gc.ca/taxdollar). But according to conference board Canada, they can add another $4 billion a year in revenue if Canadian employers can utilize the skilled immigrants to their full potential.

If you analyze the international statistics about Canadian presence at global level you will observe that most of the Canadian employers and many professional bodies may not be as visionaries as their Americans and Europeans counterparts in terms of capitalizing on international manpower out of Canadian geography. To me the one significant factor for missing the opportunity is their negligible presence on international level as compare to Americans, British, Europeans and Scandinavians. In other words, they rarely compete for international contracts or business opportunities aggressively other than offered by United States, subsequently Canadians had fewer chances of working with Chinese, Indians, Pakistanis, Filipinos and other professionals out of Canadian geography who are rapidly becoming the main source of supply for skilled professionals for Canadian labour market. Thus human resource managers are unable to reach on a true or fair judgment about their competence or talents with international credentials and experience.

327

As most of interviewers make their decisions based on outwardly obvious within half an hour interview. So the Canadian HR managers or generalist who shortlist resumes for interviews, do not reflect their faith or comfort on international education and experience. The resume of an internationally educated and experienced professional could be quickly pitched off compare to a locally less educated or less experienced candidate. Thousands of internationally educated and experienced professionals like doctors, engineers, lawyers, school teachers technologists and many more who are driving cabs and delivering pizza's are the proof of that vision. To Canadian employers and businesses the whole world is just the U.S.A as it absorbs 85% of Canadian exports (see statcan table imports & exports in part-1 page 32). That is why there are so many derogatory stereotypical associations that are harbored by many Canadian employers and professional bodies that affects the lives of internationally trained professionals and having negative impact on Canadian society and economy at large. But inspite of all disadvantages you can still be successful in Canadaian Labour market by capitalizing on positive stereotype associations. So what is a "stereotype" and how can you capitalize on positive stereotype associations and tackle the negative ones?

Lets understand what is a "stereotype". A "stereotype" is defined in Merriam Webster's Dictionary as a : "standardized mental picture that is held in common by members of a group or nation and that represents an oversimplified opinion, prejudice attitude, or uncritical judgment," The Encyclopedia Britannica describes " prejudiced" as , an "attitude", usually emotional, acquired without prior or adequate evidence or experiences." When we think of stereotypes and prejudices, we usually think of race, national origin or gender. Many people will harbor stereotypes and prejudices toward you if you wear black or pink, speak quickly or slowly, are rich or poor, tall or short, thin or fat, dowdy or fashionable, are good or poor listener, articulate or inarticulate, courteous or rude, clean or dirty, organized or disorganized – the list is endless.

Every, person you meet size you up within the first few seconds. They form impression about you who you are, what you think and how you are likely to act. And once those impressions are set in their minds, they are difficult to change.

The impression others form of you are seldom based on rational thought or independent investigation. They are the product of hundreds of associations we all make between outwardly obvious characteristics and the invisible inner qualities we believe they reflect. These stereotypes and prejudices, some positive and some negative, are an intellectual and emotional shorthand. They arises from our past experiences, social biases, promoted or perpetuated in the media and the literature we read, and from the instinctive and emotional hardwiring within our brains.

If it is a respected brand name product on a supermarket shelf, we take for granted that it is higher in both quality and price then the generic brand. If the package is attractive and inviting, we conclude the product inside must share those qualities. People make the assumptions because from past experience they believe such assumptions are warranted, and they don't have the time, energy or inclination to test their validity each time they reach for an item on the shelf.

In this article, I examined that how stereotypes and prejudices are formed and how they influence impression formation. A clear understanding of this process is critical if you hope to present yourself in the best possible light by capitalizing on positive stereotypes and nullifying unflattering ones during your job search and settlement process in Canada.

People seldom have the time or inclination to make fully informed decisions about other people. So they rely on sources that do not require case-by-case analysis and often no rational thought whatsoever. Those sources are :

Myth
Personal experience
Emotion-based stereotypes

Myth: In the Middle Ages, many Christians were told that Jews had horns and tails like the Devil. As absurd as this is, some of those who never actually met a Jew believed it to be true. Today we like to think we are more enlightened, but we continue to accept a wide assortment of myths about members of certain groups, nationalities or race. Some of these stereotypes are based on fact, but researchers find little support for many others.

Personal Experience: The most entrenched stereotypes and prejudices are those that are based on the actual experiences of the person who harbor them.

Almost everyone recognizes that all individuals who fall within a particular group do not embody the characteristics they attach generally to that group. Even the most abused young African – American males knows that all white cops aren't bad, and whites who have had consistently favorable exposure to the police recognize that there are some bad cops. But we all play the odds. If we had have consistent experiences with those who fit a particular stereotype, we conclude that others in that group are likely to think and act in the same way.

Jesse Jackson, for example, once said: " There is nothing more painful for me than to walk down the street and hear footsteps and start to think about robbery, and then see it's somebody white and feel relieved." African American Scholar Johnnetta Cole acknowledged that among black women, " one of the most painful admission I hear is :"I am afraid of my own people" .

Studies also have demonstrated that those who are themselves victims of stereotyping and prejudice are no more charitable toward members of other groups than the rest of us. In a report from the National Conference of Christians and Jews, minority groups expressed stronger prejudices then those harbored by whites toward other minority groups, as reflected in this sampling from the report cited by Dinesh D'Souza in The End of Racism: 49% of the African American and 68% percent of the Asians surveyed thought Hispanics " tend to have bigger families than they can support; 46%

of the Hispanics and 42% of the African American viewed Asian American as "unscrupulous, crafty and devious in business"; and 53% of the Asians and 51% of the Hispanics thought African Americans " are most likely to commit crimes and violence."

Keep this in mind as you evaluate the probable stereotypes and prejudices that others might harbor toward you. Don't assume that other professional women won't harbor gender-based biases against you because you too are a professional women, or that the beautiful women who obsesses about her appearance won't think you are shallow if you do likewise. Some won't but many will. Until you have gathered enough information about a person to conclude reliably that he or she has not adopted generally prevalent stereotypes, assume that he or she has.

Emotion-Based Stereotypes: Many of the schemas we form of others are based neither on myth nor conscious recall of past experience. Often the impression we form is attributed to emotion or intuition.

Intuition arises when years of experience stored behind the curtain of our subconscious percolates from those deep recesses when our memory is triggered by similar experiences. All of us stored an extraordinary amount of data in our brains about how other's behaviors relate to their beliefs and values. We know that those who smile sincerely are most often friendly; those who are great listeners are usually compassionate; and those who won't look us in the eye are frequently lying. When we see those behaviors, we seldom consciously think to ourselves: She is smiling so she must be friendly" or "She is listening so she must be compassionate," or "She is looking away so she must be lying". We just "get a feeling, which is a message from our subconscious as it taps into our stored memory of prior experiences.

Intuition usually can be explained rationally. But we make many associations that cannot. For example, dozens of studies have equated the color of clothing with people's assumptions as to someone's professionalism or honesty. Navy blue consistently scores higher than bright flashy colors, and solids receive higher ratings than plaids or dramatic patterns. In part, this can be explained rationally. Through years of experience we have found that those who are more professional and honest tend to dress more conservatively, and those who dress in flashy cloths tend to be less professional and less honest. But the same rational process can't explain why we find pastel colors more soothing, black depressing, or bright colors more invigorating and red is the color of choice to show sexuality, anger and other passions. Yet those reactions are so consistent that colors has often come to symbolize the emotions they represents. But remember, stereotypes and prejudices lie at the foundation of impression formation, whether based on myth, experience or emotional responses. They don't need to make sense to have an effect on how you are perceived.

With the above mentioned information, I hope you would have developed an idea or understanding of stereotype but "what's in it for me"? Since the last few years the influx of immigrants to Canada is from China, India, Philippines and Pakistan (top four) in independent or economic class and they are skilled workers. Considerable research indicates that even highly trained and educated skilled immigrants have a problem accessing occupations for which they have been trained in their country of origin. There are many studies that indicate a gap between wages of immigrants and native-born Canadians. Overall foreign-trained immigrants earn less than native-born residents with the same level of education they do. Recent studies show that North American and European immigrants fare better than immigrants from such countries as Asia and Central America do. Being a skilled worker professional one of the major derogatory stereotypical association that I observed and harbored by most of Canadian employers towards Asian candidates is based on their English language accent. Lets find out how you are being sized up by the Canadian employer or HR generalist during an interview and why accent is so important in impression formation. You must improve your accent and capitalize on this stereotypical association.

ACCENTS

The single most important factor during your job search or settlement in Canada that will have significant affect on your life will be your English language accent. This factor has the potential to make you employed or unemployed and subsequently rich or poor within short time-frame.

Canada's diverse, multicultural and multilingual population is affected constantly by the stereotypical associations made regarding accents and regional dialects. The stereotypes associated with particular accents are usually offshoots of the stereotypes that are directed toward race and ethnicity, although other factors also influence the extent to which accents affect impression formation.

In a study conducted by Dr. Lillian Glass and published in her book *"Talk to Win'* forty-one participants between the ages of twelve and seventy-two were asked if they like each of thirty different accents *"a lot", "a little", or "not at all"*. Dr. Glass's findings reflect that over a third of the accents listed were disliked by a majority of the respondents.

The accents that were favored were generally those incorporating sounds that are typical of English and other "romance languages." Those accents that were most disliked incorporate sounds that are not prevalent in English phonics, such as the comparatively choppy sound of Asian languages, throaty guttural sounds common to Middle Eastern languages, or the harsh sound of Germanic and Slavic languages.

This is not surprising if we consider that our emotional brains don't feel as comfortable when they process foreign data as they do when they receive familiar stimuli. *Studies showed that, with a few exceptions, the more different an accent sounds from our own, the more likely we are to equate it with lower socioeconomic class, less competence and lower intelligence. Not surprisingly, people with such accents on average receive lower pay and attain less success in the work environment. Those with non-standard accents often judge others with different nonstandard accents just as harshly as any one else.*

Those with accents that are the standard in the community, on the other hand, are perceived as more competent, confident, intelligent, friendly, ambitious and successful. They also are assumed to have a higher socioeconomic status, and what they say is thought to convey more substance. Studies also show that teachers with "standard" accents are better understood by their students, who remember what they say longer. They are also considered more dynamic.

Studies have identified three elements that most frequently trigger negative accent-related stereotypes.

The first characteristic of a poorly received accent is that it is difficult to understand. Just as others will make a broad range of negative associations if you mumble, talk too fast or otherwise make them too hard to understand what you say, so too, if your accent makes it difficult for others to understand you, they will become impatient, irritated and form derogatory associations with regard to your intelligence, capability, friendliness and competence. If you have a distinct accent that is still easy to understand, much less bias will arise.

The second factor that influences negative accent related associations is directly tied to the ever-important concept of expectations. If we meet a person from a foreign country, who has been in Canada for a relatively short period of time, and as a result, struggle with the English language and speak with a heavy and sometimes incomprehensible accent, we seldom judge the person harshly because of his accent. We expect someone who is learning a language to have difficulties. But when we encounter someone we know to have been in Canada for an extended period of time, or who has a job that requires him to be able to communicate in English without his accent presenting a barrier. The typical reaction is to assume that if he has had a reason and opportunity to learn to speak without a heavy accent, but has not, it is either because of he is not intelligent enough, industrious enough or friendly and thoughtful enough to have done so. These are strong negative associations, and perhaps even unfair, but they exist as a function of our expectations.

The final cause of negative associations with accents is that they accentuate whatever racial or ethnic biases and prejudices people otherwise harbor. Many people have significant racial and ethnic prejudice and bias, and tend to make strong stereotypical association with any members of the group who are the victims of those biases. We w'll know that there are no longer such biases when at the end of a racial joke everyone looks puzzled and say, " I don't get it, what's the guy's race got to do with the joke anyway?" Until then, racial and ethnic biases will be a reality that can be addressed with impression management.

Studies also shows that the biases often are the product of associations made at an emotional level. Heavy accents accentuate this emotional brain response. When someone has no identifiable accent, his or her race or ethnicity is much less frequently even considered. Test researchers experience against your own.

Think of individuals you know who come from particular ethnic or racial background. Focus on one or two of them who have perfect English accents, whether they are Asian, Middle Eastern, African Americans or of some other race or nationality. If you're like most people, you seldom think about their background. Then consider a few individuals you know who have heavy accents, and you probable will find that you think much more frequently about their race or ethnicity. Those who have other's minds, and with it the lingering biases other may harbor.

If you have an accent that is (1) so heavy that its difficult to understand, (2) heavier then one would expect who has had the opportunity and practical need to acquire standard English accent, or (3) reflects a racial, ethnic, regional or other background towards which strong stereotypes apply, your accent will effect the impression you make on many people.

I am not suggesting that people abandoned their cultural heritage, or that standard English accent is in any way superior to others. But we do want to impress upon those who have accents that a heavy accent will affect impression formation, particularly if the accent is associated with the racial or ethnic group toward which significant prejudice exists. If you eliminate your accent, you will decrease many of the negative stereotypes to which you are subjected. If you choose to retain your accent, you should recognize that your impression management plan should incorporate traits to offset the negative stereotypes that your accent may trigger.

With regards to stereotypical associations and other impression management techniques, I just touched the topic and showed you the tip of an iceberg that can change your life in Canada. So you must buy and read a good book on impression management several times before you migrate to Canada.

DO YOU KNOW YOUR AUDIENCE ?

Positive impression formation always requires a transmitter and a receiver that are in sync. What may impress one audience may be unimpressive to another. Think of yourself as radio station that must clearly identify its target market before it decides on a content and format of its broadcast. It is wants to appeal to a talk show audience, it emphasize lively chat. If it hopes to reach listeners at work, it adopts an easy listening music format. If its audience consists of eighteen-to-twenty-five-year – old, it plays the contemporary top forty.

Unlike radio stations, you don't have just a single audience. You have many. One moment you may want to appeal to a conservative businessman, the next to your co-workers, and a few hours later to your friends or family. To be successful in each relationship, you cant always present the same content and format. You should project the different qualities in every encounter, but how best to achieve that objective will vary from situation to situation.

The first step to knowing your audience is to identify their expectations and probable stereotypical associations. If you want to meet a client for a business lunch, you could anticipate that he would expect that you would dress and act professionally. He might also expect that you would take him to an upscale restaurant, pick up the bill and be solicitous if you were trying to curry his favour. If you dressed or acted too casually, you would disappoint those expectations, which would tend to create a negative impression.

On the other hand, if you were to make a lunch date with a high school classmate, her expectations would be very different. She would not expect you to take her to an expensive restaurant, or pick-up the cheque. She would expect a more casual, free-flowing conversation, and less formal dress and behavior. If you shown up in your new Brioni suite and kept it buttoned at the waist throughout lunch. Designer tie cinched tight, and posture as erect and formal as your speech, you disappoint her expectations. She would probably think you were full of yourself, nervous, unfriendly and boring.

There are many ways to gather information about the person or people you want to impress. Whenever possible, this information-gathering process should begin in advance of your first meeting and continue as the relationship grows.

Before a job interview, for example, you should learn as much as possible about the company. Company broachers, newspapers and the Internet provide invaluable information. If you know someone at the company, take her out to lunch and pick her brain. You may discovered that a distinctive corporate environment exist in which emphasis is placed more on one quality in its employees then on others. Stop by and visit the company before the interview. See how it's furnished. Is it stark and efficient, or luxurious and opulent? Watch the employees. All they all business, or is there a friendly patter that reflects a casual environment is usually a casual environment? Notice the working conditions. Are people cramped in small cubicles, or do they have large, private offices? Is there a staff room with plenty of space for employees to relax during breaks and lunch, or does everyone grab a quick bite at his or her desk? The corporate environment is usually a reliable reflection of the values of its decision makers. Your awareness of those values will help determine how can appeal to them if you choose to..

A friend of yours, an avid fly fisherman, put it best: "If you want to catch a trout, the first thing you have to do is to find out what they are biting. Sit on the riverbank and watch. If they are eating mosquitoes, use a fly that looks like a mosquito. If they are eating wasps, use a fly that looks like a wasp. The important think is to use whatever bait is attractive to them. You have to think like a fish, not a fisherman".

ARE YOU A PROFESSIONAL ?

You don't need to hold a graduate degree to be "professional"; nor are you "professional" just because you do. The bank teller who greets each customer with a friendly "hello, may I help you?" is professional. The telephone operator who tells the caller: " Hold your horses, I'll get you when I can" isn't. The cab driver, who keeps his car clean and neat, and seat belts readily accessible, is professional. The housekeeper who leaves the windows streaky isn't. The policeman who asks politely, "May I see your license, please?" is professional. The doctor's receptionist who asks in front of a crowed waiting room, "Are you here to see the doctor about that discharge again?" absolutely, positively isn't.

In a most recent survey respondents were asked to identify what traits most influenced their impression of someone's professionalism.

The way someone "dressed" was identified by 29.1% of the respondents as a first trait they considered. Another 6.4% listed "appearance" or "grooming". More then 35% of the respondents, therefore, identified appearance-related traits first. By comparison, body language and vocal traits tied for second place, each accounting for 14.6 % of the total responses. Only 8.2% of the respondents identified someone's job or educational level as a first characteristic they considered as they evaluated whether someone is "professional".

In the narrative portion of the participants' responses to the questionnaires, it was found that there are three themes arose most frequently as people discussed what impresses them as professional.

Appearance: The first criterion is whether you are neat, clean and appropriately dressed for your position. Whether you are a school teacher, postal worker, appliance repairman or jet pilot; whether you wear a required uniform or have complete discretion in your choice of wardrobe, don't take your decision about grooming or what to wear lightly.

Graciousness: If you are loud, pushy or discourteous, or if you embarrass, interrupt, ignore or are otherwise insensitive to other's need, you will not be viewed as professional, regardless of your academic qualifications or job status. On the other hand, if you display dignity, good manners, courtesy, respect for privacy and graciousness, you will be well on your way.

Dedication: Julius Erving described what it means to be professional as " Doing all the things you love to do on the day when you don't feel like doing them". If you have a nine-to-five attitude and just go through the motions, you won't be seen as professional. If you skip your breaks to get your job done well, or come in before nine and stay after five if that is what is required, you will. Professionalism means letting your boss, coworkers, and customers know that they can count on you to get the job done right, no matter what. It requires an outward display of commitment, responsibility and dedication.

ARE YOU A LEADER ?

What makes us turn to certain men and women for direction and inspiration? Leadership. By "leadership" we do not mean "authority". We have all known those in positions of authority may be high achievers, but they aren't leaders in the true sense of the word, they are just bosses. When we speak of leaders, we also are not referring to politicians or CEO's alone, but also to the millions of parents, teachers, little league coaches, small business owners and partners of all types.

Leadership is an invisible strand as mysterious as it is powerful, it pulls and it bonds. It is a catalyst that creates unity out of disorder. Yet, it defies definition. No combination of talents can guarantee it. No process or training can create it where the spark does not exist.

The qualities of leadership are universal: they are found in the poor and the rich, the humble and the proud, the common man, and the brilliant thinker; they are qualities that suggest paradox rather than pattern. But wherever they are found leadership makes things happen.

Researchers discovered and repeatedly identified following characteristic in true leaders.

Leaders are doers: Leaders take charge. They are proactive. They are outspoken. They volunteer. They don't wait for things to happen. They make them happen. They are willing to take risks and responsibility. They contemplate, but they don't obsess.

Leaders are confidents: Leadership requires confidence, not swaggering cockiness, but a calm, natural, effortless control.

Leaders lead, they don't push: True leaders don't force anyone to follow them; they make others want to follow them. They don't abuse their authority for ego gratification, but exercise it purposely, to benefit not just themselves but also those they lead.

Leaders watch their flock: Leaders makes others feel important and cared for. They are sensitive to their needs and desires. They do not expect their followers to respond to their own needs, but are sensitive to the needs of those who follow them.

Leaders are open-minded: Opinionated, head strong, know-it-alls are seldom successful leaders. Effective leaders recognize that the knowledge required for leadership is enhanced by a willing ear and an open mind .

Leaders support and empower others: leaders bring out the best in there followers with there support and encouragement.

Leaders appreciate others: Leaders give praise and credit freely. They are not stingy with accolades, and do not steal other's thunder.

Leaders trust others to succeed: Leaders knows when and whom to trust, and with what to trust them. They encourage other's success, and give them the incentive to strive for it.

Leaders show respect for others: Leaders don't act superior to those they lead. They recognize it is human nature to like those who like us, trust those who trust us, and respect those who respect us.

Leaders show true personal character: True leadership is not acquired by authority, but by influence. Such influence is obtained by trust in the fundamental character of a leader.

Leaders are enthusiastic: Enthusiasm energizes those who follow a leader, and injects them with the leader's commitment and dedication to his or her cause.

Leaders Inspire: Leaders inspire others with their vision, creativity, innovation and imagination. They engender a belief in a positive future, which their followers hope to achieve for their benefit, not just the leader's.

Leaders are capable: Successful leadership requires performance. Capability, in the form of intelligence, competence, confidence and professionalism, is required to instill trust that a leader will be able to create order from chaos and to guide his or her followers through both calm and tumultuous times.

Leaders lead by example: Leaders asks no more from their followers then they are willing to give themselves.

Leaders build partnership: Leaders do not sit atop the wagon pulled by others, but join them side by side to pull together toward a common goal.

HOW TO DOUBLE YOUR PRODUCTIVITY

A Secret of Success in Life

*There are many rules for success,
but none of them will work unless you do.*

(Reed Markham, American educator)

HOW TO DOUBLE YOUR PRODUCTIVITY

A Secret of Success in Life

All successful people are described as being very well organized and good time managers. Fortunately, time management skills are learnable with practice and repetition.

You can become one of the most productive people in your field by learning & following time management techniques.

What you are about to learn can change your life. These ideas, methods and techniques can increase your efficiency and effectiveness, boost your productivity, double your income, lower your stress levels and make you one of the most productive people in your field or business.

The fact is all successful people are very productive. They work longer hours and they work better hours, they get a lot more done than the average person. They get paid more and promoted faster. They are highly respected and esteemed by everyone around them.

They become leaders and role models for others, inevitably they rise to the top of their fields and to the top of their income ranges.

Every single one of these tested and proven strategies for managing your time and doubling your productivity is learnable through practice and repetition. Each of these methods if practiced regularly, will eventually become a habit of both thinking and working....lets begin

1.   Make A Decision

Every positive change in your life begins with a clear decision: either you are going to do something or going to stop doing something. Significant change starts when you decide to either get in or get out, either keep fishing or cut bait. Decisiveness is one of the most important qualities of successful and happy men and women and decisiveness is developed through practice and repetition as it becomes as natural to you as breathing in and breathing out.

The sad fact is people are poor because they have not yet decided to be rich. People are over-weight and unfit because they have not yet decided to be balanced and fit. People are inefficient time organizers because they haven't yet decided to be highly productive in everything they do.

Decide today that you are going to become an expert in time management and personal productivity. No matter how long it takes or how much you have to invest to achieve it. Resolve today that you are going to practice these principals over and over again until they become second nature. Discipline yourself to know that you need to be the very best in your field. Perhaps, the best definition of self-discipline is *"the ability to make yourself do, what you should do, when you should do it whether you feel like it or not"*. Its easy to do something when you feel like it. But when you do not feel like it and you force yourself to do it anyway, to move your life and career on the fast track

What decisions do you need to make in order to start moving toward the top of your field? Whatever they are, to get in or get out, make a decision today and then get started. This single act alone can change the whole direction of your life.

2.   Develop Clear Goals And Objectives

Perhaps, the most important word in success for you for the rest of your life is "Clarity". About 80% of your success comes about as a result of your being absolutely clear about what it is that you are trying to accomplish. Unfortunately, probably 80% or more failure or frustration comes to the people who are unclear or fuzzy about what is they want in life and how to go about achieving it. The great oil billionaire HL Hunt (reportedly the world's first billionaire) once said that there are only two real requirements for success:

First he said "decide exactly what it is you want" , most people never do this. Second he said "determine the price that you are going to have to pay to get it and then resolve to pay that price" You can have just about anything that you really want as long you are willing to pay the price and nature always demand that you pay the price in full and pay it in advance. There is a powerful seven steps formula that you can use to set and achive your goals for the rest of your life. Every single successful person uses this formula or some variation of this formula to achieve success. As a result they accomplish vastly more then the average person and so can you:

a.   Decide exactly what it is you want in each part of your life. Become a meaningful specific rather than a wondering generality . Decide how much you want to earn. Decide how much you want to weigh. Decide the kind family, relationship and lifestyle you want to enjoy. The vary act of deciding clearly, dramatically increases the likelyhood that you will achieve it.

b.   Write it down clearly and in detail. Always think on paper. A goal that is not in writing is not really a goal at all, its merely a wish and it has no energy behind it. But when you take your goals out of your imagination and crystallize them on paper, you actually program them into your subconscious mind where they take on a power of their own.

c.   Set a deadline for your goal. A deadline acts as a forcing system in your subconscious mind. A deadline motivates you to do the things necessary to make your goal come true. If it is a big goal then set sub-deadlines as well. Don't leave this to chance.

d.   Make a list of everything you can think of that you are going have to do to achieve your goal. When you think of new tasks and activities, write them of on the list until your list is complete.

e.   The 5th step in this goal setting formula for you is to organize your list into a plan. Decide what you will have to do first and what you will have to do second. Decide what is more important and what is less important and then write out your plan on paper. The same way you will develop a blueprint to build your dream house.

f.   The 6th step is for you to take action on your plan. Do something, do anything but get busy, get going and don't delay.

g.   Step seven and perhaps the most important of all is for you to do something every single day that moves you in the direction of your most important goal at the time. Develop the discipline of doing something 365 days of each year that is moving you forward. You will be absolutely astonished at how much you have accomplished when you utilize this formula every single day of your life.

Exercise:

Now here is an exercise that you can do that can change your life.

Take a blank sheet of paper and write out 10 goals that you want to accomplish in next 12 months and write each of these goals in present tense as though a year has passed and you have already achieved the goal. Start each of these goals with the word "I". For examples you can write down a goal such as

"I earned X no. of dollars this year" or
"I lost X no. of pounds in my weight" or
"I drive such and such a car"

Your subconscious mind only accepts instructions when they are phrased in present tense and when they are perceived with the word "I". Once you have your list of 10 goals, select the most important goal on that list and ask yourself "what one goal if I achieved right now will have the greatest positive impact on my life?" What ever it is put a circle around that goal and write it down at the top of a new sheet of paper, set a deadline, make a list, organize the list into a plan, take action on your plan and do something everyday until your goal is achieved.

This exercise has made more people successful than perhaps any other single exercise. From now on you should resolve to become intensely goal oriented.

Think and talk about your goals all the time. Write them and re-write them, review them everyday. Continually look for better ways to achieve them. This combination of goal setting formula and goal setting exercise will have more of a positive impact on your life than almost anything you can ever do. Give it a try.

3.   Plan Everyday in Advance

Daily planning is absolutely essential for you to double your productivity. You should practice the *6P* formula for high achievement. This formula says *"Prior Proper Planning Prevents Poor Performance"*.

Proper planning is the mark of professionals. All successful men and women take a good deal of their time to plan their activities in advance. Remember the 10/90 rule which says that the first 10% of time that you spend planning your activity before you begin will save you as much as 90% of the time necessary to perform those activities once you start work.

Always think on paper; something wonderful happens between your head and your hand when you write out your plans in detail on paper before you begin. Writing actually sharpens your thinking. It stimulates your activity and enables you to focus far better than if you are just trying to work out of your mind.

Begin by making a master list of everything you can think of that you have to do for the long term future. This master list then becomes the central control list for your life. Whenever you think of something new that you have to do, write it down on your master list. At the beginning of each month make a monthly list covering everything that you can think of that you will have to do in the coming weeks, then break your monthly list down into a weekly list and specify exactly when you are going to start and complete the tasks that you have decided upon for the month.

Finally and perhaps the most important, make a daily list of your activities. Do this the night before so that your subconscious mind can work on your list while you sleep. Always work from a list, when something new comes up during the day, write it down on your list before you do it. As you work, you tick-off each item as you finish it. This tracking gives you an ongoing sense of accomplishment and personal progress. Crossing of items one by one motivates you and actually gives you more energy. A list serves as a scorecard and makes you feel like a winner. It tells you where you are making progress and what you have to do the next day. According to the time management experts, working from a list will increase your productivity by 25% the day you begin doing it. All highly effective people think on paper and work from written lists.

4.   Set Your Priorities.

Also remember, the key to doubling your productivity is for you to spend more time doing things that are urgent and important and then working on activities which are important but less urgent. You increase your productivity by refusing to do things that are not important at all. Always ask yourself, what are the long term potential consequences of doing this task? What would happen if you did not do it at all? And whatever your answer is, let it guide you in your choice of priorities.

Use the law of forced efficiency; this law says that *"there is never enough time to do everything but there is always enough time to do most important things"*. Always ask yourself following question.

"What is the most valuable use of my time right now?"

Whatever your answer is, be sure that you are doing it most of the time. Discipline yourself to work only on your answers to the above question and this alone will double your productivity.

5.   Apply the 80/20 Rule

The 80/20 rule, the Pareto principle is one of the most important and powerful of all time management principles. This rule comes from the Italian economist and political sociologist Wilfredo Pareto (1848-1923) who divided all activities into the vital few and the trivial many. This law says that 20% of the things that you do, the vital few, will account fully 80% of the value of all the things you do. The reverse of this principle is that 80% of the things you do will account for only 20% of the value of your activities. This 80/20 rule applies to all aspects of business and personal life. In business 80% of your sales will come from 20% of your customers. 80% of your profit will come from 20% of your products. 80% of your sales come from 20% of your sales people. 80% of your income, success and advancement will come from 20% of your activities. If you make a list of ten things that you have to do in a particular day, two of those items will turn out to be worth more than all the others put together.

Your ability to identify and focus on the top 20% of tasks will determine your success and productivity as much as any other factor. Here is an idea for you:

Practice creative procrastination with the 80/20 rule. Since you can't do everything, you have to procrastinate on something, therefore discipline yourself to procrastinate on the 80% of the activities that contribute very little value to your life and your results. The average person procrastinates on high value tasks but this is not for you. You must hold your own feet to the fire and procrastinate deliberately and continuously on those low value items that have very few consequences if they are done or not. Before you start work, always check to make sure that what you are doing is in the top 20% of all the things that you could be doing. Procrastinate on the rest.

6.   Work at Your Energy Peaks

One of the most important requirements for high productivity is high levels of physical, mental an emotional energy. All highly productive, highly successful, highly paid people have high levels of energy sustained over long periods of time. To generate and maintain high levels of energy you need to practice proper eating, proper exercise and proper rest. You need to eat light nutritious high protein foods and avoid fats, sugar, white flour products, pasta, potatoes, candy, soft drinks and desserts of all kinds. You need to get regular exercise, 3-5 times per week, 30-60 minutes each time. I have always been amazed to find that marathon and tri-athlon runners, people who sometime workout several hours a day are also among highly paid and most productive people in their fields.

There seems to be a direct relationship between physical fitness and energy on one hand and high levels of productivity on the other. Be sure to get lots of rest especially if you are working hard. You need at least 7 or 8 hours of sleep per night and sometimes even more. You need to take at least one full day off each week and two full weeks off each year if you want to perform at your best. You should identify the times of day that you are the brightest and most alert. For some people this is the morning, for others it's the afternoon or evening. Whatever it is for you, you should schedule your most creative and demanding task during that time of the day when you are at your very best.

7. Practice Single-Handling With Key Tasks

Single handling is one of the most powerful of all time management techniques. This technique alone will boost your productivity by 50% or more the very first day you begin practicing it. When you make single handling a habit, you can actually double your productivity even if you do nothing else recommended above.

The way it works is really simple: you make a list of everything you have to do. You select the most important item on your list, that is the highest value use of your time then you start to work on it and you discipline yourself to stay at it until it is 100% complete.

Andrew Carnegie who became one of the richest men in the world after starting as a day laborer in a Pittsburgh steel plant attributed much of his wealth and success to this simple formula. He said it has transformed his life and the lives of everyone who ever worked for him. Remember the two keys to success are focus and concentration. Your ability to concentrate single mindedly without diversion or distraction on one thing, the most important thing and staying with it until it is complete will contribute more to your success than any other habit you will ever develop.

The fact is that if you start a task and then put it aside, coming back to it later and starting it again can eventually increase the amount of time required by 500% or 5 times. On the other hand if you pick-up a task and you discipline yourself to stay at it until it is done. You can decrease the amount of time it takes to do that task by as much as 80%. This is one of the greatest secret of time management and high productivity.

8.   Organize Your Work Space.

Highly productive people work from a clean desk and a clean workplace. Inefficient, unproductive, confused people work from a messy desk. Their workplace often looks as though a grenade has gone-off, scattering papers and files everywhere. This is not for you.

Make it a habit of cleaning off your work space and do work from a cleaned desk all the time even if you have to take everything off the desk and put it behind on the floor or on a credenza. Keep your desk clean. 30% of the working time today is spent looking for something that has been misplaced in some way. When people say that they work better from a messy desk, it turns out not to be true at all. When these same people are forced to clean up their workspace and work on one item at a time, their productivity doubles within 24 hours. It amazes them to learn the truth.

Use what is called the *TRAF formula* on all your papers. The four letters stands for **Toss, Refer, Act and File.** Your waste basket is one of the most helpful time management tools in your office. **"Toss"** away and throw everything that you possible can before you get bogged down reading through it. This is especially true with direct mail advertising, unnecessary subscriptions for magazines, newspapers or any other material that you have no need of. The **R** stands for **"Refer".** This is something that someone else should deal with. Make a note on it and send it off. Take every opportunity to delegate or refer everything that you possibly can so you have more time to do those things that only you can do. The **A** stands for

"Action" Use a red file for this purpose to make it stand out. Your action file contains everything that you have to take action on in the foreseeable future. By putting things on your action file, you deal with them and get them out of the way. And the **F** stands for **"File"**. These are papers and documents that you think you will need to have available to you at a later time. *But remember, before you file things that 80% of all the items that are filed are never referred to again.* When you make a note to file something means you are creating work for someone else. Be sure that it is necessary before you file it.

There are time management specialists today who charge several hundred dollars to help executives clear-up their desks and offices. One of the first things these experts do to help their clients go through the piles of material that the executives have been saving up to read at a later time. And here is the rule *"if you have not read it in the last six months, its junk"* throw it away. When in doubt, throw it out. This also applies to old clothes, old furniture, old toys and anything else that is cluttering-up your life. Many people are pack rats in their attitude towards saving magazines, newsletters, newspapers and other information that comes in the door. The fact is that you will never be able to read all the information you receive on a daily basis. You must discipline yourself to throw it away as quickly as you possibly can. Keep your workspace clean and keep only one thing in front of you at a time. This will dramatically increase your productivity.

9. Use Travel Time Productively

The two major forms of travel time are driving and flying. You should turn both of these forms of transition time into highly productive time. When you drive always listen to educational audio programs. The average person in North America sits in his or her car 500-1000 hours each year. This is the equivalent of the 1-2 full-time university semesters. Experts at the University of Southern California recently concluded that you can get the same educational value as full-time university attendance by simply listening to educational audio programs as you drive from place to place. Turn your car into a university on wheels. View your car as a learning machine for the rest of your career. Many people have become highly educated and moved to the tops of their fields with audio learning. You should do the same. You should resolve from this day forward that your car will never be moving without something educational playing in the car.

When you are flying, you should use this time productively as well. Time management experts have found that every hour of working in an airplane is equal to three hours of work in a busy office. The reason for this is because you can work without any interruptions at all on an airplane if you plan and organize in advance. Plan your trip in advance; prepare your work schedule, write-up an agenda for the things that you are going to accomplish when you are in the air. Once the plane takes off you can lower your table, pull out your work and begin working immediately. Resist the temptation to read the magazine in the pocket in front of you or watch the movie they play on long flights. Do not drink alcohol of any kind; instead drink two glasses of water for every hour that you are in the air. This will keep you alert and refresh and will dramatically cut down on jet lack.

Every minute counts, turn your car into a mobile classroom and turn you airline seat into your flying office. Use them both to get ahead and stay ahead of your work.

10. Work in Real Time

This is an extremely important principle for increasing your productivity. Develop a sense of urgency. Develop a fast tempo, develop a bias for action. Pick-up the pace, do it now. Today there is an incredible need for speed. People who do things quickly are considered to be better, valuable and more competent than people who do things slowly.

Make decisions quickly, 80% of all decisions can be made the moment they come up. Don't delay or procrastinate on them. Slow decision making simply plugs up your pipeline and puts a drag on your activities. Complete all quick jobs as soon as they come up. Anything that will take you less than two minutes is usually something that you should do immediately. Always think about how much time it will take you to ramp up and do the job later if you don't do it now. Take an important phone call immediately and deal with it. Have an important discussion and take a decision to solve the problem right there. Respond to requests from your boss or your customers fast. Move quickly when need or opportunity arises. Develop a reputation for speed and dependability. Your goal should be to develop a reputation of being the person who is called by your boss when something needs to be taken care of quickly. This will open more doors to you than you can imagine. This will attract more and more opportunities to you to do more and more things quickly. Doing things quickly when they come up is the vital part of doubling your productivity.

11.   Reinvent Yourself Annually

Reinvent yourself each year. We are living at the time of greatest change in all of human history. Things are changing so rapidly in all areas and all directions that you must be continually reevaluating and reinventing yourself and your life. At least once a year, you should stand back and look at every aspect of your life to determine whether or not this is something that you want to continue doing. Imagine for a moment that your company has burnt to the ground and that you have to walk across the street and start over again in a new building. What would you start-up immediately? What would you not start-up at all? Who would you bring from the parking lot to continue working in your company? Who would you leave behind in the parking lot if you had the choice?

Imagine that your job and your industry and business disappeared. Imagine that you are starting your career over again and you could go in any direction and do virtually anything. What would it be?

Evaluate where you live and how your family spends leisure time activities and vacations. Reevaluate your finances and your physical condition. If you could begin any part of your career and life over again like a painter standing before a white canvas, how would you design or reinvent your life today. When you stand back and look at your life from this point of view on a regular basis, you will begin to see all kinds of opportunities to change what you are doing; so that they are more inline with what you are really want. This is the real key to increasing your productivity.

12.   Practice Zero Based Thinking

Practice zero based thinking continuously. This is one of the best tools you will ever learn to clarify your thinking and to improve the quality of your life. Ask yourself on a regular basis "is there anything in my life that knowing what I know now, I wouldn't get into again today, if I have to do it over?" Is there anything that you are involved in today, any relationship, any investment that knowing what you now know today, you wouldn't get into, if you had to do it over? This is one of the most important questions you have to ask yourself.

When you think of time savers and time wasters, you usually think of interruptions and telephone calls. However the biggest time waster of all is for you to continue to peruse a course of action, a job, a career or a relationship that is the wrong one for you. Many people waste many years of their life working at something that they don't particularly like or enjoy and then in their thirties (30s) they have to start allover again in a completely new job, in a completely new career. Ask yourself "is there anything that you are doing today that based on your current knowledge and experience you wouldn't startup again, if you had the opportunity?

Because we are living in the time of rapid change, 70% of your decisions will turn out to be wrong in the fullness of time. This means that everyone is involved in at least one thing knowing what they now know, they wouldn't get into. The key indicator of a zero based thinking situation is "stress". Whenever you feel chronic stress, dissatisfaction or unhappiness with any person or situation that seems to go on and on, you should ask yourself, "knowing what I now know, would I get into this situation again today"? And if your answer is "No" then the next question is how can I get out of this situation and how fast?

Ask yourself these questions at least on quarterly basis, "is there any relationship in my life, business, social or personal activities that knowing what I now know, I wouldn't get into again? Is there any part of business, any product or service, expenditure or process that knowing what I now know, I wouldn't startup again today, if I had to do it over?

Remember, whatever the situation is, if it is an unhappy situation, it is probably not going to change on its own and going to verse over the time. The only question then is, "do you have the courage and character to deal honestly with your life as it really is today?" By applying the zero based thinking to every part of your life, you will be absolutely amazed that how much better your decisions become and how much more productive you become at the same time.

13.   Set Clear Posteriorities

You have heard of setting priorities Priorities are tasks that you do more of and sooner. A posteriority on the other hand is something that you do less of and later, if at all. The fact is that you are already overwhelmed with too much to do in too little time.

For you to do something new or different you must discontinue something that you are already doing. For you to do something new and different, you must begin systematically setting posteriorities on activities in your life that are no longer as important as other activities. Practice what Peter Drucker calls creative abandonment with tasks and activities that are no longer as valuable as they were when you first started doing them.

The fact is that you have too much to do already therefore before you start doing something new, you have to stop doing something old. Picking up new task requires putting down an old task, getting in means getting out, starting up means starting off. Look at your life and your work. What sort of things that you should stop doing, so you can free up enough time to do more of the things that you should be doing more of the time? The fact is that you can only get your life under control to the degree to which you discontinue lower value activities. You can only double your productivity only when you free up time to do the things that can have significant pay-off for you in future.

Whenever you feel overloaded for any reason, whenever you feel that you have to too much to do in too little time, stop. Take a deep breath and just say to yourself that "all I can do is all I can do" and then sit-down, make a list of everything you have to do and begin setting posteriorities on your time. Sometimes the word "NO" can be the best time saver of all.

14.   Keep Your Life in Balance

The reason you are working is so you can earn enough to enjoy your family, your health and the important parts of your personal life. You want to have a happy, healthy and harmonious relationship with your spouse and children. You want to be healthy and fit; you want to grow mentally and spiritually. You want to be as successful as possible in your work and career so that you have the resources to do all the things that you really care about that have nothing to do with your work

Unfortunately, most people get the cart before the horse. They become so preoccupied with their work that they loose sight of the reason for wanting to be successful at their work in the first place. This is definitely not for you. Remember that in life, relationships are everything. 85% of your success in life will come from your happy relationship with other people. Only 15% of your happiness will come from your achievements in your work.

You must keep your life in balance. This will dramatically simplify your life and reduce your work hours. This will enable you to spend more time with your family and double your income over the time, all simultaneously. The keys to balance are simple. Set your peace of mind, your happiness and your home life as your highest goals and organize the rest of your goals around them. Create blocks of time to spend with your family. Create time in the evenings, time on the weekends and time away on vacations. Remember the following formula for balance

"It is quantity of time at home that counts and quality of time at work and don't mix them up".

The simplest of all rules for balance is "put people first". Put the most important people in your life ahead of everything and everyone else. When you work, work all the time. Don't waste time with idle chatting and useless activities.

Remember that every minute you waste at work with idle socializing is a minute that you are taking away from your family and your important relationships. When you get your life in balance, you will actually accomplish more, be paid more, produce more and have vastly more time with your family. This is the whole reason for wanting to become more productive in the first place.

I believe the above 14 point formula can change your life...if practiced.

IF OUR WORLD WERE A VILLAGE OF 1000 PEOPLE

IT WOULD INCLUDE

584	Asian & Pacific Islander.
124	Africans
95	Eastern and Western Europeans.
84	Latin Americans.
55	Soviets.
52	North Americans.
6	Australians and New Zealanders.

COMMUNICATION

165	of would speak Mandarin.
86	English.
83	Hindu/Urdu.
64	Spanish.
58	Russian
37	Arabic.

The rest speak over 200 other languages, including Bengali, Portuguese, Indonesian, Japanese, German, and French.

OTHER FACTS ABOUT OUR VILLAGE.

1/3	are children.
60	are over the age of 65.
667	must drink polluted water.
70	own an auto.
335	adults are illiterate.
5	are soldiers.
7	are teachers.
3	are refugees.

IN THE LAST YEAR, THERE WERE.

28	Births.
10	Deaths, 1/3 from malnutrition.

DARE

Dare to try. Dare to love. Dare to make a commitment.
Dare to take a risk.

To laugh is to risk appearing the fool.
To weep is to risk appearing sentimental.
To reach for another is to risk involvement.
To expose your feelings is to risk exposing your true self.
To place your ideas, dreams before a crowd is to risk their loss.
To love is to risk not being loved in return.
To live is to risk dying.
To believe is to risk despair.
To try is to risk failure.
But risks must be taken, because the greatest hazard in life is to
risk nothing.
The people who risk nothing, do nothing, have nothing, are
nothing.
They may avoid suffering and sorrow, but they cannot learn,
feel, change, grow, love, live.
Chained by their attitudes they are slaves; they have forfeited
their freedom.

Only a person who risks is free.

from
The President's Newsletter, November 1982
Phi Delta Kappa
Bloomington, Indiana

KEY IMMIGRANT SERVING
ORGANIZATIONS ACROSS CANADA

Newfoundland

Association for New Canadians
P.O. Box 2031, Station C
St. John's, Nfld. A1C 5R6
Tel: 709-722-9680

New Brunswick

Multicultural Association of Greater Moncton Area
1299A Mountain Road, Suite 2
Moncton, N.B. E1C 2T9
506-858-9659

Saint John YM/YWCA
19-25 Hazen Avenue
Saint John, N.B. E2L 3G6
506-646-2389

Multicultural Association of Fredericton
123 York Street, Suite 201
Fredericton, N.B. E3B 3N6
Tel: 506-457-4038

Nova Scotia

YMCA Newcomer's Centre
3663 Dutch Village Road
Halifax, N.S. B3K 3B7
Tel: 902-457-9622

Metropolitan Immigrant Settlement Association
2131 Gottingen Street, Suite 200
Halifax, N.S. B3K 5Z7
Tel: 902-423-3607

Prince Edward Island

PEI Association for Newcomers to Canada
179 Queen Street
Mailing address: P.O. Box 2846,
Charlottetown, PEI C1A 8C4
Tel: 902-628-6009

Quebec

To contact immigrant serving organizations in the province of Quebec, contact the *ministère des Relations avec les citoyens et de l'Immigration* (MRCI). MRCI is organized by region:

Carrefours d'intégration - Island of Montréal
East Island
8000, boulevard Langelier
6e et 7e étages
Saint-Léonard (Québec) H1P 3K2
(514) 864-9191

South Island
800, boulevard de Maisonneuve Est
(Place Dupuis), rez-de-chaussée)
Montréal (Québec) H2L 4L8
(514) 864-9191

Direction régionale de l'Outaouais,
de l'Abitibi-Témiscamingue et du Nord-du-Québec
4 rue Taschereau, suite 430
Hull, Québec J8Y 2V5
819-772-3021 or
1-888-295-9095

Direction régionale de la Capitale-Nationale et l'Est du Québec
930, chemin Ste-Foy
Québec, Québec G1S 2L4
418-643-1435 or
1-888-643-1435

West Island
181, boulevard Hymus
2e et 3e étages
Point-Claire (Québec) H9R 5P4
(514) 864-9191

Direction régionale de l'Estrie, de la Mauricie et du Centre-du-Québec
740, rue Galt Ouest, bureau 400
Sherbrooke, Québec J1H 1Z3
819-820-3606 or 1-888-879-4288

Direction régionale de Laval, des Laurentides, et de Lanaudière
800, boulevard Chomedey
Tour C, bureau 200
Laval, Québec H7V 3Y4
450-681-2593 or
1-800-375-7426

Bureau de Trois-Rivières
100, rue Laviolette, R.C. 26
Trois-Rivières, Québec G9A 5S9
819-371-6011 or 1-888-879-4294

Direction régionale de la Montérégie
3ᵉ étage
2, blvd Désaulniers
St-Lambert, Québec J4P 1L2
450-466-4461 or 1-888-287-5819

Bureau de Jonquière
3950 boulevard Harvey
Jonquière, Québec G7X 8L6
418-695-8144

Ontario

Quinte United Immigrant Services
32 Bridge Street East
Belleville, Ontario K8N 5N9
613-968-7723

Newcomer Information Centre, Centre for Language
Training and Assessment Brampton Civic Centre
150 Central Park Drive, Suite 200
Brampton, Ontario L6T 1B4
905-270-6000

Brampton Neighbourhood Resource Centre
168 Kennedy Road South
Units 3 and 4
Brampton, Ontario L6W 3G6
905-452-1262

Catholic Cross-Cultural Services
37 George Street North, Suite 403
Brampton, Ontario L6X 1R5
905-457-7740

**Immigrant Settlement and
Counseling Services of Brantford**
320 North Park Street, Unit 2
Brantford, Ontario N3R 4L4
519-753-9830

YMCA of Cambridge
250 Hespeler Road
Cambridge, Ontario N1R 3H3
519-621-3250

Arab Community Centre
5468 Dundas Street West, Suite 324
Etobicoke, Ontario M9B 6E3
416-231-7746

Dejinta Beesha
8 Taber Road
Etobicoke, Ontario M9W 3A4
416-743-1286

Rexdale Women's Centre
8 Taber Road, 2nd Floor
Etobicoke, Ontario M9W 3A4
416-745-0062

Polycultural Immigrant and Community Services
3363 Bloor Street West
Etobicoke, Ontario M8X 1G2
416-233-0055

Guelph and District Multicultural Centre
214 Speedvale Avenue West, Unit 7
Guelph, Ontario N1H 1C4
519-836-2222

**Settlement and Integration Services Organization of
Hamilton**
360 James Street North
Hamilton, Ontario L8L 1H5
905-521-9917

Kingston and District Immigrant Services
322 Brock Street
Kingston, Ontario K7L 1S9
613-548-3302

Mennonite Central Committee of Ontario
50 Kent Avenue
Kitchener, Ontario N2G 3R1
519-745-8458

Kitchener-Waterloo YMCA
301-276 King Street West
Kitchener, Ontario N2G 1B6
519-579-9622

London Cross-Cultural Learner Centre
717 Dundas Street East
London, Ontario N5W 2Z5
519-432-1133

Catholic Cross-Cultural Services
90 Dundas Street West, site 204
Mississauga , Ontario L5B 2T5
905-273-4140

Dixie-Bloor Neighbourhood Resource Centre
3439 Fieldgate Drive
Mississauga, Ontario L4X 2J4
905-629-1873

India Rainbow Community Services of Peel
3038 Hurontario Street, Suite 206
Mississauga, Ontario L5B 3B9
905-275-2369

Malton Neighbourhood Services
7200 Goreway Drive
Mississauga, Ontario L4T 2T7
905-677-6270
905-672-3660

Inter-Cultural Neighbourhood Social Services
3050 Confederation Parkway
Mississauga, Ontario L5B 3Z6
905-273-4884

Northwood Neighbourhood Services (C.S.)
2528A Jane Street
Wycliffe Jane Plaza
North York, Ontario
416-748-0788

Catholic Immigration Centre
219 Argyle Avenue
Ottawa, Ontario K2P 2H4
613-232-9634

Lebanese and Arab Social Services Agency of Ottawa-Carleton
151 Slater Street, Suite 707
Ottawa, Ontario K1P 5H3
613-236-0003

Ottawa Chinese Community Service Centre
391 Bank Street, 2nd Floor
Ottawa, Ontario K2P 1Y3
613-235-4875

Catholic Community Services of York Region
21 Dunlop Street
Richmond Hill, Ontario L4C 2M6
905-770-7040

New Canadians' Centre
Windsor Essex County Family YMCA
511 Pelisser Street
Windsor, Ontario N9A 4L2
519-256-7330

South Asian Family Support Services (SAFS)
1200 Markham Road, Suite 214
Scarborough, Ontario M1H 3C3
416-431-4847

Centre for Information and Community Services of Ontario (CICS)
3852 Finch Avenue East, Suite 310
Scarborough, Ontario M1T 3T9
416-292-7510

Thunder Bay Multicultural Association
17 North Court Street
Thunder Bay, Ontario P7A 4T4
807-345-0551

Bloor Information and Life Skills Centre
672 Dupont Street, Suite 314
Toronto, Ontario M6G 1Z6
416-531-4613

Canadian Ukrainian Immigrant Aid Services
2150 Bloor Street West, Suite 96
Toronto, Ontario M6S 1M8
416-767-0036

Jewish Immigrant Aid Services of Canada
4600 Bathurst Street, Suite 325
North York, Ontario M2R 3V3
416-630-6481

Halton Multicultural Association
635 4th Line, Unit 48
Oakville, Ontario L6L 5W4
905-842-2486

Jewish Family Services of Ottawa-Carleton
1774 Kerr Avenue, Suite 230
Ottawa, Ontario K2A 1R9
613-722-2225

Ottawa Carleton Immigrant Services Organization
959 Wellington Street
Ottawa, Ontario KIY 4W1
613-725-0202

New Canadians Centre - Peterborough
205 Sherbrooke Street, Unit D
Peterborough, Ontario K9J 2N2
705-743-0882

Folk Arts Council of St. Catharines
85 Church Street
St. Catharines, Ontario L2R 3C7
905-685-6589

Tropicana Community Services Organization
670 Progress Avenue, Unit 14
Scarborough, Ontario M1H 3A4
416-439-9009

Catholic Cross-Cultural Services
780 Birchmount Road, Unit 3
Scarborough, Ontario M1K 5H4
416-757-7010

Sudbury Multicultural Folk Arts Association
196 Van Horne Street
Sudbury, Ontario P3E 1E5
705-674-0795

Afghan Women's Counseling and Integration
Community Support Organization
2333 Dundas Street West, Suite 205A
Toronto, Ontario M6R 3A6
416-588-3585

Canadian Centre for Victims of Torture
192-194 Jarvis Street, 2nd Floor
Toronto, Ontario M5B 2B7
416-363-1066

Catholic Cross-Cultural Services
10 St. Mary Street, Suite 410
Toronto, Ontario M4Y 1P9
416-324-8225

Harriet Tubman Community Organization Inc.
2975 Don Mills Road
Toronto, Ontario M2J 3B7
416-496-2044

COFTM Centre Francophone
20 Lower Spadina Avenue
Toronto, Ontario M5V 2Z1
416-203-1220

CultureLink
160 Springhurst Avenue, Suite 300
Toronto, Ontario M6K 1C2
416-588-6288

Jamaican Canadian Association
995 Arrow Road
Toronto, Ontario M9M 2Z5
416-746-5772

Mennonite New Life Centre
1774 Queen Street East
Toronto, Ontario M4L 1G7
416-699-4527

MIDAYNTA
1992 Yonge Street, Suite 203
Toronto, Ontario M4S 1Z8
416-544-1992
416-440-0520

Riverdale Immigrant Women's Centre
1326 Gerrard Street East, Suite 100
Toronto, Ontario M4L 1Z1
416-465-6021

South Asian Women's Centre
1332 Bloor Street West
Toronto, Ontario M6H 1P2
416-537-2276

Afghan Association of Ontario
29 Pemican Court, #6
Weston, Ontario M9M 2Z3
416-744-9289

Thorncliffe Park Neighbourhood Services
18 Thorncliffe Park Drive
Toronto, Ontario M4H 1N7
416-421-3054

Toronto Organization for Domestic Workers' Rights (INTERCEDE)
234 Eglinton Avenue East, Suite 205
Toronto, Ontario M4P 1K5
416-483-4554

Woodgreen Community Centre of Toronto
835 Queen Street East
Toronto, Ontario M4M 1H9
416-469-5211

Centre for Spanish-Speaking Peoples
1004 Bathurst Street
Toronto, Ontario M5R 3G7
416-533-8545

COSTI-IIAS Immigrant Services
1710 Dufferin Street
Toronto, Ontario M6E 3P2
416-658-1600

Ethiopian Association in Toronto, Inc.
2057 Danforth Avenue, 3rd Floor
Toronto, Ontario M4C 1J8
416-694-1522

Kababayan Community Service Centre
1313 Queen Street West, Suite 133
Toronto, Ontario M6K 1L8
416-532-3888

Newcomer Information Centre,
YMCA of Greater Toronto
42 Charles Street East, 3rd Floor
Toronto, Ontario M4Y 1T4
416-928-3362

Tropicana Community Services Organization
670 Progress Avenue, Unit 14
Scarborough, Ontario M1H 3A4
(416) 439-9009

Scadding Court Community Centre
707 Dundas Street West
Toronto, Ontario M5T 2W6
416-392-0335

Barrie YMCA Immigrant Services
22 Grove Street West
Barrie, Ontario L4N 1M7
705-726-6421 ext. 264

Tamil Eelam Society of Canada
861 Broadview Avenue
Toronto, Ontario M4K 2P9
416-463-7647

Toronto Chinese Community Services Association
310 Spadina Avenue, Suite 301
Toronto, Ontario M5T 2E8
416-977-4026

Vietnamese Association of Toronto
1364 Dundas Street West
Toronto, Ontario M6J 1Y2
416-536-3611

Working Women Community Centre
533A Gladstone Avenue
Toronto, Ontario M6H 3J1
416-532-2824

370

Lakeshore Area Multi-Service
Project Inc.
185 Fifth Street
Toronto, Ontario M8V 2Z5
416-252-6471

Multicultural Council of Windsor
and Essex County
245 Janette Avenue
Windsor, Ontario N9A 4Z2
519-255-1127

Youth Assisting Youth
1992 Yonge Street, Suite 300
Toronto, Ontario M4S 1Z7
416-932-1919

Social Development Council Ajax, Pickering
134 Commercial Avenue
Ajax, Ontario L1S 2H5
905-686-2661

YMCA of Metro Toronto
(Korean Community Services)
721 Bloor Street West, Suite 303
Toronto, Ontario M6G 1L5
416-538-9412

Afghan Association of Ontario
29 Pemican Court, #6
Weston, Ontario M9M 2Z3
416-744-9289

The Job Search Workshops in Ontario
1-800-813-2614

Manitoba

Jewish Child and Family Services
Suite C200-123 Doncaster Street
Winnipeg, Manitoba R3N 2B2
204-477-7430

Indochina Chinese Association of Manitoba
648 McGee Street
Winnipeg, Manitoba R3E 1W8
204-772-3107

Philippine Association of Manitoba
88 Juno Street
Winnipeg, Manitoba
204-772-7210

Success Skills Centre
616-1661 Portage Avenue
Winnipeg, Manitoba R3J 3T7
204-786-3200

Black Youth Helpline
P.O. Box 11
1631 St-Mary's Road
Winnipeg, Manitoba R2M 4A5
204-339-2769

Manitoba Interfaith
406 Edmonton Street, 2nd floor
Winnipeg, Manitoba R3B 2M2
204-943-9158

Lao Association of Manitoba
7-983 Arlington Street
Winnipeg, Manitoba R3E 2E6
204-774-1115

Immigrant Women Association of Manitoba
200-323 Portage Avenue
Winnipeg, Manitoba R3B 2C1
204-989-5800

Employment Projects for Women
990-167 Lombard Avenue
Winnipeg, Manitoba R3B 0V3
204-949-5300

Ukrainian Canadian Congress
456 Main Street
Winnipeg, Manitoba R3B 1B6
204-942-4627

Citizenship Council of Manitoba
406 Edmonton Street, 2nd Floor
Winnipeg, Manitoba R3B 2M2
204-943-9158

International Centre of Winnipeg
406 Edmonton Street, 2nd floor
Winnipeg, Manitoba R3B 2M2
204-943-9158

371

Saskatchewan

Prince Albert Multicultural Council
17 11th Street West
Prince Albert, Saskatchewan S6V 3A8
306-922-0405

Regina Open Door Society
1855 Smith Street
Regina, Saskatchewan S4P 2N5
306-352-3500

Saskatoon Open Door Society
311 4th Avenue North
Saskatoon, Saskatchewan S7K 2L8
306-653-4464

Moose Jaw Multicultural Council
60 Athabasca Street East
Moose Jaw, Saskatchewan S6H 0L2
306-693-4677

Alberta

Calgary Immigrant Aid Society
12th Floor, 910-7 Avenue SW
Calgary, Alberta T2P 3N8
403-265-1120

Central Alberta Refugee Effort (C.A.R.E.) Committee
202-5000 Gaetz Avenue
Red Deer, Alberta T4N 6C2
403-346-8818

Calgary Immigrant Development and
Educational Advancement Society
203-4310 17th Avenue SE
Calgary, Alberta T2A 0T4
403-235-3666

The Calgary Bridge Foundation for Youth
4112-4 Street NW
Calgary, Alberta T2K 1A2
403-230-7745

Changing Together - A Centre for Immigrant Women
#103, 10010 - 107A Avenue
Edmonton, Alberta T5H 4H8
780-421-0175

Edmonton Catholic Schools
10915-110 Street
Edmonton, Alberta T5H 3E3
780-426-4375

Edmonton Immigrant Services Association
11240 - 79 Street
Edmonton, Alberta T5B 2K1
780-474-8445

Edmonton Public School Board
6703-112 Street
Edmonton, Alberta T6H 3J9
780-431-5479

New Home Immigration and Settlement
572 Hermitage Road
Edmonton, Alberta T5A 4N2
780-456-4663

The Reading Network - Grande Prairie Regional College
Lower Level, 9920 - 100 Avenue
Grande Prairie, Alberta T8V 0T9
780-538-4363

Calgary Catholic Immigration Society
3rd Floor, 120-17 Avenue SW
Calgary, Alberta T2S 2T2
403-262-2006

Calgary Immigrant Women's Association
300, 750 - 11 Street SW
Calgary, Alberta T2P 3N7
403-263-4414

Calgary Mennonite Centre for Newcomers
201, 3517 - 17 Avenue SE
Calgary, Alberta T2A 0R5
403-569-0409

Catholic Social Services
10709-105 Street
Edmonton, Alberta T5H 2X3
780-424-3545

Indo-Canadian Women's Association
335 Tower II, Millbourne Mall
Edmonton, Alberta T6K 3L2
780-490-0477

Edmonton Chinese Community Services Centre
9540 - 102 Avenue
Edmonton, Alberta T5H 0E3
780-429-3111

Edmonton Mennonite Centre for Newcomers
#101, 10010 - 107A Avenue
Edmonton, Alberta T5H 4H8
780-424-7709

Millwoods Welcome Centre for Immigrants
335 Tower II, Millbourne Mall
Edmonton, Alberta T6K 3L2
780-462-6924

YMCA of Wood Buffalo
#200, 9913 Biggs Avenue
Fort McMurray, Alberta T9H 1S2
780-743-2970

Lethbridge Family Services - Immigrant Services
508-6th Street South
Lethbridge, Alberta T1J 2E2
403-320-1589
403-317-7654 (FAX)

SAAMIS Immigration Services
177 12 Street NE
Medicine Hat, Alberta T1A 5T6
403-504-1188
Fax 403-504-1211

Catholic Social Services - Red Deer
5104-48th Avenue
Red Deer, Alberta T4N 3T8
403-347-8844

Catholic Social Services
202-5000 Gaetz Avenue
Red Deer, Alberta T4N 6C2
403-346-8818

British Columbia

Burnaby Family Life Institute
32-250 Willingdon Avenue
Burnaby, BC V5C 5E9
604-659-2200

Burnaby Multicultural Society
6255 Nelson Avenue
Burnaby, BC V5H 4T5
604-431-4131

Campbell River and Area Multicultural and Immigrant Services Association
43-1480 Dogwood Street
Campbell River, BC V9W 3A6
250-830-0171

Chilliwack Community Services
45938 Wellington Avenue
Chilliwack, BC V2P 2C7
604-792-4267

Comox Valley Family Service Association
1415 Cliffe Avenue
Courtenay, BC V9N 2K6
250-338-7575

Cowichan Valley Intercultural and Immigrant Aid Society
3-83 Trunk Road
Duncan, BC V9L 2N7
250-748-3112

Kamloops Cariboo Regional Immigrant Services Society
110-206 Seymour Street
Kamloops, BC V2C 2E5
250-372-0855

Multicultural Society of Kelowna
100-1875 Spall Road
Kelowna, BC V1Y 4R2
250-762-2155

Langley Family Services Association
5339-207th Street
Langley, BC V3A 2E6
604-534-7921

Central Vancouver Island Multicultural Society
114-285 Prideaux Street
Nanaimo, BC V9R 2N2
250-753-6911

Lower Mainland Purpose Society for Youth and Families
40 Begbie Street
New Westminster, BC V3M 3L9
604-526-2522

North Shore Multicultural Society
102-123 East 15th Street
North Vancouver, BC V7L 2P7
604-988-2931

Penticton and District Multicultural Society
508 Main Street
Penticton, BC V2A 5C7
250-492-6299

Immigrant and Multicultural Services Society of Prince George
1633 Victoria Street
Prince George, BC V2L 2L4
250-562-2900

Richmond Multicultural Concerns Society
210-7000 Minorou Boulevard
Richmond, BC V6Y 3Z5
604-279-7160

Family Services of Greater Vancouver
250-7000 Minorou Boulevard
Richmond, BC V6Y 3Z5
604-279-7100

Richmond Connections
190-7000 Minorou Boulevard
Richmond, BC V6Y 3Z5
604-279-7020

Surrey Delta Immigrant Services Society
1107-7330 137th Street
Surrey, BC V3W 1A3
604-597-0205

Options: Services to Community
100-6846 King George Highway
Surrey, BC V3W 4Z9
604-596-4321

Progressive Intercultural Community Services Society
109-12414-82nd Street
Surrey, BC V3W 3E9
604-596-7722

Family Services of the North Shore
101-255 West 1st Street
Vancouver, BC V7M 3G8
604-988-5281

Collingwood Neighbourhood House
5288 Joyce Street
Vancouver, BC V5R 6C9
604-435-0323

Kiwassa Neighbourhood House
2425 Oxford Street
Vancouver, BC V5K 1M7
604-254-5401

MOSAIC
1522 Commercial Drive, 2nd Floor
Vancouver, BC V5L 3Y2
604-254-9626

Ray-Cam Cooperative Centre
920 East Hastings Street
Vancouver, BC V6A 3T1
604-257-6949

South Vancouver Neighbourhood House
6470 Victoria Drive
Vancouver, BC V5P 3X7
604-324-6212

Frog Hollow Neighbourhood House
2131 Renfrew Street
Vancouver, BC V5M 4M5
604-251-1225

Pacific Immigrant Resources Society
385 South Boundary Road
Vancouver, BC V5K 4S1
604-298-4560

West End Community Centre Association
870 Denman Street
Vancouver, B.C. V6G 2L8
604-257-8333

Victoria Immigrant and Refugee Centre
305-535 Yates Street
Victoria, BC V8W 2Z6
250-361-9433

Mennonite Central Committee of BC
31414 Marshall Road, Box 2038
Abbotsford, BC V2T 3T8
604-850-663

Immigrant Services Society
530 Drake Street
Vancouver, BC V6B 2H3
604-684-7498

Jewish Family Service Agency
300-950 West 41st Avenue
Vancouver BC V5Z 2N7
604-257-5151

Little Mountain Neighbourhood House
3981 Main Street
Vancouver, BC V5V 3P3
604-879-7104

The People's Law School
150-900 Howe Street
Vancouver, BC V6Z 2M4
604-688-2565

Riley Park Community Association
50 East 30th Avenue
Vancouver, BC V5V 2T9
604-257-8641

SUCCESS
28 West Pender Street
Vancouver, BC V6B 1R6
604-684-1628

Hispanic Community Centre
Society of BC
4824 Commercial Street
Vancouver, BC V5N 4H1
604-872-4431

Vancouver Association for the Survivors of Torture (VAST)
3-3664 East Hastings Street
Vancouver, BC V5K 2A9
Tel: 604-299-3539

Vernon and District Immigrant Services
100-3003 30th Street
Vernon, BC V1T 9J5
250-542-4177

Intercultural Association of Victoria
930 Balmoral Road
Victoria, BC V8T 1A8
250-388-4728

Abbotsford Community Services
2420 Montrose Avenue
Abbotsford, BC V2S 3S9
604-859-7681

374

NEWS RELEASES

Surging Resource Prices Stimulate Growth in Western Provinces

OTTAWA, May 3, 2005 – Elevated primary resource prices, combined with healthy fiscal situations, are making Alberta and British Columbia two of the fastest growing provincial economies in Canada, according to the Conference Board's *Provincial Outlook – Spring 2005.*

"Sizzling global demand for mining resources is driving economic growth across western Canadian provinces," said Marie-Christine Bernard, Associate Director, Provincial Outlook. "With oilsands investments and strong energy exploration activity, Alberta's economy is firing on all cylinders. B.C. is enjoying healthy gains in most sectors, as well as strong construction activity leading toward the 2010 Winter Olympics. Saskatchewan will ride high commodity prices to a second consecutive year of strong growth."

Saskatchewan and British Columbia enjoyed strong GDP growth in 2004. They are expected to match each other in 2005, achieving growth of three per cent.

Alberta's real gross domestic product (GDP) growth of 3.5 per cent in 2005 will lead all provinces. The province's growth is expected to ease to three per cent in 2006, second only to Newfoundland and Labrador. The provincial budget showcased an admirable fiscal situation, as soaring energy royalties helped eliminate Alberta's accumulated debt.

Manitoba's real GDP is expected to increase by 2.3 per cent in 2005. The province's goods sector is solid, led by non-residential investment in energy projects—and future prospects look bright with hydroelectric power generation being promoted under the federal government's Kyoto implementation plan.

377

Even with strong consumer spending, real GDP growth (at market prices) of 2.1 per cent is expected in Ontario this year. After navigating a turbulent period in which the stronger dollar punished exports, a rebound is in sight for later this year and into 2006.

Weakening housing starts and more moderate retail sales growth will dampen domestic demand in Quebec. As a result, real GDP growth (at market prices) will fall to two per cent in 2005. Stronger construction activity in 2006 is expected to lead to growth of almost three per cent.

Together, the Atlantic provinces will grow by two per cent in 2005. Stronger mining production and an expansionary provincial budget will boost Newfoundland and Labrador's 2005 real GDP growth to 2.3 per cent. With a full year of production at White Rose and Voisey's Bay in 2006, real GDP growth is expected to soar to 5.4 per cent, the highest in Canada.

At 1.8 per cent growth, Nova Scotia's economy is expected to be the country's weakest in 2005, but manufacturing and the service sector have better prospects for next year. New Brunswick will experience broad-based gains this year, with construction and manufacturing doing well. For Prince Edward Island, sizzling construction activity will help the economy, but budget cuts will erode some of those gains.

The *Provincial Outlook* provides a quarterly economic outlook for all 10 Canadian provinces.

═══════════════ News Release ═══════════════

Government of Canada Announces Internationally Trained Workers Initiative

OTTAWA, April 25, 2005 — The Government of Canada today launched the Internationally Trained Workers Initiative, delivering on the commitment made in the Speech from the Throne to improve the integration of immigrants and internationally trained Canadians into the work force. The launch was held simultaneously in Toronto and Vancouver.

"For Canada to succeed in the 21st century economy and ensure our quality of life, we must continually improve the quality of our work force," said the Honourable Lucienne Robillard, President of the Queen's Privy Council for Canada, Minister of Intergovernmental Affairs, and Minister of Human Resources and Skills Development, in announcing the comprehensive strategy in Toronto. "We look forward to working with partners to ensure that everyone can use their skills and abilities, no matter where they received their training, so that they—and Canada—can benefit to the fullest."

Today's announcement includes the following:

- The launch of the Government of Canada's initiative to help address shortages of health-care professionals by providing $75 million over the next five years to improve the integration of internationally trained doctors, nurses and other health-care professionals into the Canadian system;

- The launch of the Government of Canada's Foreign Credential Recognition program, with $68 million in funding over six years to facilitate the assessment and recognition of foreign qualifications for both regulated and non-regulated occupations;

- The launch of the Government of Canada's on-line Going to Canada Immigration Internet Portal, to be implemented in cooperation with the provinces and territories. This is part of a $100 million commitment to an improved and integrated service delivery strategy. The portal will help prospective immigrants make informed decisions about coming to Canada and prepare for the Canadian labour market and society before they arrive;

- A commitment to provide $20 million a year in ongoing funding to the Enhanced Language Training initiative, which helps immigrants acquire the language skills necessary to obtain and retain jobs commensurate with their level of skill and experience. This initiative complements the $140 million a year being spent to provide basic language training to immigrants outside of Quebec; and

- The government's recently launched Action Plan Against Racism, with $56 million over five years for a series of measures to combat the discrimination Canadians sometimes face, including in the workplace, and to help realize Canada's vision of an inclusive and equitable society.

"With this initiative, we are addressing many of the challenges that immigrants and internationally trained Canadians face when starting a career in Canada," said the Honourable Hedy Fry, Parliamentary Secretary to the Minister of Citizenship and Immigration, in Vancouver. "When the Prime Minister asked me to lead this comprehensive and integrated interdepartmental initiative, it became clear that the Government of Canada could not accomplish this alone. We need to build on partnerships with stakeholders who have jurisdiction in many of the areas that require intervention if we are to achieve common success."

These actions are part of a coordinated strategy to bring the skills and experience of internationally trained professionals into the Canadian labour market. Provincial and territorial governments are essential partners. The Government of Canada will also work with cities and communities, service providers, employers, labour, professional and regulatory bodies, post-secondary educational institutions, the business community itself, and other stakeholders to find national, coherent solutions to this challenge.

"Immigration is vital to our economic and social development, but for a variety of reasons some immigrants face difficulties integrating into the work force and society," the Honourable Joe Volpe, Minister of Citizenship and Immigration, told representatives of professional associations, regulators, employers, educators and immigrants in Toronto. "The Internationally Trained Workers Initiative reflects this government's commitment to equality of opportunity and our understanding that Canada's diversity is a source of strength and innovation."

"We are taking direct action to fulfill the commitment we made last September when the First Ministers unanimously agreed on the Ten-Year Plan to Strengthen Health Care," said the Honourable Ujjal Dosanjh, Minister of Health, in Vancouver. "This initiative will help address shortages of health-care professionals and improve Canadians' access to high-quality care. It supports our efforts with the provinces and territories to renew the health system and ensure it is sustainable."

On March 21, the Minister of State (Multiculturalism), Raymond Chan, launched Canada's first-ever Action Plan Against Racism. "We have just unveiled, as part of our Action Plan Against Racism, the Racism-Free Workplace Strategy," said the Honourable Raymond Chan, in Vancouver. "The goal of this strategy is to eliminate all discriminatory barriers to employment and to ensure full inclusion in the workplace. To this end, we have also initiated projects through the multiculturalism program that actively involve internationally trained workers in overcoming barriers based on foreign credential recognition. Only by working together can we ensure that everyone has the opportunity to achieve their potential and contribute fully to Canadian society."

The Internationally Trained Workers Initiative has been developed in partnership with a broad variety of stakeholders, who have been consulted in a series of roundtables across Canada by the

Honourable Hedy Fry. Some 14 federal departments and agencies are working on the initiative in close collaboration with provincial and territorial governments, regulators and various stakeholders.

════════════════ News Release ════════════════

Investment in Enhanced Language Training Pays off

TORONTO, April 25, 2005 — As part of the Internationally Trained Workers Initiative, Citizenship and Immigration Canada is helping newcomers acquire the language skills they need to reach their full potential in the Canadian labour market, Citizenship and Immigration Minister Joe Volpe announced today.

"Language is one of the main barriers to integration into the workplace for many immigrants to Canada," said Minister Volpe. "This investment will help engineers, trades people, doctors, nurses and workers in many other fields who received their training outside of Canada to find and keep good jobs that match the skills and experience they bring to Canada."

While most newcomers have adequate conversational language skills upon arrival in Canada, many employers report gaps in the specialized workplace language skills and vocabulary that are required in many trades and professions. The Enhanced Language Training (ELT) initiative will provide job-specific language training to enable immigrants to gain the language skills they need to flourish in the workplace.

"I am pleased to report the progress we have made to date on this important initiative and share with you the list of projects that have been implemented across the country in 2004–2005," added the Minister. "This would not have been possible without the successful partnership we established with Ontario, Saskatchewan, Manitoba, Nova Scotia and British Columbia on the delivery of ELT projects in these provinces."

The government currently spends about $140 million a year on basic language training for about 50,000 adult immigrants outside of Quebec. The Enhanced Language Training initiative accounts for an additional $20 million annually, and provides bridge-to-work assistance, including mentoring, work placement and other assistance in accessing the labour market.

The ELT initiative is an important component of the Government of Canada's efforts to attract highly skilled workers and ensure more successful integration of immigrants into the economy and communities. Other measures include working with regulatory bodies and sector councils to facilitate the development of effective processes for the recognition of foreign credentials and prior work experience, and the development of the Going to Canada Immigration Portal to provide better information to immigrants before they come to Canada.

═══════════════════ News Release ═══════════════════

Health Minister Dosanjh Announces $75 Million Initiative To Bring More Internationally Educated Professionals into Health Care System

VANCOUVER - Health Minister Ujjal Dosanjh today announced a $75 million federal initiative that is expected to assist more than 2,000 internationally educated health care professionals to put their skills to work in Canada's health care system.

"The whole country benefits when immigrants and internationally educated Canadians are able to make full use of their knowledge and experience," said Minister Dosanjh. "This initiative will strengthen our health system by helping to increase the supply of health care professionals, which will improve access to quality health care and reduce wait times."

The $75 million, which was included in Budget 2005, will be provided over five years. During this period, it is estimated the funding will assist in the assessment and integration into the workforce of up to 1,000 physicians, 800 nurses and 500 other regulated health care professionals. The numbers will vary, however, according to the priorities of provincial and territorial governments.

"This fulfils the Government of Canada's commitment at the First Ministers Meeting last September to accelerate and expand the assessment and integration of internationally educated health care professionals," said Minister Dosanjh. "This complements a series of other measures we are taking in collaboration with provinces and territories and the health care community to provide cities and rural areas across this country with the health care workers they need."

Strengthening the health care workforce is a key objective of the Ten-Year Plan to Strengthen Health Care, which all First Ministers signed in September 2004. The Government of Canada is supporting the training and hiring of more health care professionals through the $5.5-billion Wait Times Reduction Fund. In addition, the Pan-

Canadian Health Human Resource Strategy provides $20 million per year to improve health care workforce planning, promote the use of interdisciplinary health care teams and increase recruitment and retention of needed health care professionals.

Minister Dosanjh also noted that today's $75 million announcement is part of a wider Internationally Trained Workers Initiative, involving 14 federal departments and agencies.

"The Initiative will improve the integration of immigrants and internationally trained Canadians into the labour force so they can contribute their full potential to Canada and share in its prosperity," said Minister Dosanjh.

The $75 million initiative on internationally educated health care graduates will build on work that is already underway. As part of that work, which received $8.5 million in earlier funding from the Government of Canada, Minister Dosanjh today announced:

- The launch of a national website that will help international medical graduates prepare to become licensed to practice in Canada. The Association of International Physicians and Surgeons of Ontario, with funding of $126,356 from Health Canada, took the lead in preparing the online Canadian Information Centre for International Medical Graduates (www.IMG-Canada.ca). The site is a central point of information for international medical graduates, providing comprehensive information on the Canadian health care system and medical licensure requirements, education and training services in different provinces and territories. It also provides information on alternative health care careers. The Website will enable international medical graduates to assess their options and opportunities even before they come to Canada and will be linked to Citizenship and Immigration's "Going to Canada" immigration portal. Minister Dosanjh officially launched the site Monday with Dr. Dale Dauphinee, executive director of the Medical Council of Canada.

- A National Credential Verification Agency will be established by the Medical Council of Canada to provide a streamlined process for verifying the credentials of international medical graduates. After this verification, these graduates can then take an evaluation exam or other steps toward becoming licensed to practice in Canada. The single-source verification service will prevent these graduates from having to get their credentials verified in each province or territory in which they seek licensure. This $1.86 million project is funded by Human Resources and Skills Development Canada.

- The Medical Council of Canada will make its evaluation exam more readily accessible to international medical graduates in a $1.34 million project funded by Human Resources and Skills Development Canada. This exam is the first stage in the licensing process for international medical graduates in Canada. The exam will be put into an electronic format to enhance its availability.

- The Canadian Post M.D. Education Registry is receiving $834,625 from Human Resources and Skills Development Canada to create a pan-Canadian database with information about international medical graduates that will improve planning for the assessment, training and integration of these graduates.

════════════════ News Release ════════════════

AN IMMIGRATION SYSTEM FOR THE 21st CENTURY

OTTAWA, April 18, 2005 — The Honourable Joe Volpe, Minister of Citizenship and Immigration, today announced a series of measures aimed at improving service delivery and the efficiency of Canada's immigration and citizenship programs.

"Canada's immigration system is a model for the world and today's measures allow us to maintain and enhance our position. We will do this by reducing application processing times for permanent residents who want to become Canadian citizens and sponsored parents and grandparents who want to be reunited with their family in Canada. International competition for talented international students is fierce and today's announcement moves Canada even further ahead," said Minister Volpe.

Today's measures include an investment of $69 million over two years to restore, by 2007–2008, processing times to an average of 12 months for a grant of citizenship and four months for a proof of citizenship. Citizenship and Immigration Canada (CIC) is also exempting citizenship applicants from undergoing language ability and knowledge-of-Canada tests at 55 rather than 60 years of age, while in no way reducing the rigorous security screening requirements that all applicants for Canadian citizenship must go through before becoming citizens of Canada.

The measures to speed up the processing of sponsorship applications for parents and grandparents coming to Canada as family class immigrants include tripling the number of parents and grandparents who can immigrate to Canada from 6,000 to 18,000 a year in 2005 and in 2006. Also, the issuance of multiple-entry visitor visas will be facilitated so that parents and grandparents can visit their families in Canada while their applications are in process. The Government of Canada will invest $36 million a year for two years to cover the costs of processing and integrating parents and grandparents.

CIC is expanding two pilot initiatives for international students to enhance the competitiveness of Canada's education industry. The first will allow international students across Canada to work off-campus while completing their studies and the second will allow them to work for a second year after graduation. This second initiative will apply outside of Montreal, Toronto and Vancouver to help spread the benefits of immigration to more regions in Canada. The Government of Canada is investing $10 million a year for five years to support this strategy.

The measures announced today demonstrate action on commitments laid out by by Minister Volpe in his January 2005 six-point plan for addressing critical issues in the citizenship and immigration programs.

For more information on today's announcements, please visit CIC's Web site at www.cic.gc.ca.

================= News Release =================

New Initiatives: Off-campus Work and Post-graduation Employment

Off-Campus Work

MAY 13, 2005: The off-campus work program allows foreign students at public post-secondary institutions to work off-campus while completing their studies.

Off-campus work is an option for students studying at institutions in provinces that have signed agreements with CIC. These provinces are as follows:

- Manitoba
- New Brunswick
- Quebec. The census metropolitan areas of Montréal and Québec are currently excluded. The agreement will soon be amended to include them.

As new agreements are reached, more provinces and territories will be added to the list. Watch the CIC Web site for updates.

Students who come to Canada under the Canadian Commonwealth Scholarship and Fellowship Plan or under the Government of Canada Awards Program funded by Foreign Affairs Canada or by the Canadian International Development Agency are not eligible for off-campus work.

Post-Graduation Employment

As of May 16, 2005, the post-graduation work program will allow certain students to work for up to two years after their graduation. Previously, students were only allowed to work for one year.

Foreign students are eligible for a post-graduation work permit only for employment in their field of study. They must still have a valid study permit and apply for the work permit within 90 days of receiving written confirmation (transcript, letter, etc.) from their institution indicating that they have met the requirements of their program.

Once students have one of these documents, they can apply for a work permit. Post-graduation work permits are only available to graduates of a program at a Canadian university, a community college, a CEGEP, a publicly funded trade or technical school or a Canadian private institution authorized by provincial statute to confer degrees.

To be eligible for a two-year work permit (rather than just a one-year permit), foreign students must have

- successfully completed a program of at least two years of full-time studies;

- received written confirmation (transcript, letter, etc.) from the educational institution indicating that they have met the requirements of the program of study;

- studied at and graduated from an institution located outside of the Communauté métropolitaine de Montréal (CMM), the Greater Toronto Area (GTA) or the Greater Vancouver Regional District GVRD);

http://www.cic.gc.ca/english/study/work-locations.html

Note: If you complete your studies at a campus located inside the **CMM,** the **GTA** or the **GVRD,** but at an institution whose headquarters for that campus are located outside those areas, you are not eligible for a two-year work permit under this program.

- found employment outside of the **CMM, GTA** or **GVRD.**

- **Note:** Foreign students who graduate from an institution located inside one of those areas are not eligible for a second year of work, even if the employment is located outside of those areas.

Foreign students who currently hold a one-year post-graduation work permit and who meet the eligibility criteria for a two-year permit can apply for a one-year extension of their work permit.

Important Information About Work Permits For Students:

Do not work without being authorized to do so. If you do, you will be in contravention of the law and may be asked to leave Canada. Students who qualify for the new initiatives still require a work permit, but they will be able to apply for one without having to obtain a labour market opinion from Human Resources and Skills Development Canada. Students must not begin to work until they have received their work permit.

Find out about work opportunities for foreign students at http://www.cic.gc.ca/english/study/work-opps.html

Guru's Knowledge

I think there is a world market for maybe five computers.
(Thomas Watson, chairman of IBM, 1943)

Computers in the future may weigh no more than 1.5 tons.
(Popular Mechanics, forecasting the relentless march of science, 1949)

I have traveled the length and breadth of this country and talked with the best people, and I can assure you that data processing is a fad that won't last out the year. (The editor in charge of business books for Prentice Hall, 1957)

There is no reason anyone would want a computer in their home.
(Ken Olson, president, chairman and founder of Digital Equipment Corp., 1977)

This 'telephone' has too many shortcomings to be seriously considered as a means of communication. The device is inherently of no value to us.
(Western Union internal memo, 1876.)

The wireless music box has no imaginable commercial value. Who would pay for a message sent to nobody in particular?
(David Sarnoff's associates in response to his urgings for investment in the radio in the 1920s.)

The concept is interesting and well-formed, but in order to earn better than a 'C,' the idea must be feasible."
(A Yale University management professor in response to Fred Smith's paper   proposing reliable overnight delivery service. (Smith went on to found Federal Express Corp.))

Who the hell wants to hear actors talk?
(H.M. Warner, Warner Brothers, 1927.)

I'm just glad it'll be Clark Gable who's falling on his face and not Gary Cooper.   (Gary Cooper on his decision not to take the leading role in "Gone With The Wind.")

A cookie store is a bad idea. Besides, the market research reports say America likes crispy cookies, not soft and chewy cookies like you make.
(Response to Debbi Fields' idea of starting Mrs. Fields' Cookies.)

We don't like their sound, and guitar music is on the way out.
(Decca Recording Co. rejecting the Beatles, 1962.)

Heavier-than-air flying machines are impossible.
(Lord Kelvin, president, Royal Society, 1895.)

Professor Goddard does not know the relation between action and reaction and the need to have something better than a vacuum against which to react. He seems to lack the basic knowledge ladled out daily in high schools. (1921 New York Times editorial about Robert Goddard's revolutionary rocket work.)

Drill for oil? You mean drill into the ground to try and find oil? You're crazy. (Drillers who Edwin L. Drake tried to enlist to his project to drill for oil in 1859.)

Stocks have reached what looks like a permanently high plateau. (Irving Fisher, Professor of Economics, Yale University, 1929.)

Airplanes are interesting toys but of no military value. (Marechal Ferdinand Foch, Professor of Strategy, Ecole Superieure de Guerre).

Everything that can be invented has been invented. (Charles H. Duell, Commissioner, U.S. Office of Patents, 1899.)

Louis Pasteur's theory of germs is ridiculous fiction. (Pierre Pachet, Professor of Physiology at Toulouse, 1872)

The abdomen, the chest, and the brain will forever be shut from the intrusion of the wise and humane surgeon." (Sir John Eric Ericksen, British surgeon, appointed Surgeon-Extraordinary to Queen Victoria 1873.)

640K ought to be enough for anybody." (Bill Gates, 1981)

The level of human knowledge in every known field to them whether it is science, technology or culture have not yet reached to its embryonic stage. (Tariq Nadeem - Author, 2005)

GLOBAL CAREER & EMPLOYMENT WEBSITES

Following websites has been compiled for the benefit of professionals and students who are interested in work or a career overseas. It aims to serve as a quick and easy guide to some of the most useful employment websites on the Internet. However, due to the extremely fast rate of change on the web, the accuracy of all websites cannot be guaranteed. Please let us know if you are aware of any additional sites which merit inclusion.

Generic employment websites

Bilingual Jobs	http://www.bilingual-jobs.com/
Career Builder	http://www.careerbuilder.com
Career Magazine	http://www.careermag.com
Escape Artist	http://www.escapeartist.com
Employment Resources on the Net	http://www.noncon.org/insight/jobs
Hobsons Global Careers & Education	http://www.hobsons.com
Idealist.Org	http://www.idealist.org
J-Hunter	http://www.j-hunter.com
Job Hunt	http://www.job-hunt.org
Jobnet	http://www.jobnet.com.au
Jobs Abroad	http://www.jobsabroad.com
Monster Work Abroad	http://workabroad.monster.com
Monster Worldwide	http://www.monsterworldwide.com
News Directory	http://www.newsdirectory.com
Newspapers Online	http://www.newspapers.com/
Overseas Jobs	http://www.overseasjobs.com/
Quintessential Careers	http://www.quintcareers.com/
TMP Hudson Global Resources	http://www.hudsonresourcing.com
The Riley Guide	http://www.rileyguide.com/
What you need to know about International Resources	http://jobsearch.about.com/cs/internationaljobs1/

Africa

African Development Bank	http://www.afdb.org/
Africa Online	http://www.africaonline.com/
Career Junction	http://www.careerjunction.co.za/
Careers.Org - South Africa	http://www.careers.org/reg/cint-safrica.html
Find a Job in Africa	http://www.findajobinafrica.com/
I-Africa Careers	http://careers.iafrica.com/
Job Navigator	http://www.jobs.co.za/

Asia

Adecco Asia	http://www.adecco-asia.com/
Asia Business Daily	http://www.asiabusinessdaily.com/
Asian Development Bank	http://www.adb.org/
Asia Employment Centre	http://jobs.asiaco.com/jobbank/
Asia Inc Online	http://www.asia-inc.com/
Asia Job Search Resources	http://www.escapeartist.com/jobs7/asia.htm

Asia Net	http://www.asia-net.com/
Asia Pacific Economic Cooperation	http://www.apec.org/
Asia Partnership	http://www.asiapartnership.com/
Asia Times	http://www.asiatimes.com/
Asiaweek	http://www.asiaweek.com/asiaweek//
Careerbuilder.com	http://www.careerbuilder.com/
Far Eastern Economic Review	http://www.feer.com/
J-Hunter	http://www.j-hunter.com/
Job Asia	http://www.jobasia.com/
Job Culture	http://www.jobculture.com/
Jobs Database	http://www.jobsdb.com/
Job Street Australasia	http://www.jobstreet.com/
Recruit Asia	http://www.recruitasia.com/
Wang & Li Asia Resource Online	http://www.wang-li.com/

Australia

Austrade	http://www.austrade.gov.au/
Australian Business Limited	http://www.australianbusiness.com.au/
Australian Federal Government	http://www.fed.gov.au/
Australian Job Search	http://www.jobsearch.gov.au/
Australian Financial Review	http://afr.com/
Australian Stock Exchange	http://www.asx.com.au/
Australian Universities	http://www.avcc.edu.au/
Career Guide	http://www.yourcareerguide.com/
Career One	http://www.careerone.com.au/
CPA Australia	http://www.cpaaustralia.com.au/
Dep't of Foreign Affairs & Trade	http://www.dfat.gov.au/
Fairfax Classifieds	http://www.market.fairfax.com.au/
Gradlink	http://www.gradlink.com.au/
Graduate Opportunities	http://www.graduateopportunities.com/
Institute of Chartered Accountants	http://www.icaa.org.au/
Job Watch	http://home.vicnet.net.au/
Monster	http://www.monster.com.au/
My Career	http://www.mycareer.com.au/editorial/graduate/
My Future	http://www.myfuture.edu.au/
SEEK	http://www.seek.com.au/
SEEK Campus	http://campus.seek.com.au/
The Age	http://www.theage.com.au/
The Australian	http://www.theaustralian.com.au/
Victorian Government	http://www.vic.gov.au/
Visa Requirements	http://www.immi.gov.au/
WageNet	http://www.wagenet.gov.au/

Austria

Adecco Austria (German)	http://www.adecco.at/
Hill Woltron Recruitment (German)	http://www.hill-woltron.com/
Job Direct (German)	http://www.job-direct.co.at/
Jobnet Austria (German)	http://jobnet.uibk.ac.at/
Job Pilot Austria (German)	http://www.jobpilot.at/
Manpower Austria (German)	http://www.manpower.at/
Trenkwalder	http://www.trenkwalder.at/

Bangladesh

Bangladesh Internet Resources	http://www.bdcenter.com/
The Independent	http://independent-bangladesh.com/

Belgium
Belgian job directory (Dutch)	http://www.info123.be/
Job@ (Dutch)	http://www.jobat.be/
Jobs and Careers Belgium	http://www.jobs-career.be/
Jobs today	http://www.jobstoday.be/
Vacature (Dutch & French)	http://www.vacature.be/
VDAB	http://www.vdab.be/

Brunei
Brunei Government Site	http://www.brunei.gov.bn/
Brunei News	http://www.bruneinews.net/

Cambodia
Business in Cambodia	http://www.business-in-cambodia.com/
Cambodia News	http://www.cambodia-web.net/

Canada
Monster	http://monstor.ca
BC Workinfo Net	http://workinfonet.bc.ca/
CACEE	http://www.cacee.com/
Canada Careers	http://www.canadiancareers.com/
Canada Employment Weekly	http://www.mediacorp2.com/
Canadian Public Service	http://www.psc-cfp.gc.ca/index_e.htm
Career & Immigration Tips	http://www.careertips.com
Dep't of Foreign Affairs & Trade	http://www.dfait-maeci.gc.ca/
Work Site Canada	http://www.worksitecanada.com/
Workapolis	http://www.workapolis.com/

Caribbean
Caribbean Hello	http://www.caribbeandaily.com/
The Daily Herald	http://www.thedailyherald.com/

China
Beijing Review	http://www.bjreview.com.cn/
Business Directory of China	http://www.china-business-directory.com/
Career Agent China	http://china.career-agent.net/
China Daily	http://chinadaily.com.cn/
China News Digest	http://www.cnd.org/
China Vista	http://www.chinavista.com/
China HR	http://www.chinahr.com/
China Window	http://www.china-window.com.cn/
Chinese Newspapers Online	http://www.lib.duke.edu/ias/eac/chnsp.htm
Fujian	http://www.fz.fj.cn/
Guangzhou Ribao	http://www.gmw.com.cn/
Inside China Today	http://www.einnews.com/china/
People's Daily	http://www.snweb.com/
South China Morning Post	http://www.scmp.com/
Wen Hui Daily	http://www.whb.com.cn/
Zhaopin	http://www.zhaopin.com.cn/

Czech Republic
CV Online (Czech) http://www.cvonline.cz/
Czech Jobs (Czech) http://www.jobs.cz/
Department of Foreign Affairs http://www.czech.cz/
Hot Jobs (Czech) http://www.hotjobs.cz/
Job European Job Sites http://1job.net/
Jobmaster (English and Czech) http://www.jobmaster.cz/

Denmark
EURES (English & Danish) http://www.eures.dk/
Job Bank (Danish) http://www.jobbank.dk/
Job Denmark (Danish) http://www.jobdanmark.dk/
Job guide (Danish) http://www.job-guide.dk/
Job Index (Danish) http://www.jobindex.dk/

Europe
Career Builder http://www.careerbuilder.com/
Careers Europe http://www.careers.co.uk/
EURES http://www.europa.eu.int/jobs/eures/
Euro-graduate http://www.eurograduate.com/
European Union http://europa.eu.int/
IAgora - iWork http://www.iagora.com/
Job Pilot http://www.jobpilot.com/
Job Site http://www.jobsite.co.uk/
Step Stone http://www.stepstone.com/

Fiji
Fiji Online http://www.fiji-online.com.fj/
Fiji Trade Contacts http://www.fiji-online.com.fj/business/

Finland
Aamulehti Newspaper (Finnish) http://www.aamulehti.fi/tyopaikat/
Academic Career Services in Finland http://www.minedu.fi/
Academic Careers Service http://www.aarresaari.net/english/
Ministry of Labour http://www.mol.fi/tyopaikat/
PIB http://www.pib.fi/

France
ANPE (French) http://www.anpe.fr/
Experian en France http://www.experian.fr/carriere/job.htm
French-Aust. Chamber of Commerce http://www.facci.com.au/
French Employment Directory http://www.jobpilot.fr/
French News and Employment http://wanadoo.fr/

Germany
Berlitz (Teaching English) http://www.berlitz.com/
Die Zeit Jobs http://www.jobs.zeit.de/
Job Exchange http://www.hueber.de/german/jobs/index.asp
Stellen Market (German) http://www.stellenmarkt.de/
Student Employment in Germany http://www.careernet.de/

Greece
Athens News   http://athensnews.gr/
OAED   http://www.oaed.gr/mainenglish.htm
Skywalker Job Search   http://www.skywalker.gr/

Hong Kong
Career Times Hong Kong   http://www.careertimes.com.hk/
Chinese University of Hong Kong   http://www.cuhk.edu.hk/
Classified Post   http://www.classifiedpost.com.hk/
Gemini Personnel Ltd   http://www.gemini.com.hk/
HKU Careers Service   http://www.hku.hk/cepc/
Hong Kong Jobs   http://www.hkjobs.com/
Hong Kong Polytechnic University   http://www.polyu.edu.hk/
Hong Kong Trade Dev't Council   http://www.tdctrade.com/
Hong Kong Uni Employers   http://www.hku.hk/cepc/service/com_name.htm
Ming Pao Daily News   http://www.mingpaonews.com/
Recruit Online with Panda Planet   http://www.pandaplanet.com/
Sing Tao   http://www.singtao.com/
South China Morning Post Careers   http://careers.scmp.com/
Ta Kung Pao   http://www.takungpao.com.hk/

Africa Iceland
Jobs Iceland   http://www.job.is/atvinnutorg/

India
Jagran   http://www.jagran.com/
Deccan Chronicle   http://www.deccan.com/
Deccan Herald   http://www.deccanherald.com/
Economic Times   http://www.economictimes.com/
Express India   http://expressindia.com/
India Connect   http://www.indiaconnect.com/
India Government Homepage   http://alfa.nic.in/
India Server   http://www.indiaserver.com/
India World   http://www.indiaworld.com/
INDOlink   http://www.indolink.com/
Jobs Ahead   http://www.jobsahead.com/
Kerala Home Page   http://www.keral.com/
Naidunia   http://www.naidunia.com/
Net Guru India   http://www.netguruindia.com/
News India-Times   http://www.newsindia-times.com/
Sanjevani   http://www.sanjevani.com/
The Hindu   http://www.hinduonline.com/
The Statesman   http://www.thestatesman.net/
The Telegraph   http://www.telegraphindia.com/
Times of India Jobs and Careers   http://www.timesjobsandcareers.com/

Indonesia
Australia Indonesia Business Council http://www.aibc.net.au/
Bali Post Online   http://www.balipost.co.id/
Bisnis Indonesia   http://www.bisnis.com/
Bernas   http://www.indomedia.com/bernas/
Indobiz   http://www.indobiz.com/
IndoWEB   http://www.indoweb.com/
Dep't of Foreign Affairs Indonesia   http://www.dfa-deplu.go.id/
Indonesia Government Homepage   http://www.ri.go.id/

Indonesia Professional Associations   http://www.dnet.net.id/ipa/
Kompas Cyber Media   http://www.kompas.com/
Living in Indonesia – for Expatriates   http://www.expat.or.id/
Media Indonesia Online   http://www.mediaindo.co.id/
Pikiran Rakyat   http://www.pikiran-rakyat.com/
Republika Online   http://www.republika.co.id/
Suara Merdeka   http://www.suaramerdeka.com/

Ireland

AA Ireland   http://www.aaireland.ie/jobs/
Irish Jobs   http://www.irishjobs.ie/
NI Jobs   http://www.nijobs.com/
Nixers   http://www.nixers.com/
Recruit Ireland   http://www.recruitireland.com/
The Irish Times   http://www.ireland.com/

Israel

Marksman International Personnel   http://www.marksman.co.il/
The Jerusalem Post Daily   http://www.jpost.co.il/

Itlay

Adecco Italia   http://www.adecco.it/
Corriere della Sera (Rome)   http://www.corriere.it/
Italian and international jobs   http://www.joblinks.f2s.com/
Job Pilot (Italian)   http://www.jobpilot.it/
Job Online   http://www.jobonline.it/
Talent Manager   http://www.talentmanager.it/

Japan

Agara   http://www.agara.co.jp/
Asahi Shimbun (Tokyo)   http://www.asahi.com/
Chugoku Shimbun (Hiroshima)   http://www.chugoku-np.co.jp/
Gaijinpot   http://www.gaijinpot.com/
Hokkoku Shimbun   http://www.hokkoku.co.jp/
Ingenium   http://www.ingeniumgroup.com/indexe.asp
InterCareer Net Japan   http://www.intercareer.com/japan/
Japan Newspapers & Media Online
http://www.sabotenweb.com/bookmarks/newspapers.html
Japan Times (Tokyo)   http://www.japantimes.co.jp/
Job Dragon   http://www.jobdragon.com/index_e.asp
Mainichi Interactive   http://www.mainichi.co.jp/
Nara Shimbun   http://www.nara-shimbun.com/
Nikkei   http://www.nikkei.co.jp/
Nikkan Koyko Shimbun   http://www.nikkan.co.jp/
Nishinippon Shimbun   http://www.nishinippon.co.jp/
O Hayo Sensei (Teaching)   http://www.ohayosensei.com/
Okinawa Times   http://www.okinawatimes.co.jp/
Pacific Stars and Stripes   http://www.estripes.com/
Ryukyu Shimpo   http://www.ryukyushimpo.co.jp/
Tokyo Stock Exchange   http://www.tse.or.jp/
Yomiuri Online   http://www.yomiuri.co.jp/

Latin America
Jobs in Latin America   http://www.latpro.com/

Luxembourg
HVB Luxembourg   http://www.hvb.lu/en/jobs/
ADEM   http://www.etat.lu/adem/

Malaysia
Graduan   http://www.graduan.com.my/
Daily Express   http://www.infosabah.com.my/
JARING   http://www.jaring.my/
Jobstreet   http://www.jobs.com.my/
Kuala Lumpur Stock Exchange   http://www.klse.com.my/
Malaysia Online   http://www.mol.net.my/
Manfield in Malaysia & Singapore   http://www.manfield.com.sg/
Sarawak Tribune   http://www.sarawaktribune.com.my/
Star Jobs   http://star-jobs.com/
Wencom Career Guide   http://www.jaring.my/wencom/career.htm

Mauritias
L'Express   http://www.lexpress.mu/
Le Mauricien   http://www.lemauricien.com/mauricien/

Middle East
Bayt   http://www.bayt.com/
Careers Emirates   http://careeremirates.com/
Gulf Job Sites   http://www.gulfjobsites.com/

Nepal
Nepalese Newspapers   http://www.south-asia.com/

Netherlands
Dambusters Recruitment   http://www.dambustersrecruitment.com/
English Language jobs in Holland   http://www.englishlanguagejobs.com/
Jobs Today Directory (Dutch)   http://www.jobstoday.nl/
Jobnews (Dutch)   http://www.jobnews.nl/
JobTrack (Dutch)   http://www.jobtrack.nl/
Van Zoelen Recruitment   http://www.vz-recruitment.nl/

New Zealand
Best Jobs New Zealand   http://www.bestjobsnz.com/
Kiwi Careers   http://www.careers.co.nz/

Norway
EMB Net   http://www.no.embnet.org/Jobs/index.php3
FINN   http://www.finn.no/
Norge Jobbguiden   http://www.jobbguiden.no/
RekrutteringssystemerAS   http://www.rekrutteringssystemer.no/

Pakistan

Business Recorder	http://www.brecorder.com/
News International	http://www.jang-group.com/thenews/
The Dawn	http://dawn.com/

Philippines

Business World	http://bworld.com.ph/
Chinese Commercial News	http://www.siongpo.com/
Filipino Express	http://www.filipinoexpress.com/
Filipino Online Job Hunting	http://www.trabaho.com/
Manila Bulletin	http://www.mb.com.ph/
Philippines Times	http://www.philippinespost.com/
Philippine Star	http://www.philstar.com/
Visayan Daily Star	http://www.visayandailystar.com/

Portugal

Emprego (Jobs) (Portuguese)	http://emprego.aeiou.pt/
IEFP	http://www.iefp.pt/
Jobs Express (Portuguese)	http://www.expressoemprego.pt/
Portugal Jobs	http://portugal-info.net/jobs/deletejob.htm
Talent 4 Europe	http://www.talent4europe.com/Portugal/jobs.htm

Poland

Job Pilot (Polish)	http://www.jobpilot.com.pl/
Polandjobs.com	http://www.polandjobs.com/
Top Jobs (Polish)	http://www.topjobs.pl/

Romania

Best Jobs Romania	http://bestjobs.neogen.ro/
Jobsearch Romania (Romanian)	http://www.jobsearch.ro/index.cfm
Romania jobsearch portal	http://addbusiness.hypermart.net/employment/

Russia

Human Resources Online Russia	http://www.hro.ru/
Russia Today	http://www.russiatoday.com/
St Petersburg Times	http://www.sptimes.ru/

Singapore

Asia One	http://www.asia1.com.sg/
Alpha Maps	http://www.alpha-maps.com/
Business Times	http://business-times.asia1.com.sg/
Career Zone – Jobs in Singapore	http://www.careerzone.com.sg/
Contact Singapore	http://www.contactsingapore.org.sg/
Job Bank	http://www.adpost.com/sg/job_bank/
Lianhe Zaobao	http://www.asia1.com.sg/zaobao/
Manpower Singapore	http://www.manpower.com.sg/
Nanyang Polytechnic	http://www.nyp.edu.sg/
National University of Singapore	http://www.nus.edu.sg/
Singtao Times	http://www.singtao.com/
Shipping Times	http://business-times.asia1.com.sg/shippingtimes/
Singapore Chamber of Commerce	http://www.sicc.com.sg/
Singapore Government	http://www.gov.sg/
Singapore Information Map	http://www.sg/
Singapore Stock Exchange	http://www.ses.com.sg/

The Straits Times	http://straitstimes.asia1.com.sg/
9to5 Asia	http://coldfusion.9to5asia.com/

South Korea

Chosun Daily News	http://www.chosun.com/
Chungang Ilbo	http://www.joins.com/
Dong A Ilbo	http://www.donga.com/
Han-Kyoreh Shinmum	http://www.hani.co.kr/
Korean News Service	http://www.nowcom.co.kr/
Korea Post	http://www.koreapost.com/
Korea Times	http://www.korealink.co.kr/times/times.htm
Maeil Shinmun	http://www.m2000.co.kr/
Munhwa Ilbo	http://www.munhwa.co.kr/
The Korea Herald	http://www.koreaherald.co.kr/

Spain

Terra (Spanish)	http://www.terra.es/
Trabajos (Spanish)	http://www.trabajos.com/
Todo Trabajo (Spaish)	http://www.todotrabajo.com/
Trabajo.org (Spanish)	http://www.trabajo.org/

Sri Lanka

Daily News	http://www.dailynews.lk/
Lanka Academic Network	http://www.lacnet.org/
Sri Lanka Server	http://www.lanka.net/
Tamil Eelam News (Tamil)	http://www.eelam.com/news/tamil/

Sweden

AMS	http://www.ams.se/englishfs.asp?
I see Head hunting & Consulting	http://www.isee.se/
Jobline	http://www.jobline.se/
Manpower Sweden (Swedish)	http://www.manpower.se/
Proffice (Swedish)	http://www.proffice.se/
Swednet Job Search	http://www.swednet.org.uk/
Temporary Office Work in Sweden	http://www.proffice.com/

Switzerland

Emploi Switzerland	http://emploi.ch/
Job Engine	http://www.jobengine.ch/
Swiss Info	http://www.swissinfo.org/
Swiss Jobs	http://www.swissjobs.ch/
Swiss Web Jobs	http://www.jobs.ch/
Top Jobs Switzerland	http://www.topjobs.ch/

Taiwan

China Economic News Service	http://cens.com/
China Times	http://www.chinatimes.com.tw/
JobsDB.com	http://www.jobsdb.com.tw/
SinaNet Taiwan News	http://sinanet.com/
Taiwan Jobs Center	http://jobs.asiaco.com/taiwan/
Taiwan Stock Exchange	http://www.tse.com.tw/
Taiwan Tribune	http://www.taiwanese.com/

Thailand

Bangkok Post Jobs	http://www.bangkokpostjobs.com/

Business Day	http://bday.net/
Phuket Gazette	http://www.phuketgazette.net/
Siam Jobs - resume/jobs database	http://www.siam.net/jobs/
Thai Aust. Chamber of Commerce	http://www.austchamthailand.com/
Thailand Business	http://www.accessasia.com/xroad/xrthbus.html

United Kingdom

Academic Jobs	http://www.jobs.ac.uk/
ASA Education (Teaching in UK)	http://www.asaeducation.com/
BBC News Online	http://news.bbc.co.uk/
Celsian Group	http://www.celsiangroup.com/
Daily Record	http://www.dailyrecord.co.uk/
Financial Times	http://www.ft.com/
Fish 4 - Jobs	http://www.fish4.co.uk/
IC Resources	http://www.ic-resources.co.uk/
Job Mall	http://www.jobmall.co.uk/
Jobsearch	http://www.jobsearch.co.uk/
JobServe	http://www.jobserve.co.uk/
Microscape Recruitment Ltd	http://www.microscape.co.uk/welcome.asp
Net Job	http://www.netjobs.co.uk/
Planet Recruit	http://www.planetrecruit.com/
Prospects	http://www.prospects.ac.uk/
SEEK UK	http://www.seek.com.au/if.asp?loc=ukjobs
Technojobs UK	http://www.technojobs.co.uk/
Telegraph Newspaper Online	http://www.telegraph.co.uk/
The Guardian -Jobs	http://jobs.guardian.co.uk/
The Monster Board, UK	http://www.monster.co.uk/
The Times	http://www.timesonline.co.uk/
Top Jobs	http://www.topjobs.co.uk/

USA

Adguide's College Recruiter	http://www.adguide.com/
Financial Times	http://www.usa.ft.com/
Internship Programs	http://internships.wetfeet.com/
Job Hunt	http://www.job-hunt.org/
Jobweb	http://www.collegejournal.com/
Nation Job Network	http://www.nationjob.com/
Net Temps	http://www.net-temps.com/
The New York Times	http://www.nytimes.com/
The Wall Street Journal – College	http://www.collegejournal.com/
USA Today	http://www.usatoday.com/
US Government official site	http://www.usajobs.opm.gov/

Vietnam

| Vietnam Works | http://www.vietnamworks.com/ |

United Arab Emirates

| Jobs in Dubai | http://www.jobsindubai.com/ |
| The Emirates Network | http://www.theemiratesnetwork.com/business/jobs.htm |

International Organizations

OECD	http://www.oecd.org/
Inter-American Development Bank	http://www.iadb.org/
International Labour Organisation	http://www.ilo.org/
International Monetary Fund	http://www.imf.org/
Red Cross	http://www.redcross.org/
UNESCO	http://www.unesco.org/
United Nations	http://www.un.org/
The World Bank Group	http://www.worldbank.org/
World Health Organisation	http://www.who.org/
World Trade Organisation	http://www.wto.org/
Worldwide Corporate Information	http://www.corporateinformation.com/

Few More North American Job search Websites

ACCOUNTING/BANKING/FINANCE --
ACCOUNTING AND FINANCE JOBS – http://www.accountingjobs.com
ACCOUNTING.COM -- http://www.accounting.com
ACCOUNTING.NET -- http://www.accounting.net
AMERICAN BANKER ONLINE'S CAREERZONE -- http://www.americanbanker.com/careerzone
BLOOMBERG – http://www.bloomberg.com
CFO'S FEATURED JOBS -- http://www.cfonet.com/html/cfojobs.html
FINANCIAL, ACCOUNTING, AND INSURANCE JOBS PAGE --
http://www.nationjob.com/financial
FINCAREER -- http://www.fincareer.com
JOBS FOR BANKERS ONLINE -- http://www.bankiobs.com
NATIONAL BANKING NETWORK – http://www.banking-financejobs.com
ADVERTISING/MARKETING/PUBLIC RELATIONS –
ADWEEK ONLINE – http://www.adweek.com
DIRECT MARKETING WORLD – http://www.dmworld.com
MARKETING JOBS – http://www.marketingjobs.com

AEROSPACE
AVIATION AND AEROSPACE JOBS PAGE – http://www.nationjob.com/aviation
AVIATION EMPLOYMENT – http://www.aviationemployment.com
SPACE JOBS – http://www.spacejobs.com

ARTS AND ENTERTAINMENT
THE INTERNET MUSIC PAGES -- http://www.musicpages.com
ONLINE SPORTS -- http://www.onlinesports.com/pages/CareerCenter.html

BIOTECHNOLOGY/SCIENTIFIC
BIO ONLINE – http://www.bio.com
SCIENCE PROFESSIONAL NETWORK – www.recruitsciencemag.org

CHARITIES AND SOCIAL SERVICES
THE NONPROFIT TIMES ONLINE -- http://www.nptimes.com/classified.html
SOCIAL SERVICE – http://www.socialservice.com
SOCIAL WORK AND SOCIAL SERVICES JOBS ONLINE –
http://www.gwbweb.wustl.edu/jobs/index.html

COMMUNICATIONS
AIRWAVES MEDIA WEB – http://www.airwaves.com/job.html
THE JOBZONE – http://www.internettelephony.com/JobZone/jobzone.asp

COMPUTERS
COMPUTER – http://www.computer.org/computer/career/career.htm
THE COMPUTER JOBS STORE – http://www.computerjobs.com

COMPUTERWORK – http://www.computerwork.com
DICE – http://www.dice.com
DIGITAL CAT'S HUMAN RESOURCE CENTER – http://www.jobcats.com
IDEAS JOB NETWORK -- http://www.ideasjn.com
I-JOBS -- http://www.I-jobs.com

JOBS FOR PROGRAMMERS -- http://www.prgjobs.com
JOBS.INTERNET.COM -- http://jobs.intemet.com
JOB WAREHOUSE -- http://www.jobwarehouse.com
MACTALENT -- http://www.mactalent.com
SELECTJOBS -- http://www.seIectjobs.com
TECHIES -- http://www.techies.com

EDUCATION
ACADEMIC EMPLOYMENT NETWORK -- http://www.academploy.corn
ACADEMIC POSITION NETWORK -- http://www.apnjobs.com
AECT PLACEMENT CENTER -- http://www.aect.org/employment/empIoyment.htm
THE CHRONICLE OF HIGHER EDUCATION CAREER NETWORK – http://chronicle.com/jobs
DAVE'S ESL CAFÉ – http://www.eslcafe.com
HIGHEREDJOBS ONLINE – http://www.higheredjobs.com
JOBS IN HIGHER EDUCATION -- http://www.gsIis.utexas.edu/~acadres/jobs/index.html
LIBRARY & INFORMATION SCIENCE JOB SEARCH – http://www.carousel.lis.uiuc.edu/~jobs
THE PRIVATE SCHOOL EMPLOYMENT NETWORK – http://www.privateschooljobs.com
TEACHER JOBS – http://www.teacherjobs.com

ENGINEERING
ENGINEERJOBS -- http://www.engineerjobs.com

ENVIRONMENTAL
ECOLOGIC -- http://www.rpi.edu/dept/union/pugwash/ecojobs.htm
ENVIRONMENTAL JOBS SEARCH PAGE –
http://ourworld.compuserve.com/homepages/ubikk/env4.htm
WATER ENVIRONMENT WEB – http://www.wef.org
GOVERNMENT
CORPORATE GRAY ONLINE -- http://www.greentogray.com
FEDERAL JOBS CENTRAL -- http://www.fedjobs.com
FEDERAL JOBS DIGEST -- http://www.jobsfed.com
FEDWORLD FEDERAL JOB ANNOUNCEMENT SEARCH --
http://www.fedworld.gov/jobs/jobsearch.htmI
THE POLICE OFFICERS INTERNET DIRECTORY -- http://www.officer.com/jobs.htm

HEALTHCARE
HEALTH CAREER WEB -- http://www.heaIthcareerweb.com
HEALTH CARE JOBS ONLINE -- http://www.hcjobsonIine.com
HEALTH CARE RECRUITMENT ONLINE – http://www.healthcarerecruitment.com
MEDHUNTERS -- http://www.medhunters.com
MEDICAL-ADMART -- http://www.medicaI-admart.com
MEDICAL DEVICE LINK -- http://www.devicelink.com/career
MEDZILLA -- http://www.medziIIa.com
NURSING SPECTRUM CAREER FITNESS ONLINE – http://www.nursingspectrum.com
PHYSICIANS EMPLOYMENT – http://www.physemp.com
SALUDOS HISPANIS WEB CAREER CENTER – http://www.saludos.com/cguide/hcguide.html
HOTELS AND RESTAURANTS
ESCOFFIER ONLINE – http://www.escoffier.com/nonscape/employ.shtml

AMERICAN JOBS -- http://www.arnericanjobs.com
BEST JOBS USA – http://www.bestjobsusa.com

We would appreciate your help in keeping this resource up to date! mail your feedback at tariq_nadeem@selfhelppublishers.com

List of Suggested Job Search Web Sites in Canada

Canada Job search	www.canadajobsearch.com
Canada Wide	www.canada.com
Canada Work Info Net (B)	http://workinfonet.ca
Canada Work Infonet	www.workinfonet.com
Canadian Career Page	www.canadiancareers.com
Career Bookmarks	www.careerbookmarks.tpl.toronto.on.ca
Career Exchange	www.creerexchange.com
Career Mosaic	www.careermosaic.com
Career Networking	www.careerkey.com
Contractors Network Corporation	www.cnc.ca
Culture Net Announcement Board	www.culturenet.ca
Electronic Labour Exchange	www.ele-spe.org
E-Span	www.espan.com
Head Hunter	www.HeadHunter.net
HEART/Career Connections	www.career.com
Hot Jobs	www.hotjobs.com
HRDC Canada(B)	www.hrdc-drhc.gc.ca
Job Bus Canada	www.jobbus.com
Job Find	www.jobfind2000.com
Job Hunters Bible	www.jobhuntersbible.com
Job Search Canada	www.jobsearchcanada.about.com
Job Search Engine	www.job-search-engine.com
Job Shark	www.jobshark.com
Monster Board	www.monster.ca
Net Jobs	www.netjobs.com
Ontario Government (B)	www.gojobs.gov.on.ca
Public Service Commission of Canada(B)	http://jobs.gc.ca
SERN	www.sern.net
Toronto HRDC Jobs and Links	www.toronto-hrdc.sto.org
Toronto Job Ads	www.workwaves.com
University of Toronto Job Board	www.utoronto.ca/jobopps
Work Search (B)	www.worksearch.gc.ca
Workink(B)	www.workink.com
Work Insight	www.workinsight.com
Workopolis	www.workopolis.com

HI TECH

Hi Tech Career Exchanges	www.hitechcareer.com
IT Career Solutions	www.vectortech.com
Position Watch	www.positionwatch.com
Ward Associates	www.ward-associates.com

ENGINEERING

Canadian Society for Mechanical Engineers	www.csme.ca
Engineering Institute of Canada	www.eic.ici.ca

NON PROFIT ORGANIZATION

Canadian International Development Agency	www.acdi-cida.gc.ca
Charity Village	www.charityvillage.com
Human Rights-Job Bank	www.Hri.ca/jobboard/joblinks.shtml
Law Now's Resource for Charity/Non Profit	www.extension.ualberta.ca/lawnow/nfp
Online Resource for Non Profit	www.onestep.on.ca

HEALTH

Canadian Medical Placement Service	www.cmps.ca
Hospital News	www.hospitalnews.com
Med Hunters	www.medhunters.com

EDUCATION

Jobs in the Educational Field	www.oise.utoronto.ca/~mpress/jobs.html

WOMEN

Wired Women	www.wiredwoman.com

MULTI MEDIA

MultiMediator	www.multimediator.com

TOURISM AND HOSPITALITY

Cool Jobs Canada	www.cooljobscanada.com
Hospitality Careers	www.hcareers.com

AGRICULTURE

Caffeine	www.caffeine.ca
The Farm Directory	www.farmdirectory.com/employment.asp

ARTS AND ENTERTAINMENT

Acting	www.madscreenwriter.com
ACTRA (film)	www.actra.com
Canadian Actor Online	www.canadianactor.com
Canadian Actors Equity Association	www.caea.com
Canadian film @ TV Production Association	www.cftpa.ca
Canadian Film Centre	www.cdnfilmcentre.com
Mandy	www.mandy.com
National Film Board	www.nfb.ca
Ontario Theatre	www.theatreontario.org
Playback Magazine	www.playbackmag.com

SPECIALIZED

Canadian Federation of Chefs & Cooks	www.cfcc.ca
Canadian Human Resource Counsellors	www.chrp.ca
Contact Point – Counsellors	www.contactpoint.ca
Oil and Gas Industry	www.pcf.ab.ca
Social Workers of Toronto	www.swatjobs.com

PEOPLE WITH DISABILITIES

Canadian Council for Rehabilitation & Work	www.ccrw.org
Canadian Hearing Society	www.chs.ca
Canadian Mental health Association	www.cmha.ca
Canadian Paraplegic Association	www.canparaplegic.org
Job Accommodation Network	http://janweb.icdi.wvu.edu
TCG for People with Disabilities	www.tcg.on.ca
U of T Adaptive Tech ERC	www.utoronto.ca/atrc

WEB SITES FOR YOUTH AND RECENT GRADUATES

Bridges	www.bridges.com
Canadian Youth Business Foundation	www.cybf.ca
Canadian Youth Business Foundation (B)	www.cybf.ca
Career Owl	www.careerowl.ca
Career Planning	www.alis.gov.ab.ca
Cdn.International Development Agency(B)	www.acdi-cida.gc.ca
Fedeal Student Work Experience Program (B)	www.jobs.gc.ca
MazeMaster	www.mazemaster.on.ca
National Graduate Register	http://ngr.schoolnet.ca
Strategies Business Info – By Sector (B)	Strategis.ic.gc.ca/sc_indps/en gdoc/homepage.html
Summer Jobs	www.summerjobs.com

Work Web (B)	www.cacee.com
Youth Canada (B)	www.youth.gc.ca
Youth Info-Job (B)	www.infojob.net
Youth Opportunities Ontario (B)	Youthjobs.gov.on.ca
Youth Opportunities Ontario (B)	www.edu.gov.on.ca

NEW COMERS

Citizenship and Immigration Canada	www.cic.gc.ca
Settlement.org	www.sttlement.org
Skills for change	www.skillsforchange.org
World Educational Services/Foreign Credentials Assessment	www.wes.org/ca

CAREER PLANNING AND JOB SEARCH STRATEGIES

Bridges	www.cxbridges.com
Career Cruising	www.careercruising.com
Counsellor Resource Centre (B)	http://crccanada.org
Essential Skills	www.essestialskills.gc.ca
Job Futures	http://jobfutures.ca
National Occupational Classification (NOC)(B)	www.hrdc.gc.ca/noc
Toronto Public Library	http://careerbookmarks.tpl.vrl.toronto.on.ca
What Colour is your parachute:	www.jobhuntersbible.com

LABOUR MARKET / INDUSTRY INFORMATION

Canada News Wire	www.newswire.ca
Canada Work InfoNet (B)	www.workinfonet.ca
HRDC Metro Toronto(B)	www.toronto-hrdc.sto.org
HRDC Sector Studies (B)	www.on.hrdc-drhc.gc.ca/english/lmi
Industry Canada	http://strategis.ic.gc.ca
Labour Market Information: Salary Ranges	www.Canadavisa.com/documents/salary.htm
Ontario Wage Information	www.on.hrdc-drhc.gc.ca
Workwaves Toronto	www.workwaves.com

NEWSPAPERS/MAGAZINE

Eye Magazine	www.eye.net/classifieds.
Globe and Mail	www.theglobeandmail.com
National Post	www.careerclick.com
Newswire	www.neweswire.ca
Toronto Star	www.thestar.com
Toronto Star / Globe and Mail	www.workpolis.com

Toronto Sun	www.canoe.ca

SMALL BUSINESS INFORMATION

Business Development Bank of Canada (B)	www.bdc.ca
Canada Business Service Centres (B)	www.cbsc.org
Canadian Company Capabilities (B)	Strategis.ic.gc.ca/engdoc/main.html
Canadian Women's business Network	www.cdnbizwomen.com
Educated Entrepreneur	www.educatedentrepreneur.com
Enterprise Toronto	www.enterprisetronto.com
Self Employment Assistance	http://www.sedi.org/html/prog/fs1_prog.html
Toronto Business	www.city.toronto.on.ca/business/index.htm

WEB SITES WHERE YOU CAN POST YOUR RESUME

Electronic Labour Exchange	www.ele-spc.org
Job Canada	www.jobcanada.org
Job Shark (B)	www.jobshark.com
Monster Board (B)	www.monster.ca
National Graduate Register (B)	www.campusworklink.com
NetJobs	www.netjobs.com
Worklink	www.workink.com
Workopolis	www.workopolis.ca

TRAINING

Can Learn	www.canlearn.ca
Ellis Chart/Apprentice Training Programs	www.hrdc.gc.ca/hrib/hrpprh/redseal/ndex.shtml
Interactive Training Inventory (B)	www.trainingiti.com
Ministry of Eduction & Training	www.edu.gov.on.ca/eng/welcome.html
Onestep	www.onestep.on.ca
Ontario Universities' Application Centre	www.ouac.on.ca
Scholarships and Exchanges (B)	www.homer.aucc.ca
School finder(B)	www.schoolfinder.com

TUTORIAL SITES

Internet Stuff	www.webteacher.com
Learn the Net	www.learnthenet.com

| Microsoft Office: word, excel, powerpoint | www.utexax.edu/cc/training/handouts |
| Mouse Tutorial | www.albright.org/Albright/computer-Lab/tutorials/mouse/ |

RELEVANT INFORMATION

City of Toronto	www.city.toronto.on.ca
Employment Resource Centres	www.tcet.com/ercs
Possibilities Project	www.possibilitiesproject.com

VOLUNTEER SITES

Charity Village	www.charityvillage.com
Rehabilitation	www.voc-reb.org
Volunteers	www.volunteer.ca

FREE EMAILS SITES

Excite	www.excite.com
Hotmail	www.hotmail.com
Mail City	www.mailcity.com
Yahoo	www.yahoo.com

SINGLE SEARCH ENGINES

www.google.com	www.altavista.com
www.excite.com	www.go.com
www.hotbot.com	www.yahoo.ca

META SEARCH ENGINES

www.search.com	www.profusion.com
www.megaweb.com	www.metacrawler.com
www.dogpile.com	

TIPS:

- Post your multiple versions of resume on-line where ever possible and register with as many recruiting agencies as you can. Services of these agencies are free for candidates because they are being paid by the employer if they find them an employee of their choice.

- Your resume should not be more then 2 pages of MS Word. The average time spent by an employer in Canada to shortlist resume is 10-15 seconds. So the first page of your resume should carry the most important information that you want to be noticed by HR managers.

- Access your resume by response, If you apply against 100 jobs and you receive 5-10 interviews that mean your resume is fine and you are doing a good job.

- After arriving in Canada attend job search workshops and trainings organized by your nearest HRDC (Human Resource Development Canada) office or by HRDC sponsored agencies free of charge. You will learn how job search techniques are different in Canada from rest of the world.

- When you are in Canada, do your networking, let as many people know as possible that you are looking for a job and learn making cold calls. These are the highly successful and result oriented methods of job search in Canada.

- Mail at least 5-10 resume and make 5 cold calls everyday for quick results.

- www.workopolis.com, www.monster.ca & www.hotjobs.com are the most commonly visited websites for job search.

Some Useful Toll-Free Numbers
For USA and Canada only

Information on the Government of Canada	1 800 622-6232
Canada Business Service Centres	1 800 576-4444
Canada Child Tax Benefit	1800 387-1193
Canada Education Saving Grant	1 888 276-3624
Canada Saving Bonds	1 800 575-5151
Citizenship and Immigration Canada	
In Montreal (local call)	1 54 496-1010
In Toronto (local call)	1 416 973-4444
In Vancouver (local call)	1 604 666-2171
Elsewhere in Canada	1 888 242-2100
Customs Information Service	1 800 461-9999
Employment Insurance and Social Insurance Number	1 800 206-7218
Old Age Security and Canada Pension plan	1 800 277-9914
Passport Office	1 800567-6868
Tax Enquiries-personal	1 800 959-8281
Youth Info Line	1 800 935-5555

Snow Fall

I like Snow

Rainbow Bridge (Canada on left USA on right)

A Sunset in Toronto

Ice Fishing

Can you do this?

Canadian Train

Skywalk Toronto

City of Montreal

I want to migrate to Canada too, under skilled worker class. I am trained to work at airports and I will prepare my application by myself. I heard that my rights are very well defined and respected in Canada.

INDEX

About the Author

The author has an electro-mechanical engineering background in turnkey thermal power station contracting business. He has more than 14 years of experience with multi-national companies especially in site/project management and coordination by leading multi-discipline engineering teams. He was also a Cisco certified network and design professional (CCNP, CCDP, A+). He arrived in Canada as a skilled worker immigrant and faced numerous surprises and challenges as well as suffered a number of losses.

The author has a flare to help and teach. He wishes to save new immigrants from potential losses and miseries by sharing the wealth of information that he has gathered while immigrating and settling in Canada. After interviewing hundreds of new immigrants, especially internationally trained professionals from various countries, the author has come to the conclusion that the root cause of all the problems and loss of hard earned money and precious time is the lack of information and training before arriving to Canada.

In this book, the author provides everything to new or potential immigrants to not only prepare and submit their immigration application under skilled worker class in a professional manner but to start working towards their eligibility for employment in Canada. He encourages them to explore employment opportunities or secure a job offer while their applications are in process.

For the people who are interested in starting their own small business in Canada, he also published a book titled "How to Start a Small Business in Canada" which is the 5th book under his belt. In this book he provides all the necessary tools, guidance and information to men and women who are on paid jobs and wishes to start their own small business. He encourages and motivates foreign trained professionals to be self-employed, who are facing numerous barriers during their job search efforts and struggling for an opportunity where they can utilize their talent and skills to their full competence.

He also voluntarily helps clients from all over the world via e-mail, phone and personally. He provides people with necessary guidance and advises by answering to their questions about Canadian immigration, settlement, employment search and starting a small business in Canada.

The Author can be reached at ***tariq_nadeem@sympatico.ca*** or *info@selfhelppublishers.com* for advice or feedback upon his publications.

He has published this book with the approval of Citizenship and Immigration Canada (CIC) under a licensing agreement with Public Works and Government Services Canada 350 Albert Street, 4th Floor Ottawa ON K1A 0S5.

Bibliography

Statistics Canada information is used with the permission of Minister of Industry, as Minister responsible for Statistics Canada. Information on the availability of the wide range of data from Statistics Canada can be obtained from Statistics Canada's Regional Offices, its World Wide Web site at http://www.statcan.ca and its toll-free access number 1-800-263-1136

Introduction to Canada, facts and figures – CIA -The world fact book 2005

Fact sheet, http://www.cicic.ca/professions/indexe.stm
Cultural Shock: An introduction to KSA

Top Ten Ways to Get Canadian Experience - Do You Have International Experience By Shawn Mintz of A.C.C.E.S www.accestrain.com.

NOTES

Printed in the United States
39072LVS00001B/16